Blackstudies
792.789
Fr

M
BlK.St.

The Negro units of the Federal Theatre Project – highly controversial, cutting-edge expressions of New Deal philosophy at work within the Works Progress Administration's Arts Projects – brought to the forefront one of the central problems in American democratic culture: the representation of racial difference. As Harry Hopkins, the head of the WPA, and Hallie Flanagan, the director of the FTP, and writers like Richard Wright and Theodore Ward attempted to make art more relevant and more accessible to more people, they often found themselves compelled to negotiate a high-minded sense of what art could accomplish against the demands of their audience for popular entertainment. At a time when the tradition of black entertainment had come to seem suspect to many of the black intelligentsia and black artists, the question of how political or entertaining black theatre should be rendered judgments of what an audience might need or want especially problematic. Those working in the profession quickly discovered the inescapable ideological responsibilities that come of opening a curtain on any sort of show, whether apparently entertaining or political in nature.

Blueprints for a Black Federal Theatre explores the historical context of its subject while examining the liberal idealism of the thirties and the critical debates in black journals over the role of a national theatre for African Americans. Surveying the difficulties of writing new plays that broke with old stereotypes, the conflicting demands audiences made for different kinds of dramas, and the role of the "essentially dramatic" black actor, the book also offers broader reflections on the issues of cultural separatism and multiculturalism engaging the arts today.

CAMBRIDGE STUDIES IN AMERICAN LITERATURE AND CULTURE

Blueprints for a Black Federal Theatre, 1935–1939

CAMBRIDGE STUDIES IN AMERICAN LITERATURE AND CULTURE

Books in the series
79. Alan Filreis, *Modernism from Right to Left*
78. Michael Staub, *Voices of Persuasion: The Politics of Representation in 1930s America*
77. Katherine Kearns, *Robert Frost and a Poetics of Appetite*
76. Peter Halter, *The Revolution in the Visual Arts and the Poetry of William Carlos Williams*
75. Barry Ahearn, *William Carlos Williams and Alterity: The Early Poetry*
74. Linda A. Taylor-Kinnahan, *Poetics of the Feminine: Authority and Literary Tradition in William Carlos Williams, Mina Loy, Denise Levertov, and Kathleen Fraser*
73. Bernard Rosenthal, *Salem Story: Reading the Witch Trials of 1692*
72. Jon Lance Bacon, *Flannery O'Connor and Cold War Culture*
71. Nathaniel Mackey, *Discrepant Engagement, Dissonance, Cross-Culturality and Experimental Writing*
70. David M. Robinson, *Emerson and the Conduct of Life*
69. Cary Wolfe, *The Limits of American Literary Ideology in Pound and Emerson*
68. Andrew Levy, *The Culture and Commerce of the American Short Story*
67. Stephen Fredman, *The Grounding of American Poetry: Charles Olson and the Emersonian Tradition*
66. David Wyatt, *Out of the Sixties: Storytelling and the Vietnam Generation*
65. Thomas Strychacz, *Modernism, Mass Culture, and Professionalism*

Continued on pages following the Index

Blueprints for a Black Federal Theatre, 1935–1939

RENA FRADEN
Pomona College

CAMBRIDGE
UNIVERSITY PRESS

Published by the Press Syndicate of the University of Cambridge
The Pitt Building, Trumpington Street, Cambridge CB2 1RP
40 West 20th Street, New York, NY 10011-4211, USA
10 Stamford Road, Oakleigh, Melbourne 3166, Australia

© Cambridge University Press 1994

First published 1994

Printed in the United States of America

Library of Congress Cataloging-in-Publication Data
Fraden, Rena.
  Blueprints for a Black federal theatre, 1935–1939 / Rena Fraden.
    p.   cm. – (Cambridge studies in American literature
  and culture : 80)
  Includes bibliographical references and index.
  ISBN 0-521-44359-8
  1. Federal Theatre Project (U.S) – History.   2. Afro-American
theater.   3. Theater – United States – History – 20th century.
I. Title.   II. Series.
PN2270.F43F73   1994
792'.08996073 – dc20   93-31189
                             CIP

A catalog record for this book is available from the British Library

ISBN   0-521-44359-8 hardback

for my parents

"Byron Webb (Technical Director) and Perry Watkins (Set Designer), *Haiti,* seen here pouring over blueprints." LCFTP. New York City. February 28, 1938.

Contents

List of Illustrations	*page* viii
Preface	xi
Acknowledgments	xvii
Introduction	1
1 A New Deal (or Not) for Culture	21
2 Critical Directions: Toward a National Negro Theatre	49
3 Producing New Dramas: The Politics of Choice	88
4 The Unpredictable Audience	136
5 Acting Properly	168
Afterword	196
Notes	207
Index	239

Illustrations

All illustrations from the Library of Congress Federal Theatre Project Collection George Mason University (LCFTP)

Cover and illustration. LCFTP. New York City. February 28, 1938. "Byron Webb (Technical Director) and Perry Watkins (Set Designer), *Haiti,* seen here pouring over blueprints."   *page* vi

1. LCFTP. New York City. "A fervent appeal, *Sweet Land.*"   90

2. LCFTP. Seattle, WA, June 1936. "Tense standoff, *Stevedore.*"   90

3. LCFTP. New York City. "Convicts and power, *Hymn to the Rising Sun.*"   91

4. LCFTP. Chicago, IL, April 6, 1938. "At home, *Big White Fog.*"   92

5. LCFTP. Chicago, IL, April 6, 1938. "Money to the Garveyites, *Big White Fog.*"   92

6. LCFTP. Chicago, IL, April 6, 1938. "Last act – a new beginning, *Big White Fog.*"   93

7. LCFTP. "Crowds."   137

8. LCFTP. "Celebrities."   138

9. LCFTP. "Mrs. Roosevelt and Mayor La Guardia at *Swing Mikado,* New York City."   139

10. LCFTP. "Dancing at the *Swing Mikado.*"   140

11. LCFTP. "Crowds at voodoo *Macbeth*."   141

12. LCFTP. New York City. "Dancing, *Androcles and the Lion*."   142

13. LCFTP. Los Angeles, July 21, 1938. "Church Revival, *Run, Little Chillun*."   169

14. LCFTP. Los Angeles, July 22, 1938. "African Chants, *Run, Little Chillun*."   170

15. LCFTP. New York City. "Voodoo Men, *Macbeth*."   171

16. LCFTP. Seattle, WA. "Voodoo Man, *Black Empire*."   172

17. LCFTP. Chicago/New York City. "The Mikado and Chorus, *Swing Mikado*."   173

18. LCFTP. Chicago/New York City. "Pooh–Bah (William Franklin), Ko–Ko (Herman Green), Pish Tush (Lewis White) in *Swing Mikado*."   174

Preface

This study does not attempt to chronicle the complete production history of the Negro units of the Federal Theatre Project.[1] Instead, through a critical discussion of issues embedded in, and articulated and implied by the efforts to establish a black theatre within the setting of a national "people's" theatre, I write about the Negro units as an instance of cultural politics at work – in regard to race.

I came to this study first through the sound of voices, quite literally, the voices of people who had worked on the Negro units of the FTP and who had been recorded on tape (and some of the tapes transcribed) by researchers at George Mason University. By a twist of fate, I had found myself one summer in Washington, D.C., surrounded by people working in the short but intensely lived American National Theatre under the direction of Peter Sellars. There I learned first hand just how weird and contentious and exciting theatre can be. The Kennedy Center housed this latest attempt at a national theatre – a huge building, imposing, but hardly conducive to experimental or critical or even (some would say) entertaining theatre with its red carpet and chandeliers and immense ceilings. The bureaucracy of that government institution, the tyranny of auditoriums too big or too small, of jealous curtain pullers made me sympathetic to the trials of the Federal Theatre of fifty years earlier. From the beginning, Sellars and his cohorts received a good deal of criticism because they had been given the title "National." How can one theatre represent this pluralistic country? Regional theatres (regional theatres said) are the true national theatre of America. And given how short lived ANT was – in two short years it lost $5 million and never found an audience in Washington, D.C. – perhaps the regional theatres were right.

It was in conversations there that I first learned about the FTP and the archival material gathered at George Mason. Since I had already begun to teach courses on the thirties, I thought a look at the library would yield, at the very least, a few stories for my students. How the archives got to *be* at George Mason is the first story to recount. Professors Lorraine Brown and John O'Connor tracked down the missing papers of the FTP in the early seventies to an airplane hangar in Baltimore. The FTP's leftist cultural politics had caused its banishment from the archival center of Washington, but the politics no longer seemed so threatening in the seventies. The FTP was now safely historical, and its voluminous records could be gathered together and arranged at George Mason, including six thousand playscripts and radio scripts, playreading reports, production notebooks, photographs, designs, audience surveys, clippings, reviews.

What I first encountered in the archives, what first entranced me, were the sounds of the conversations and memories invoked in oral interviews collected by Brown, O'Connor, and other researchers. People told marvelous stories – passionate, sardonic, wry, proud, angry – of hopes and disappointments. I felt immediately surrounded by, I cannot think of another name for it, authenticity. I want to quickly add that the stories weren't authentic because they were all the same; indeed, the stories contradicted each other and sometimes themselves. The nature of oral interviews, gathered many years later, is bound to be marked by forgetfulness, mistaken memories, or willed cover-ups, as well as by the influence of ensuing years in which the New Deal programs have been celebrated or denigrated. Some of the storytellers celebrated the FTP as a shining example of democratic representation; others chronicled the lack of opportunities open to them. In their differences, they seemed to reveal to me some of the choices, prejudices, popular preconceptions, and willful and unconscious blindnesses that both centrally and incidentally shape the history of this cultural movement.

The National Archives in Washington holds the rest of the FTP's historical records. There one can find the bureaucratic decisions, the memos in triplicate, letters from supervisors to superiors, descriptions of meetings between protestors and officials. And there too one finds contradictions and historical gaps. Partly this has to do with the shortcomings of historical sources. For instance, in spite of the massive amount of paperwork the government demanded from the FTP, there seems to be no detailed recording of who first had the idea to set up the Negro units. I do rely on many oral interviews, which, of course, may be full of historical inaccuracies. But I use them not so much for the "facts" they provide as for the gestures they make toward the past.

What people choose to remember or have remembered, how they interpret the past and see their part in the cultural experiment, interests me. I
wish also I had more information about what, in fact, "the people" *did*
think about the FTP and the Negro units. There is some evidence in the
form of audience questionnaires that the FTP circulated and collected,
but here too, the information is filtered through data collectors who
collated results, as well as through audience members who may have
been influenced by what they thought the FTP bureaucrats wanted to
hear. There are reviews by critics, of course, and one can surmise what
was popular and not popular (sometimes) depending on how long a
production ran. But information about what either the people or individuals thought is so often frustratingly indirect. Although at times I
wished I could find a reply to a letter or an account of a particular
meeting, I was not temperamentally persuaded that a chronology of the
Negro units would help make the kind of cultural argument I wished to
construct. A chronology might, inadvertently, cover up some of the
contradictions and gaps I wished to expose because my sense of cultural
history is that it is made up of contradictions, mixed desires, revisionary wishes.

Still, the archives gave up all kinds of sounds I had never listened to
before. For me, that archival moment of discovery when I heard voices
I wanted to learn more about, voices that seemed to move me, has led
me to question in all sorts of ways my own claims, my authority,
sincerity, and authenticity. In the first place, that I found myself in an
archive was strange and a bit suspect considering my training as an
undergraduate learning how to read from young and old New Critics
and as a graduate student under the uneasy influence of deconstruction.
Archival work seemed unnecessary to New Critics, concentrating on
words, and equally uninteresting to theorists. But for someone like me
who had always been interested in history and biography, reading other
people's voices not in "texts" but in letters and memos seemed, somehow, to make room for a different sort of criticism, neither purely
formal nor theoretical, but cultural.

I do not mean to claim that in letting people "tell" their tale, I am
somehow removed from the picture, outside the framework. Because,
of course, I've chosen certain voices and left others out. If we ask
on what basis those self-appointed representatives from the past made
decisions about what was culturally proper, we must also ask ourselves
as historians, readers, or consumers of the past how we choose from
among representations and thus become involved in the struggle to
shape culture according to our desires. For someone like myself, someone who had not yet found a satisfactory critical voice, not in New

Criticism, or the newer (at that time – late 1970s, early 1980s) theories, the pleasure in this work and the pain was inextricably bound up with the way I found myself finding my voice by questioning the way others had found theirs. I was in the curious position of a writer experiencing some of the same doubts and difficulties that the people I was writing about experienced. As I questioned my rights and ability, my knowledge and experience to represent a historical subject, to penetrate communities and histories foreign to me, I saw that this was exactly the subject I sought to write about.

Who can authentically represent an aesthetic? I look at how people decide what constitutes a community and who can represent it. White critics sometimes refused to suggest what the Negro units should produce because they felt unqualified, in the dark, out of touch with the Negro community. They would say, "Go ask a member of that community." Sometimes white critics like Hallie Flanagan, the director of the FTP, felt perfectly capable of telling the black community what it should like; at other times she hesitated. Black critics, who felt they were in touch by virtue of their race even when they were at odds with some part of a black audience's sense of culture, struggled anyway to impose their desires for a certain sort of cultural politics and a certain kind of community. Intellectuals often felt they had both the right and duty to pronounce and persuade about the proper course of culture, but often both black and white intellectuals shared the problem of feeling estranged from "their" black and/or white people.

Rather than analyze specific artists or styles, or judge the merit of certain works, I write about the way the work was managed and culture practically negotiated. Often in the case of the FTP, the process of negotiation was articulated by intellectuals operating as critics, or by artists and bureaucrats who worked as critics, managers, canon makers, politicians, and cultural creators. In their pronouncements and decisions, in their policing of the canon and making new traditions, these representatives interpreted and cajoled, persuaded and constructed communities to fall into a particular line. I show how certain voices were appropriated, repressed, or liberated and the way people resisted, rejected, accommodated, or presented alternatives. I think that it is not enough to focus solely on the rhetoric of the hierarchy of the FTP in attempting to chart its influence; nor is it enough to see only how the Negro units responded to such rhetoric. It is in the interpenetration of ideas and rhetoric, theory and practice that cultural exchange occurred.

I have shaped this book thematically then, rather than chronologically, and I should warn the reader here that I take almost two chapters to arrive at the material directly related to the FTP Negro units.[2] In so doing I have deliberately embedded this little-known four-year experiment in ethnic theatre into a wider historical context. In Chapter 1, I examine the rhetoric of liberal politics that inspired Harry Hopkins, the director of the WPA, and Flanagan, as well as race leaders like W. E. B. Du Bois and Charles Johnson. Sometimes they used the same vocabulary but meant different things: Du Bois's call for renewed commitment to segregated institutions in the thirties was not what Flanagan had in mind when she created the segregated Negro units. At a certain point, I don't think Du Bois cared whether anybody other than the Negro community came to his theatre, but Flanagan always had to worry about what white people and the Negro people would think in a theatre that was *never* to be segregated by audience. In Chapter 2, I detail the rich and varied debates within the black community, from the teens, twenties, and thirties, over the proper sort of New Negro and the politically and artistically correct theatre that should portray him and her.[3] Black cultural critics turned their attention to the theatre, not music or the fine arts, as a crucible for a new nationalism, a new Negro national theatre, "about, by, for, and near" them. I investigate at length some of the critical debates by black critics in black journals in order to show how the Negro units were shaped by and responded to ongoing debates about race, art, ideology, and how the theatre came to seem an appropriate medium for creating a new identity, a Negro, or black, or African, or African American, or American identity of resistance and pride during the FTP. The discussions of the rhetoric of liberalism and the debates about the New Negro prepare the way for the rest of the book in which I examine the cultural understandings and misunderstandings that mark my interest in the Negro units of the FTP. In Chapter 3, I concentrate on political misunderstandings and struggles that occurred between individuals and groups of individuals within and between the races. In spite of Popular Front politics that informed much of the government Art Projects, communities were often deeply divided over just how they wanted to be represented at large; the production of Theodore Ward's *Big White Fog* in Chicago brings some of these problems to light. The idea of the audience, who they were, how they came to be known or represented, who they thought they should be becomes the thematic center of Chapter 4. Sometimes celebrated, sometimes a puzzlement, sometimes scorned, the audience is a necessary part of the "people's theatre," but cultural leaders, both black and white, often found themselves at a distance from the people they were representing. In Chapter 5, I discuss what was considered appropriate material for black actors. What is proper, what is property, what is appropriation are all questions that frame the work of black actors; here, two productions are examined in detail, Hall Johnson's *Run, Little Chillun* and *Swing Mikado*.

Finally, I would want to argue two things. First, groups who are appropriated or commodified or aestheticized stand to lose a great deal – they can be misrepresented, humiliated, dispossessed, and decimated – but they have also been able to manipulate the appropriators and create something we (and I mean that pronoun to be as inclusive as a culture can imagine) might treasure. Second, in our postmodern world, cultural borrowings and appropriations of all sorts are impossible to escape; no culture can be sure of being purely, of, by, and for. I don't believe it is possible to create a theatre "about, by, for, and near" any one particular group in the thirties or in postmodern America. Since I believe that American culture consists of always-changing cultures, mixing, overlapping, appropriating and appropriative, and therefore that no "subculture" remains pure for long, I think that a politics or critique of multiplicity that tries to deny cultural hybridization is futile, even undesirable. What is appropriate, who gets to properly represent cultural property, remains a contested arena, as contested as the idea of a single national American culture. It may be that the struggles over what is properly national, what must be included and excluded, will create the most vibrant American culture possible.

Acknowledgments

When it comes time to sit down and compose the acknowledgments, it is, I admit, with a certain surprise that I find myself not alone – which is how I have often felt as an academic – but richly accompanied. Indeed, where should an acknowledgment begin, where must it stop?

Certainly this book would not have been completed without institutional support from the Graves Foundation, the National Endowment for the Humanities, and most of all from Pomona College; from my chair, Thomas Pinney, who said to me early on in my career, "Do what interests you," from the various research committees over the years who never said no, and from the Pew Charitable Trusts, which funded, at Pomona, reading groups – course releases and conversation – indispensable gifts to me as I began to write.

Nor could I have framed this project without the archives. The National Archives were fundamental, but I was lucky in that three others had such wonderful curators who generously granted me permission to quote from their collections: James Hatch of the Hatch–Billops Collection, Esme Bahn at Howard University, and all the people at the George Mason University Federal Theatre Project Special Collections not only were courteous, they made the collections come alive, unlocked treasures, told me stories, and always brought me one more folder.

Thanks to all of my colleagues who read and listened to bits and pieces of my book. Early on, Henry Louis Gates, Jr., and Lorraine Brown wrote letters on my behalf; Richard Ohmann at the Wesleyan Humanities Center kindly invited me to participate as a senior fellow at a critical time in the process of writing this book; Michael Roth asked me the kinds of pointed questions he is famous for and was always encouraging and full of solid, friendly advice. Laura Kalman read a chapter in her guise as New Deal historian, and Gayle Greene read the

xvii

whole manuscript with her sharp editor's eye; Eric Sundquist, Barbara Melosh, and an anonymous reviewer at Cambridge pointed out ways to rethink questions at the final stage; and two research assistants, Belle Richmond and Shauna Mulvihill, helped me with library searches and notes.

Then there is the network of good and patient nonacademic friends who lived in New York and Washington, where I did most of my research: Pamela Wilson, Tom Rychman, Nancy Dittes, Paula Becker, Barry Brown, and especially Geoffrey Aronow and Melinda Halpert. These people put me up for extended periods of time, fed me, and made me feel, much of the time, that I was in a better place than home.

Finally, the circle shrinks to encompass those people for whom any acknowledgment would be insufficient: my writing group – Betsy Emerick, Betty Farrell, Joanna Worthley – who jump started me, allowed me to complain, consoled and cheered me on; Richard Millington, to whom I gladly ceded Hawthorne so long as we could still talk American, which we do to my immense benefit; Robert Dawidoff, who has provided me with examples of practical and theoretical liberation and insight and given me so much attention during my ten years in Claremont; Abbe Blum, who is my dearest friend and critical conscience; Ruthie and Eva King, my newest loves, and Davies King, who has surrounded me with his eccentric sense of the world, on and off the stage, who surprises and reassures me time after time that there is so much more to be acknowledged.

A portion of Chapter 3 first appeared as "The Cloudy History of *Big White Fog:* The Federal Theatre Project, 1938," *American Studies* 29.1 (Spring 1988): 5–28.

Introduction

Imagine that you enter a parlor. You come late. When you arrive, others have long preceded you, and they are engaged in a heated discussion, a discussion too heated for them to pause and tell you exactly what it is about. In fact, the discussion had already begun long before any of them got there, so that no one present is qualified to retrace for you all the steps that had gone before. You listen for a while, until you decide that you have caught the tenor of the argument; then you put in your oar. Someone answers; you answer him; another comes to your defense; another aligns himself against you, to either the embarrassment or gratification of your opponent, depending upon the quality of your ally's assistance. However, the discussion is interminable. The hour grows late, you must depart. And you do depart, with the discussion still vigorously in progress.   – Kenneth Burke[1]

I

In 1935, Congress mandated that under the auspices of the Works Progress Administration (WPA), four Arts Projects should be created so that unemployed writers, musicians, artists, and actors could do the work for which they had been trained. Although the money appropriated for the Arts Projects would be a very tiny portion of the WPA budget (less than 1 percent of the WPA allocation was spent on the Federal Theatre Project, i.e., out of $5 billion, $27 million were set aside for all of the arts), even this small amount was a controversial step for the U.S. government. Whereas before the thirties "the arts were considered elitist and as such undeserving of direct public support," the New Deal policy would claim that artists and the arts were an integral part of a democratic people and a democratic culture.[2] Desperate times seemed to demand radical measures: economic catastrophe made it politically possible for sympathetic people in the government to force Congress to act openly and directly as a producer of culture, to dispense it

1

freely so that rich and poor alike might enjoy an evening's entertain-ment.[3] In becoming a part of the WPA (later renamed Works Project when the emphasis on "progress" seemed politically dangerous), the directors of the Writers', Art, Music, and Theatre Projects hoped that such government support meant that the idea of American culture itself was changing. Federal art encompassed "high" and "low" forms, classi-cal music and jazz, Shakespeare and Shaw, social realism and minstrel shows.

Hallie Flanagan, the director of the FTP, went to work immediately once the WPA Arts Projects were funded. From the $6,784,036 she was given, she hired twelve thousand people.[4] Ninety percent of the appropriations were to be spent on wages and all but 10 percent of the personnel had to be culled from relief rolls. Although the Arts Projects were given a special allowance to hire 25 percent nonrelief personnel who could help them get started, this allowance was reduced to the intended 10 percent by 1936. The stated goal of the FTP was to take theatre professionals who were on relief and put them to work doing what they did best. Sometimes the FTP would retrain actors; ultimately, though, the idea was that actors from the FTP would be hired back by an increasingly strong private industry.[5] In addition, the FTP aimed to bring the theatre to the people by making the shows free to the public and by introducing theatre to localities outside urban centers.

The structure of the FTP was unwieldy, but then, after all, this was a government project. Under Flanagan there was a deputy national direc-tor who oversaw procedural and administrative questions and an assis-tant director who coordinated royalties and equipment. Then there were seven regional directors, who included the city directors of New York, Los Angeles, and Chicago and regional directors of the East, West, Midwest, and South. All ten directors met to organize a national plan, deciding on plays and policies every four months. In this way, Flanagan hoped to spread theatre far and wide. The National Service Bureau offered such services as the Play Service, in which scripts were submit-ted and classified, translated or edited; loan services for personnel and equipment; and research services, which included lectures and traveling exhibits. The special production units in New York included radio, information, and a children's theatre. Flanagan and Harry Hopkins, her boss and director of the WPA, agreed that the FTP should not compete with commercial theatre, and hence Flanagan stressed other sorts of theatre: marionette, dance, productions for high schools, and a caravan theatre. Different kinds of units existed in each region depending on the talent available and the local audience: a Spanish unit in Miami, Yiddish units in New York and Los Angeles, French and Italian units, a South-west unit in Los Angeles, as well as classical units, vaudeville, and a circus all in New York. The Community Drama Division played schools, settlement houses, and hospitals. The FTP covered the territory from North to South, in English and other languages for audiences who might never have afforded the price of a ticket. In doing so, the directors hoped to demonstrate how they believed art could work: to comfort, teach, entertain, and delight, to create communities and identify enemies, and to stimulate others to celebrate culture and analyze its failings.

Finally, there were the famous Negro units located in several cities as a way to put to work the many black professionals – including vaudevillians and musicians – who were on relief.[6] Flanagan set up a meeting in September 1935 with Rose McClendon, a well-respected black actress who had performed on Broadway, John Houseman, who had directed Virgil Thomson's *Four Saints and Three Acts,* and a group of eight other black artists to talk about the formation of a "negro theatre. All . . . enthusiastic."[7] Whether the initiative came from Flanagan or McClendon is unclear, but the mutual enthusiasm was there from the beginning. By October 1936, seventeen Negro units had been established: three in the South, Birmingham, Durham, and Okmulgee, Oklahoma, the latter two teaching units; three units in the Midwest, a drama unit and an "all-colored" minstrel unit in Chicago, and a musical revue unit in Peoria; in New York City, drama, choral, youth, operetta, and marionette units; units in Boston, New Jersey, and Connecticut; and on the West Coast, in Oakland, Los Angeles, and Seattle.[8] By January 1939, there were ten units: the Hartford unit with about twenty-five blacks were still putting on plays and making occasional tours around Connecticut; forty people were still employed on the Boston Negro unit; in addition, Newark, Philadelphia, Raleigh, North Carolina, Los Angeles, Seattle, New York, Chicago, and San Francisco still were in operation.[9] There were four projects in New York City alone: a unit at the Lafayette Theatre in Harlem, the Negro youth unit, African dance unit, and a vaudeville unit.

Flanagan was the most outspoken of all the directors in her belief that art should represent and reflect America in all its diversity, seemingly undaunted by U.S. theatre history, by the field already sown. She believed she could start anew, self-consciously cultivate a culture, to create it in order to identify it, to grow it in order to name it. The FTP came to be recognized almost immediately as the most politically engaged of all the projects. She applauded regional plays and historical pageants and instituted ethnic and language-based units, and her celebration of a localized America with differences in language, customs, and histories never seemed to conflict with her idea that she was sponsoring a uniquely national American culture. No one discounts the impressive accomplishments of the FTP. Between 1935 and 1939, the FTP helped to sustain theatrical folk in New York, Chicago, Los Angeles, and other major urban centers, presenting 830 major titles and countless other productions. Since the tickets were free or of a nominal charge and because theatres, at least early on, managed to exist beyond the confines of Broadway, the FTP brought shows to over 30 million people, many of whom had never been to the theatre before, seeming thereby to earn its nickname – the "people's theatre." Playwrights, directors, and scene designers who might have had to drop out of the profession altogether were able not only to survive but to experiment and perfect their art.

Yet any investigation of the New Deal Arts Projects quickly reveals the high hopes and frustrations, good intentions and inevitable limitations that attend institutions designed to nurture and create culture for the American people. Indeed, the very notion of a singular "people" becomes a problem when various peoples begin to speak. In this regard, the creation of the Negro units in sixteen cities has always been considered one of the more controversial acts of the FTP. The fact that the U.S. government was actively supporting minority theatre was so extraordinary that in the FTP's own press releases and in much of the history written about these projects, the emphasis has been, understandably, a celebration of just this act. Hallie Flanagan took much pride in the successes of the Negro units. Some of the best work, the most popular at the time and most memorable over time, was conceived and produced in these units, such works as the voodoo *Macbeth* at the Lafayette Theatre in Harlem and the *Swing Mikado* in Chicago. The FTP gave African American theatre professionals and amateurs new opportunities. Some for the first time gained technical training and joined theatre craft unions; writers wrote plays that departed from minstrel stereotypes; and directors chose Shaw and Shakespeare for Negro units, allowing actors a chance to play parts very different from the usual maid or field hand. By providing the opportunity for young actors to train and giving older actors roles to match their talents, the FTP helped foster an ongoing black theatre. Certainly a different set of people who had never been able to afford it or who did not live near the centers of culture were granted access to listen and look and sometimes create because of the institutions of the New Deal Arts Projects.

But one of the central problems that plagued the Negro units and the FTP (and by extension those who believed in the idea of a national culture itself) was that nobody *knew* who "that" Negro audience was; they couldn't even be sure a or any Negro audience would show up at the theatre. Similarly, nobody knew just who the Negro artist was. The idea of "a race" seemed to provide cultural planners, critics, bureaucrats, and politicians a singular and unified entity, a necessity for attempting to make political demands on behalf of a group of people, though it also meant ignoring many of the divisions within the Negro audience. From excerpts of audience surveys, it is clear that there were various tastes influenced by class, region, and education. In at least some of the plays written for the FTP's Negro units, differences of skin color, class, ideology, and nationality are central to the plots. When critics and bureaucrats generalized about race on the basis of what was "authentically" racial and ignored political differences and personal tastes, they often created fixed and single roles for individuals and groups, closing off rather than opening up the possibility for a transforming culture. Those who worked within the FTP's Negro units continually ran up against differences within African American culture, and yet the preconception of single racial interests was so established that actual differences were simply not seen, ignored, or assumed by progressives to be attributable to racism. The rhetoric of racial identity is so basic that it supercedes all other influences in the cultural analysis of the times. Everyone involved with making a theatre for blacks made assumptions about who that black audience was, but these assumptions were generated by political and aesthetic motives, by personal jealousies and ambitions, and by cultural beliefs so established that nothing could shake them. In fact, the problems of creating a national Negro theatre were similar to those involved in creating a national people's theatre. Although the FTP acknowledged the importance of regional and ethnic differences and accommodated varying tastes for entertainment from the classical to experimental to minstrelsy, too often the institution forgot about difference and appealed to Americans, the people, the Negro as if they were single identities.

The FTP constantly elided, as much from ignorance as from elitism, the differences in taste, cultural, and class allegiance within the Negro units, while some race leaders ignored differences in order to further political cohesion and therefore cultural recognition. It was also wishful thinking and somewhat disingenuous on the part of the FTP bureaucracy to believe that one could establish a theatre for others and not also exercise control over it. What sort of control and who would control it – how the Negro units could be "of, by, and for" themselves – were played out in practice in specific and not easily generalized or recognizably theorized ways.

II

African Americans had been the subject of an American conversation about the theatre that had been going on for years. One task for black intellectuals and artists in the first few decades of the twentieth century was how to begin to take part as subject, as critic, actor, director, playwright, and thereby change the course of the conversation and the course of theatre. Black music had always been at the center of popular American culture. Could African Americans turn to the theatre and begin to write new parts for themselves, ones that would be serious and central not just to popular but to formal American culture? Community theatre and black universities provided some alternatives for blacks in the teens and twenties. The FTP provided another opportunity to figure out new terminology, characters, plays, identities, and ways to create formal culture. Artists and bureaucrats would have to negotiate with audiences of various persuasions; they would have to figure out whether old plays should be rewritten or new ones composed, whether old actors should be trained anew or whether directors should adapt to old ways. They would have to negotiate with multiple interests and competing ideals.

From W. E. B. Du Bois's manifesto of 1926 in which he called for a theatre "of, by, for, and near" Negroes, to an administrator of the FTP, who wrote, "As you know, it is the desire of the Federal Theatre Project to establish the negro unit in the Lafayette Theatre in New York as a negro theatre for negroes, rather than as a Harlem attraction for downtown whites," attempts were made to define an audience by including some and excluding others.[10] Du Bois believed that only an alternative to the commercial theatre, wholly controlled by the community, would succeed in creating dramatic types different from the norm. Both he and Flanagan recognized the way Broadway had enticed the best and the brightest from the black community, and both hoped that a separate theatre, resolutely not commercial, would reverse the trend.

But a "separate" theatre meant something different for Du Bois and Flanagan. Du Bois's separate nationalism, Flanagan's American liberalism, and good old white racism all could be and were accommodated by the FTP's Negro units. Du Bois wanted a national race theatre for Negroes. The FTP wavered between the desire to promote an American theatre with an ethnic slant and an autonomous race theatre. It was not always clear how the FTP believed a separate ethnic theatre was related to American theatre or American culture. The organizational structure of the Negro units may have allowed for a certain amount of autonomy, but it was enforced by various forms of segregation. While on the one hand the FTP refused to let Negro units perform in theatres that segregated audiences, the Negro units seemed to ensure that black actors would not be integrated into any other FTP units. Rarely were blacks lent to white casts in other units, and there was always trouble when whites were imported to black shows. Maurice Clark, who directed the play *Haiti* in Harlem, tells the story of a white actress sent to him by the FTP casting pool who refused to act in the mixed cast because, she said, Negroes smelled differently to her. She was not given a role.[11]

Though segregated on stage, Negro productions were popular with mixed audiences. The FTP was never able to prevent white audiences – ("downtown" whites) – from traveling uptown to Harlem when a particular show seemed to appeal, nor were they discouraged from going. It should also be noted that black audiences in Chicago seemed to prefer to see Negro unit plays on the Loop in interracial company rather than in a high school in their community on the South Side of the city. White and black theatregoing communities were never culturally autonomous the way, for instance, the Yiddish theatre was at the turn of the century. There the difference in languages and the abrupt and relatively recent history of Jewish immigration from Eastern Europe allowed a separate Jewish theatre to flourish without the threat of appropriation and to take up issues of assimilation on their own terms, on their own ground, in their own theatres, in their own language. The Jewish immigrants used the theatre as a protected space to explore the experiences of being American without being caricatured by the dominant society, but blacks had no such protected theatrical space. The history of black performance has never been so segregated.

So much "black" theatre in the United States had been written by whites for whites in blackface that one of the larger questions governing this study is whether or under what circumstances Negroes could become "New" and independent through the cultural medium of the theatre. If it is true, as Michael Rogin argues, that the United States was built on the backs of the Indians (the West) and blacks (the city/popular culture), what will it take to stand up and be counted on their own?[12] I can understand both the desire on the part of that white bureaucrat to give black theatre over, let this be a theatre all their own, not an attraction for downtown whites, and Du Bois to want to take it over, let it be about us, by us, for us, and near us. But the "gift" was not without strings attached; cultures could not be so simply cut loose from each other. The white bureaucracy of the FTP never could relinquish its almost complete control, down to what plays would be produced, for how long, and in which theatres, and the most successful plays in the Negro units were heralded by both black and white press reviews and audiences.

I want to argue that those who wished to maintain a separate national Negro theatre and those who thought a place could be found for such a theatre within the auspices of an uplifting and noncommercial American theatre miscalculated the popular strengths of American culture and certainly the history of American theatre. What I find remarkable is how similar black and white intellectual critics of the theatre were in their hopes of using the theatre to educate and uplift the masses. Very often the black and white intellectual believed in the same principles of bourgeois culture: it should educate, uplift; it should be opposed to popular culture's pandering to entertaining and easy listening. One of the problems for certain cultural critics from the middle of the nineteenth century through the present, has to do with what they feel to be a disappointing level of taste in popular audiences. In the twenties and thirties, some black and white middle-class critics tried to impose certain critical standards by policing not only the canon but the way people should behave in public spaces like the theatre. Often the middle-class critic and bureaucrat – black and white – who had everything to do with the Negro units and the FTP shared a desire to attract "the people" to the theatre and a disdain for them at the same time. They hoped to embed a thirst for uplifting culture in the hearts of the masses and so make artistic culture (and thereby everyday life) more sustaining, a crucial piece of American life. The mistake many of the intellectuals made lay in their unwillingness to understand the urban mass audience's language of desire. Too many intellectuals, black and white, thoroughly disdained commercial culture, but it would not go away, and indeed it won over most of the nation. The FTP too often missed its chance to take seriously the pleasures popular culture gave. But liberal and leftist participants in the FTP and Negro units were reacting against popular theatre that in the United States had been deeply racist. The question was how to pay homage to the popular and not repeat its racist forms and assumptions.

Black entertainers and blackface performance mark the national American difference. Any national American theatre would have to include black entertainers and at the same time incorporate popular forms, paying attention to the ways "race" has been theatrically portrayed. A national Negro theatre could not afford to exclude white audiences if it hoped to build a strong racial theatre, but it too would have to redirect the racism embodied in popular theatre. New Deal liberalism gave African Americans some greater cultural space to experiment in, but they were only able to experiment up to a point. Certain topics were taboo for some; Flanagan worried about portraying miscegenation and violence on stage, and some black middle-class professionals were worried about antagonizing a white audience, offending a middle-class black audience, and boring both. The experimentation was hedged in by concerns for a mixed racial audience and by, in some quarters, dismissal of popular theatre, in other quarters, fear of political theatre.

The choice between cultural separation and integration continue to structure the way we think about American culture. In literary criticism a kind of separatism has been advanced under the name of "vernacular criticism" most eloquently argued by Henry Louis Gates, Jr. Gates distances himself from Du Bois's moralizing tone, recognizing the ways in which Du Bois sacrificed form for content. Nevertheless, Gates follows Du Bois's strategy for empowerment by emphasizing a separate and unique African American tradition.[13] Vernacular criticism is the latest incarnation of cultural separation talk, a strategy to empower difference. Of course, such believers in separate traditions must be firm policers of new canons, deciding what is appropriately included and excluded. It is easy to see the way forms of separatism may empower a people. In Michael Awkward's view, black studies has been founded on the principle of difference, and to attack difference is to attack a whole intellectual and political enterprise of empowerment.[14] But difference can easily shade over into a kind of racial chauvinism. Paul Gilroy has written about the "progression from vulgar to cultural racism," from "crude biologism" to nationalism. As a justification of apartheid,

> culture is conceived along ethnically absolute lines, not as something intrinsically fluid, changing, unstable, and dynamic, but as a fixed property of social groups rather than a relational field in which they encounter one another and live out social, historical relationships. When culture is brought into contact with race it is transformed into a pseudobiological property of communal life.[15]

Cultural separatism thus can be used to excuse racism or to rationalize it. On the basis of national cultures, an "authentic" Englishman might consider someone from a former colony now living in England "inauthentically" English. A dominant group in the United States may use the same argument to purify its shores, to make sure everyone learns English in schools and not some other "secondary" language. I'd like to think that there is a way out of such a narrow formulation of culture as separation or integration. Such an either – or opposition makes any third act impossible, unimaginable; it freezes depictions of culture.

I want to argue for an idea of American culture that relies more on Cornel West's and Paul Gilroy's notion of "hybridization." Cornel West believes that it is important to "construct more multi-valent and multi-dimensional responses that articulate the complexity and diversity of Black practices in the modern/postmodern world." In the modern world of the thirties and the postmodern world of the nineties, whiteness and blackness depend on notions of the other, and as West argues, "race," "ethnicity," and "nationality" are all "profoundly hybrid."[16] Perhaps the choices one makes as critic, artist, or audience may be broadened to allow for a greater fluidity and a transgressive culture. To be separate denies the possibility of creative influence; to assimilate risks losing precious differences. In the critique of essentialism and authenticity, Gates knows that the "essential" black subject is a constructed entity, though no less real in its political and cultural effects. The differences between black subjects and the critique against the ideology of race itself have blown apart that single black subject some assumed to exist in the thirties and some continue to believe exists today. In the proliferation of difference, might not cultural, even racial identity be seen as always in the process of borrowing, adopting, adapting, appropriating, changing?

The desire for a separate Negro theatre does not necessarily entail racial essentialism, but rather a strategic desire to build institutions for particular communities where people could be nurtured and taught certain skills. One understands all of the historical reasons why some wanted to nurture a separate cultural theatre for African Americans, to attempt to achieve some political and cultural autonomy. Trying to create a space for a separate Negro theatre was a noble aim of the FTP and of certain black critics, given the historical racism and lack of opportunity for black performers, directors, and technicians in American theatre. But in the end, for either a Negro or an American national theatre to succeed, the institution would have to include rather than exclude, to acknowledge in this postcolonial, postmodern world that the African in the United States has been so intertwined with and appropriated, mirrored, and defined by what is distinctively American that to separate theatrical traditions cannot be managed. Some may find that a tragedy, and certainly there are painful and tragic instances of powerful appropriations of a people's cultural traditions. But culture dynamically operates back and forth against such interests. To fix the boundaries around only what is distinctive misses all of the ways – for good and for bad – the American culture has been constituted by crossovers of all sorts.

III

Achieving some sort of separate status motivated both FTP officials and those involved in the Negro units. So did an equally important cultural belief: that they could discriminate between authentic and inauthentic voices, that there was an authentic culture free from the debasement of commercial influences, free of provincialism, free of the victimization of history. Discriminating between the authentic and inauthentic becomes the central task of a critic and an audience when judging a cultural performance. A basic assumption for those who promoted "the people's culture" within the Federal Arts Projects was that not only do the people have a right to have their stories told, but their stories are their own to tell. The essentialism of democratic representation goes something like this: "Since this is who I am, I must know how I am feeling. And who can tell me differently?" "Let blacks have their own theatre so they can tell their story their own way, more authentically than Gershwin's *Porgy and Bess*." What both white and black critics agreed on and what the FTP hoped to produce was a new group of African American playwrights who by virtue of their race could claim their art was authentically, essentially Negro. The challenge to black playwrights did not, all of a sudden, arise in 1935. Throughout the twenties, during the Harlem Renaissance, black artists had been invited to speak in their own voices. Eugene O'Neill, who had achieved a kind of notoriety and fame for his "race" plays, *Emperor Jones* and *All God's Chillun Got Wings,* published a piece in 1925 in the socialist Negro journal the *Messenger*. In it he summed up the belief that only Negroes could tell their own story truly, authentically:

> I have read a good number of plays written by Negroes and they were always *bad* plays – badly written, conceived, constructed – without the slightest trace of true feeling for drama – *unoriginal* – and, *what revolted me the most, bad imitations in method and thought of conventional white plays!*
>
> If I have one thing to say – (and I grant that "I" is a presumption) – to Negroes who work, or have the ambition to work, in any field of artistic expression, it is this: Be yourselves! Don't reach out for *our* stuff which *we* call good! Make *your stuff* and *your good!* You have within your race an opportunity – and a shining goal! – for new forms, new significance. Every white who has sense ought to envy you! *We* look around with accustomed eyes at somewhat jaded landscapes – at least too familiar – while to *you* life ought to be as green – and as deep – as the sea! There ought to be a Negro play written by a Negro that no white could ever have conceived or executed. By this I don't mean greater – because all art is equally great – but *yours, your own,* an expression of what is deep in you, *is* you, *by* you!!
>
> If the above sounds rather strong – and impertinent! – why I

have no excuses except that I appreciate the Negro too well ever
to want him to be white – in the arts which have no "line" of
here or there – and I do urge him to dig within and not
without![17]

As the sociologist and great promoter of the Harlem Renaissance
Charles Johnson wrote, "An artist can express best the life which he
knows and in that life which is the Negroes', any Negro artist has the
advantage."[18] Other famous and influential writers like W. E. B. Du
Bois and Pearl Buck would agree. Certainly Flanagan believed that her
mission was to enable true stories to be told.[19] It was a common belief,
and common sense to believe it, that blacks will tell their story differently from whites and that historical differences will translate into artistic differences. But there are also contradictions in this common-sense
plea for new voices, based on racial differences. O'Neill wants race to
matter and not to matter, for a great black play can only be written by
an authentic black man, but great art knows no color line. No standard
except racialism can calibrate authenticity, yet greatness should transcend such lines. If all black writers could be granted essential authenticity in writing their own story, the problem still remained about judging
the greatness and even the authenticity of the individual portrayal.

The connection between democratic essentialism and authenticity,
between authenticity and direct representation, is clear: if you let a
group of people, in this case, black people, tell it their way, then they
will produce the authentic, honest, true history, and America will be
better for it. But the notion of "the people" must be continually tested
and contested. Stuart Hall and David Held have written about the
inevitable tension in the Left's position on

> citizenship, since it both requires and can be threatened by the
> state. One tendency of the Left has been to resolve or bypass
> this difficulty by, so to speak, dissolving the whole question
> into that of democracy itself. The extension of popular democ-
> racy, it is thought, will resolve all these knotty problems. Hence
> the Left's advocacy of collective decision-making and demo-
> cratic participation as a resolution to all the problems of citi-
> zenship.

But as Hall and Held ask:

> Will the fact that we are all members of the great collective
> democratic subject – "the people" – provide a guarantee of the
> rights and liberties of the individual citizen? Not necessarily.
> "The people" is, after all, also a discursive figure, a rhetorical
> device, a mode of address. It is open to constant negotiation,

> contestation, and redefinition. It represents as a "unity" what
> are in fact a diversity of different positions and interests. . . .
> "The people" has also functioned so as to silence or marginalize
> the conflicts of interests which it claims to represent.[20]

This study concentrates on the conflicts of interests between peoples and within a people that have been suppressed in some version of the WPA Arts Projects' history.

New Dealers like Harry Hopkins and Hallie Flanagan believed that in allowing the people to speak "for themselves," they were tapping into a central artery of America. People in the FTP administration, white and black, believed from the beginning to the end that the guidebooks, documentary living newspapers, photographs, and collections of folk songs expressed the voice of the people, and when they were also by the people, those representations embodied the true America. In his book *Documentary Expression and Thirties America,* William Stott argues that Federal Arts Project artists experienced "American Stuff" (the title of one Federal Writers' Project book) first hand, and therefore they were able to see things more honestly: "The arts projects kept the revolution honest: in touch with real facts about America rather than merely sentimental myths, and in touch with literally tens of millions of Americans."[21] This sentence encapsulates, I think, the animating belief of the Federal Arts Projects: that "real facts" came to be represented because the artists on the projects were "in touch" with millions of people. But there may be an illogical leap from asserting that everyone can and should represent themselves to arguing that when they do so they are necessarily closer to the truth, in touch with real facts, and can avoid sentimental myths. Indeed, politics may *depend* on sentimental myths: there are different stories you have to tell people to get them to do things. The rhetoric of authenticity can be honored as a strategy of political and social survival, as a politically potent story. People certainly believed in it and it became a judgment, a way of recognizing what was politically good and what wasn't, a New Negro or an Uncle Tom. It inevitably included some people in the conversation and excluded others – or in Hall's and Held's language, silenced and marginalized the conflicts of interests it claimed to represent.

The idea of a collective identity seems to carry within it both a feeling of authenticity in memoirs and oral interviews about the thirties and a nostalgia for such a time and such a touch. One official of the FTP reminisces:

> But these were the things that bound us together, this constant – we lived in a world that was falling apart – and we were
> constantly ourselves under the pressure of not knowing whether

next year we would have a project or whether Congress would vote you funds or whatever it was.[22]

"Bound . . . together," "in touch," "real facts" – how metaphorical, how literal should we take these statements to be? Can we know who, specifically, was "in touch" with whom? Many people testify that they saw audiences responding to performances by banging their feet on the floor; they were touched and voted with their feet to say so. This kind of rhetoric, so prevalent in writings of the period as well as in memoirs written much later, seems clearly to reinforce the idea that some unified central communication existed between the artists and the American people. But when you look at individual case histories, at individuals within "the people," the ways in which they felt themselves to be touched are not always so literally a happy transaction. If some were bound together, others found themselves unwillingly bound to roles and conceptions they could not escape. While some remember the FTP as a time of people coming together and forming communities, often the stories they or others tell reveal in the details that the communities were a fractious bunch of separate interests.

For black race leaders, it was clearly a political necessity to present their people as unified with singular needs. Without organizing around the idea of a single community, African American leaders could not expect to pressure the WPA or any other government organization for a fair share of the goods. And partly due to prejudice and partly due to ignorance born out of prejudice, hegemonic culture needed to believe that there was only one body, without difference, "the Negro." The Negro was certainly easier to deal with if singular. But when a Negro stood up to represent all the others, invariably some of the others claimed they were being *mis*represented. This happens again and again. W. E. B. Du Bois's idea that "the talented tenth" (i.e., people like himself) best represent the interests of his people may not represent fully the desires of those he considered untalented and uncultured. One of the problems with the essentialist position – only the author can tell you what it means to be a certain way – is that when one moves from representing only oneself to representing a group, that is, when one tries to talk as a representative of the people or of one's "own" people, then one runs up against conflicting voices and conflicting ideas about what *is* authentic. When the focus is not on the political process in which it can at least be determined how many voted but on the cultural realm, then the issue of who legitimately represents whom is more doubtful. Who or what decides that representation is fair, accurate, inclusive, authentic?

Not only in the records of the FTP, but in the cultural debates about authentic black culture by black critics in black journals, one often sees a conflict between the democratic notion that everyone should tell their own stories and the elitist despair with the story heard. Du Bois's power to represent his people never lay in the idea that he was representing their present desires; he believed he should represent their need to be uplifted and transformed. But when audiences (or actors) decide to vote with their feet for a play that Du Bois would hold worthless, what then? Were audiences in Harlem laughing at the figure of the Emperor Jones because they weren't properly acculturated or because they found the Emperor's clothes irrelevant and silly? The project constantly shifted between representing a democratic essentialist notion that the "people" should decide and efforts to tell the people what they should think.

The discourse of authenticity regarding African American culture in some ways remained constant and in other ways changed from the twenties to the thirties. The vogue of the "primitive" Negro, which was articulated and promoted by white culture throughout the Harlem Renaissance of the twenties and which lasted into the thirties and beyond, connected the notion of human authenticity with the idea of the primitive. African Americans were said to be more spiritual, more sensual, more natural, more "in touch" with nature, and therefore more authentically human. Black artists sometimes self-consciously cultivated "primitive" rhythms and themes because white patrons made it worth their while to do so and sometimes because they believed that their artistic power was indeed generated from either the "African" tradition or more commonly the "folk" tradition of African Americans. Black critics theorized too about the technicalities of primitivism, and some championed folk arts in the twenties while others scorned them for their provinciality. But by the thirties, many black and white critics located authenticity no longer in the primitive but in the style of social realism.

The value of "authenticity," however, was never in question, only what, in any particular instance, merited the term. It still today retains its meaning as a commercial sign of value (e.g., that which is authentic is worth more in museums) as well as a moral sign (that which is inauthentic is scorned as debased).[23] It clearly had its political place, especially in the case of African Americans who were struggling to counter what they considered harmful *in*authentic stereotypes about their people. Authenticity was both a way for black race leaders to rally around a new, more radical identity in the twenties and thirties and to organize around a resistance politics against the inauthentic old stereotype. Black cultural critics depended on notions of authenticity and appropriation in their understanding of the way theatre represented or failed to represent black culture as they saw it. Even in writing about

the dramatic performance, people continued to appeal to authentic performances, authentic writers. But they often disagreed about just where
the authentic voice of "their people" was located. Black and white critics
and artists continued to feel they could represent an unproblematic
collective of black identity but continually came up against the rumbling
dissonance from other artists as well as within audiences. Cultural politics was carried on in the struggle to win over "the people" – black and
white – to various individual authentic visions of "the true New
Negro."

Bringing together a theoretical discussion about the claims of authenticity with a historical account and a personal story, I critique the op-
pressive power authenticity has by privileging one voice over another,
but I also want to recognize the political force it has had to empower the
disempowered, to rally around a new type. So while today the concept
of authenticity is almost entirely discredited by some intellectuals who
believe it is a constructed category, not a universal given, historically –
in the claim of the New Deal Arts Projects that "the people" could
speak more authentically and so could represent themselves better than
anyone else and again in the claims of the black arts movement of the
sixties – the formative power of authenticity was and remains enormous
and cannot be denied. It would be historically anachronistic to suggest
that the critics from the twenties and thirties really did not believe in
authenticity but only employed it as a strategy. Since the critics, reviewers, and audiences I have investigated all trust the category, I continue
to invoke authenticity as a political, aesthetic, and cultural category,
preferring it to "discourse," or "aura," or "sentiment," although I hope
to show what is repressed in the name of authenticity as well as to show
its value.

IV

To know what seems new is easy: it is less easy to know
how to evaluate and determine that a particular cultural form is truly
alternative, truly oppositional, assuming that opposition can exist without being subsumed into the hegemonic. This book looks at the bases
by which people judged what was most representative of that entity,
"the New Negro," and what sort of New Negro art would signify a
significant break with tradition. Some people praised a particular Negro
production as progressive while others criticized it as already co-opted.
The voodoo *Macbeth,* produced by the Negro unit in Harlem, was
condemned as a capitulation to stereotypes, the primitive black men
superstitious and afraid, and praised for the chance it offered black

men and women to perform Shakespeare. Aesthetic judgment always depended on the kind of power one hoped to bestow or deny "the Negro." To investigate what forms the stories take, how groups try to justify or consolidate their power, argue for a story's progressive nature and against other stories, groups, and forms of power is to ask questions about rhetoric as well as about the social constitution of power. Richard Wright thought the Negro unit in Chicago could foster a revolutionary cultural theatre. But he was to be deeply disappointed when the troupe refused to perform a Paul Green play about a southern chain gang because they felt it wasn't properly entertaining. Wright's condemnation of the unit's actors as stupid, victims of racism and of popular culture's demand that they conform to vaudeville's form, did not take into account that his idea of what constituted progressivism simply may not have fit the particular circumstances of the black troupe in urban Chicago.[24] The desire to "entertain," usually condemned as Uncle Tom behavior, victimization, co-optation, in this case, may have been an expression of something oppositional: these were actors doing a job, taking pride in what they did best (or what people paid them for) – to entertain. Actors and playwrights sometimes accommodated black stereotypes and continued to play the old Negro, resisting what may have seemed not only elitist but inartistic notions of uplift and propaganda, and thus rejecting the very sense of opposition intellectuals, artists, and critics hoped to promote.

Some critics are not as optimistic about the possibility of making a clear break with hegemonic forces. In *Criticism and Social Change,* Frank Lentricchia puts the case bleakly:

> Our identities are very nearly hopelessly complicated (beyond self-conscious control) by a hegemonic process that would enroll us in a range of corporate identities, some concentric, others in conflict. The results of such complicating and proliferating coordinations and corporations of identity is to clog and solidify identity to the point where change of the radical sort is almost unimaginable.[25]

Consensual histories show how hegemonic structures have been able to defuse, subvert, or negate any form of revolutionary change. Certainly one story of the New Deal traces the ways Roosevelt's rhetoric, as much as his policies, operated as a safety valve, acting to subvert more radical changes. By making the dispossessed feel that they were being cared about, Roosevelt secured their allegiance to a capitalist system that had virtually starved them. Though I agree that instances of "radical rupture" in cultures may be hard to imagine, I do not believe they are entirely unimaginable. Surely progressive change may occur throughout history. Kenneth Burke locates such changes in the "stealing back and forth of symbols," in the way, for instance, the concept of "rights" and "freedom" have been appropriated by one class or one group after another in order to grasp their share of power.[26] I think this stealing back and forth of symbols occurs throughout the New Deal's Federal Arts Projects and particularly in the representation of race. Here a dispossessed people, African Americans, were given some opportunities to define their concept of freedom – artistic and political. There was no radical rupture in theatrical representation, certainly not in the reception of blacks on stage at this time; the short-lived four-year history of the FTP was part of a much longer attempt by blacks to negotiate a greater freedom of expression on that American stage that had been so severely marked by racist assumptions. But the New Deal provided some greater measure of freedom for African American artists and, thus, I would argue, a measure of progressive change.

Raymond Williams has argued that in the world of advanced capitalism, when the means of production and reception have become thoroughly mass-produced and mass-marketed, when everything has become a commodity, it is almost impossible to find pockets of culture that are not dominated by the hegemonic.[27] He asserts that there are acts that significantly break with the dominant, that even though they may "*in part* be neutralized, reduced, or incorporated," they still retain an "active" element, "independent and original." Williams continues his remarks about the kind of history a cultural critic might write by noting that we will be better able to discern where those breaks in culture occur "if we develop modes of analysis which instead of reducing works to finished products, and activities to fixed positions, are capable of discerning, in good faith, the finite but significant openness of many actual initiatives and contributions." Williams also emphasizes the way Gramsci's theory of the hegemonic allows for moments of resistance as well as domination by consent, insisting that the hegemonic is made up of *both* domination and resistance. Hegemony "does not just passively exist as a form of dominance. It has continually to be renewed, recreated, defended, and modified. It is also continually resisted, limited, altered, challenged by pressures not at all its own."[28] It is, I hope, with good faith that I look at specific moments, "actual initiatives," in order to question and open up what is so often "fixed" and "finite" about cultural positions. May not an investigation of the particular make room for a critic to practice oppositional cultural criticism? Further, may not opposition sometimes lie even in the most co-opted of forms: in a desire to "entertain"? When Williams speaks of the oppositional, he means social movements and social formations, but I have shifted from an investigation of the whole – the FTP, the Negro units – to the particular – a particular play, a particular director – to demonstrate that opposition as well as "actual initiatives and contributions" can come in unexpected ways, not always conforming to neat political positions or to broader social movements.

The FTP and Negro unit story has been told most often in two modes: the story of failure and the story of celebration. The few histories written about the Federal Arts Projects celebrate discrete aspects of the organizations, the ways in which groups who had never been supported were encouraged to produce art. And these histories always analyze the reasons for the failure of the whole: the lack of a tradition in the United States of public support for the arts; the contradiction built into a relief program for the arts in which the standard of artistic quality might be superseded by economic need; the conflict of interest between a government acting as a cultural producer and one acting to protect its national interests. I don't dwell on the institutional failures of the FTP, partly because the reasons for them have been analyzed thoroughly by others. As for the Negro units, to speak about failure, as Houston Baker has argued, makes failure come to seem inevitable and thus closes off other ways of seeing or analyzing.[29] Celebratory rhetoric can have the same effect, of course. The FTP certainly issued a lot of press releases on its own behalf and on behalf of the Negro units praising its own highmindedness. I respect and admire the impulse to try to make a culture more sustaining, inclusive, pluralistic, and more liberating. But it should come as no surprise to the student of cultural history that liberation is never complete or without costs.

To argue as I do that neither the FTP nor the Negro units were wholly autonomous cultural entities but deeply circumscribed by history, tradition, and the dominant hegemony does not mean that I do not wish to recognize the innovation found there or honor certain strategies for change. But if framing a problem by failure makes failure inevitable, celebrating a movement doesn't inevitably ensure its success. In shifting the focus away from failure or celebration, I want to emphasize the struggles and contestations, both inter- and intraracial, that mark this cultural movement. I am interested in the complications and contradictions of this particular cultural project, the attempt on the one hand to allow for pluralism and diversity but also to insist on the universalism of difference, to create something separate and call it American. I want to suggest that it may be more fruitful to look beyond the discourse of either failure or celebration to contradiction and cultural struggle for it may be here that the seeds for a new strain of culture might grow, new ways of seeing and new cultural habits.

Like Houston Baker, I am interested in the ways black intellectuals attempted to nurture a national culture based on race. I too want to "revise" the stories of the past, but while Baker has in his sights the "distinctive" practices of "black expressive culture and criticism," I want to juxtapose that black culture and criticism with hegemonic culture in order not only to refigure the boundaries of what lies within the Harlem Renaissance or the Negro units of the FTP, but to show how the boundaries of a national Negro and a national American culture are fluid, always changing, and always transformative.[30]

The motivating purpose of recording this story has been to give voice to those voices in a critical context, one that places their contradictory and contestatory voices back to back to give them further hearing. I also believe that at least one way to think about our national identity is to focus on our interracial, different theatrical cultural selves. In tracing the ways different traditions were co-opted or, more benignly, learned from one another, it is possible to see how communities defined themselves against others and within themselves and sometimes tried to cover over divisions. I write a history of American culture that juxtaposes voices as a way to begin a conversation among white and black critics, artists, administrators, and audiences, showing the way they have been overhearing each other, repeating with a difference, plagiarizing, struggling to be original, ignoring, appropriating, denigrating, revering that "other," which is sometimes the voice of those in power, sometimes that of those who are not, always trying to locate the authentic conversation going on in the far corner, sometimes in the center of the room. The conversation, like this history, is never finished, but goes on, mishearing, borrowing, repeating what was never said, making room for other voices. If we can listen to other voices, we may hear our own with a saving difference; our own might change in response, to create, what seems, for the moment, something truer.

1

A New Deal (or Not)
for Culture

In an age demanding an image – or a myth or symbol – did the social and
political movements provide one effective enough?   – Warren Susman[1]

Most historians of the New Deal pose the same questions. Was
it a New Deal or just a fancy reshuffling of the deck? Was it a revolution
or a last-ditch defense against revolution? Was it a new dream or the
same old dream dressed up in clothes that masked its true nature? Did
the New Deal break with the past to include new originary forces or did
it reinforce traditional moments? What part was truly new, who benefited, who was left out? Reformation, transformation, revolution, or
preservation – which is it to be? The New Deal sometimes provided
images and symbols, programs and policies that reformed, even transformed culture, but at other moments preserved old ways of seeing. In
focusing on the very particular case of African American participation in
one very small part of the New Deal, I hope to show how ideology,
institutions, and old and new ways of seeing constantly interacted,
limiting choices *and* making change possible. In part, liberal rhetoric
made possible Negro participation in the New Deal, and in return, that
participation invigorated and challenged New Deal rhetoric, exposing
its practical limits.

In this chapter, I set forth some of the rhetoric of inclusion that
helped spawn the creation of the WPA, headed by Harry Hopkins,
and especially the Federal Theatre Project, directed by Hallie Flanagan,
focusing on Hopkins's ideas of social work and cultural work and on
Flanagan's belief that a noncommercial "people's theatre" could create a
new sort of cultural politics for all Americans. This was the promise of
the New Deal's Art Projects: that it meant to include the forgotten
workers, the artists. The Arts Projects were designed to serve *all* the

21

people, to reach out especially to those who had been excluded by the commercial arts, because of expense or location or disinterest. Not for the elite and not an elitist luxury, New Deal art should appeal to the masses as a necessary part of their lives. Many black and white intellectuals connected to the theatre believed that, at the very least, theatre should provoke discussion and debate about current policies and social conditions. But very often, black and white cultural workers found themselves at odds with the people's taste for popular forms. Certain cultural workers believed they could produce an appetite in the people for a politically engaged or experimental theatre on an everyday basis if given a space protected from commercialism. The New Deal provided them with that space and a short period of time to create new cultural desires, a formidable task indeed.

The inclusion of African Americans in the FTP would be one gauge to how well the New Deal lived up to its promise of inclusion in practice. Struggles for inclusion marked the FTP and especially the Negro units, where the cultural politics seemed so contradictory. Separate Negro units were largely directed by whites and still dependent on white reviewers and white audiences for popular success. The Negro units would feel particular pressure from certain whites and blacks to continue to provide popular entertainment and from others to become a national race theatre. No other ethnic group in the FTP had this range of purpose. In examining New Deal rhetoric of inclusion – heady, excitable stuff – I want to be alert to some of its contradictions in its relation to the practical institutional requirements of the WPA, and in relation to customs, prejudices, and deeply held beliefs about "the people." These contradictions will inform the various conflicting expectations for the Negro units as a theatrical experiment in cultural change.

I

If liberalism has been scorned recently by conservatives, rejected by some leftists, even avoided by ideologues of the middle, in part for its caution and compromises and sometimes for its championship of the principle of inclusion, New Deal liberalism has been on trial for all of these things since its heyday in the thirties. Roosevelt's liberalism was notoriously vague. Arthur Schlesinger describes Roosevelt as a man without clear ideas except a desire to rescue public policy from the "debasing consequences of business domination," a belief in the strength of democracy to adapt to historical circumstance and faith that the "forgotten man" must be taken care of in any just and decent society.[2]

This desire to include those who have been "forgotten," to represent *all* Americans, no matter how poor or how unskilled, fueled Roosevelt's Democratic party and inspired Harry Hopkins and Hallie Flanagan in their attempt to provide work and culture for the greater American public.

Precisely on this issue of inclusion have historians judged the New Deal's promise. The New Left historians of the sixties argue that the New Deal cannot be said to have helped those who most needed a new deal, the poorest unskilled workers, sharecroppers, servants. Even supporters of Roosevelt's policies agree with radical historians that the New Deal did not change the "fundamentals. Social power and wealth were basically in the same hands at the end of the New Deal as they had been at the beginning."[3] Who or what was to blame?

New Left historians sometimes blame the rhetoric of liberalism, which "seduces" people into thinking liberal politics was designed to help them. Certainly a majority of African American voters thought they were being offered a better deal, thus switching allegiance from the Republican party of Lincoln to the Democratic party of Roosevelt.[4] Barton Bernstein writes, "Perhaps this is one of the crueller ironies of liberal politics, that the marginal men trapped in hopelessness were seduced by rhetoric, by the style and movement, by the symbolism of efforts seldom reaching beyond words."[5] Of course, this wouldn't be the first or the last time marginal men (and women) would be seduced by rhetoric, and we also know that it wasn't only the marginal who were seduced, either here in America or abroad during the thirties. Another historian of the New Deal, Otis Graham, counters that powerful institutions rather than ideology made radical change impossible. Graham's insistence on the obduracy of institutions corrects some of the imbalance created by emphasizing the faults of liberal ideology. He goes on to argue that much radical history on the New Deal has not "conclusively defined how much more was possible and where lies the responsibility for the remarkable persistence of the old habits and social arrangements."[6]

Have the New Left historians proved that there is something particularly and especially devious about *liberal* political rhetoric? I happen to think not, although certain contradictions inherent in liberalism plagued Hopkins and Flanagan as they attempted to create a more inclusive culture. First, to include blacks and others previously marginalized did not necessarily mean that the way others thought about them would change. Second, quite often the rhetoric of inclusion or "giving" opportunities to others did not take into account history, that which was already there. Flanagan records what Hopkins told her just before he

made the announcement of her appointment and the establishment of
the FTP:

> Mr. Hopkins talked about everything – about engineering,
> about the building of airports, about the cities and countryside
> through which we were passing; but no matter what we started
> to talk about, it ended up with what was at that time the core
> and center of his thinking – the relationship of government to
> the individual. Hadn't our government always acknowledged
> direct responsibility to the people? Hadn't it given away the
> national domain in free land to veterans and other settlers?
> Hadn't it given away vast lands to railroad companies to help
> them build their systems? . . .
>
> The new work program, Mr. Hopkins believed, would ac-
> complish these same ends by giving of the nation's resources in
> wages to the unemployed, in return for which they would help
> build and improve America.[7]

The rhetoric of "giving" runs throughout the New Deal philosophy.
This New Deal rhetoric has the characteristic charm and elitism that
marks the administration's belief in "Progress." Hopkins believed that
the government had freely given land away, but didn't recognize that it
had been taken from Native Americans. Hopkins never worried about
the sins of appropriation, of historical theft. It is unclear how much
Flanagan knew about the history of blacks in American theatre – their
centrality and their appropriation and their attempts to create a separate
tradition. Although both Hopkins and Flanagan embraced the way politics and culture became overtly intertwined in the WPA Arts Projects,
they underestimated the deep suspicion such a marriage would generate.
Flanagan believed that art had to be political, by which she meant
current, local, *interested,* and part of people's everyday life. But such
artwork might be considered by some to be too particular, too local,
too partisan to be "great" or "universal."

So often the principle of inclusion overlooked history and the divisions within groups of people. In the excitement of creating new institutions like the WPA and the Arts Projects, liberals innocently, naively, or
hopefully ignored the uneasy relationship between politics and culture.
Warren Susman has tried to question the popular idea of the thirties as a
decade committed to ideological struggles:

> Ideology may indeed have been important in the Thirties, but
> many of the most brilliant and long-lasting contributions
> to political analysis written in the period were distinctly anti-
> ideological. . . . Rather, what appears to have been the stunning

weakness of the decade was that innocence *replaced* all ideological sense, when *both* may in fact be essential."[8]

It may have been America's peculiar innocence to think that everyone could be included satisfactorily and that any one institution could represent all of the people happily without serious contention. It may also be that very innocence that helped include some people who hadn't been included before and yet made other sorts of representation impossible.

Throughout the course of American history, one of the test cases for fundamental change has been both political and social policies, habits, and arrangements toward African Americans. Arthur Schlesinger argued that when Roosevelt began in 1934 to appeal to groups of people outside the traditional Democratic party – immigrants, labor, intellectuals – the inclusion of the Negro "struck vitally at the conception" of the party, constituting the "most dramatic and risky innovation in the New Deal design."[9] In a famous speech Harold Ickes gave to the Baltimore chapter of the National Association for the Advancement of Colored People (NAACP), he said: "I am convinced that the liberal-minded and far-seeing among us will eventually realize that, as a people, we can be no happier or stronger than our most miserable and weakest group."[10] Although Ickes acknowledged that "the prejudices that have been fostered and built up for 60 years cannot be done away with over night," he believed that the New Deal provided the "greatest advance since the Civil War toward assuring the Negro that degree of justice to which he is entitled."[11]

Black critics of the government at the time protested the inequities of the system a good deal more strongly than Ickes did, believing that their people deserved a bigger portion of the New Deal than they were getting. Historians have agreed that inequities in hiring and salary persisted against African Americans throughout the entire New Deal. The resistance to seeing, much less giving up, prejudicial practices was fierce and deep set, not only in the South, but among the most progressive liberals who inhabited the most progressive parts of the New Deal, even by those who ran the Arts Projects. The stereotype of the Negro as an untutored but natural entertainer made countertypes seem odd and risky, not artful but political, not quite American. To include a new type of Negro, artful *and* political and still recognizably American, would be one of the tests of the New Deal cultural experiment.

II

The WPA's Arts Projects came into being at the height of Roosevelt's popularity. But the WPA and especially the Arts Projects were always viewed with suspicion, as not quite American. Even at the moment of Roosevelt's greatest political success, his party's overwhelming victory in 1934, when the Republican presence in Congress was weaker than at any time since the Civil War, and in spite of the urban mass support for Roosevelt's national Democratic coalition and the ideology attached to the word "liberal" – which according to Raymond Moley came to describe the enlargement of power of the federal government into welfare programs like the WPA – when Congress decided to risk $5 billion for relief in 1935, the administration still had to assure Congress that "liberalism," if this is what the WPA stood for, was also, absolutely, true-blue American.[12] Harry Hopkins had to try to change the American people's attitude toward government aid to workers and especially to artists. The government's responsibility to supply relief for workers could be seen as a necessary consequence of a terrible depression, but it was less clear that people would accept the production of art as valuable work or culture as necessary for their psychic and economic welfare.

As a work relief project, the WPA challenged certain assumptions held up to that point about the unemployed. Like so much else in the New Deal, it tried to take a "middle course" and therefore failed to satisfy anyone completely.[13] Hopkins, whose background was in social work, believed that the masses of unemployed during the Depression needed to be treated with respect. The psychological burden of unemployment was something that work projects must alleviate. Instead of a handout or direct relief in cash or kind, Hopkins and other social workers championed work projects because they believed the work would bolster a man's (and sometimes even a woman's) self-respect. "Give a man a dole and you save his body and destroy his spirit . . . give him a job and pay him an assured wage, and you save both the body and the spirit," Hopkins wrote.[14]

Work projects were presented as embodying the American way of doing things, of maintaining individual initiative and self-help, and the projects were never meant to compete with the private sector but to, in the end, fold back into a stronger capitalistic economy.[15] How to make the projects useful, to bolster the morale of workers and maintain public support while not making the projects so attractive that people wouldn't want to return to private industry, was Hopkins's dilemma. Social workers believed the WPA failed on all counts. It never provided work to all those who needed it because neither Roosevelt nor Hopkins were willing to address the problems of the chronically unemployed; consequently "at no time did they employ more than one third of the nation's jobless people." Often the projects were make-work and not useful.

Finally, there were means tests so that workers felt they were being handed charity.[16] When even Roosevelt, in his 1935 State of the Union address, denounced relief as a narcotic, there could be little hope that the general public's suspicion toward work relief might be changed.[17] Nevertheless, to many people, especially many African Americans who were hired by the WPA and the Arts Projects and given the chance to develop and practice their skills, the WPA boosted morale and provided life-saving funds as well.

Of all the sorts of work relief generated, the Federal Arts Projects – Writers', Art, Music, and Theatre – seemed to Congress most expendable. Here Hopkins would have to change the very old American idea that artistic production was not work and that consumption of art was a luxury. Of course, popular art continued to be consumed by the working class and the poor even through the toughest of economic times. Popular art seemed safely embedded in everyday American life, but it was "high art," art that had cost too much and that only the rich could afford that Hopkins wanted to bring to the American people, to make it, along with popular art, part of the daily diet. He believed that more of the American public deserved more art and that the arts could stir a spiritual as well as an economic recovery. In his book *Spending to Save* (1936), Hopkins set out his hopes for the professional work projects; not only laborers would be put to work building bridges, but writers, teachers, and actors would get their chance to practice their arts and enrich American culture. The "greatest contributions" to American life and culture would be made by professionals, those workers who constitute the "upper fraction of the people who lead the way of history." Although culture will still be produced by a minority, that "upper fraction," Hopkins planned to spread it around more widely than ever before. "Throughout history, nations have set their approval upon the practice of the arts and sciences by making them the reward of the few. Government is now taking a hand on behalf of the many."[18] This democratization of culture is sounded again and again by the promoters of the WPA. Leisure should not belong only to the few because all Americans deserve to partake of the fruits of culture.

Using the same rhetoric of cultural uplift that so many other progressive Americans resort to, including, as we will see, W. E. B. Du Bois, Hopkins argues that culture is somehow different from the competitive struggles of everyday life yet should be included in it: "This renascence of the arts" without precedent in American history,

> betokens a deep spiritual change and re-estimate of what is valuable in American life. . . . The quickening of the audience,

the new desire to fill life with something more than the competitive struggle for existence, undoubtedly accelerates the process.
And this demand itself, both on the part of the performer and
the one who enjoys the performance, points to a new upward
movement of labor.

Hopkins implicitly reasons that the artist is a worker, producing goods
like any other worker, but that the consumer consumes art differently
from any other commodity. Bread sustains the body; art provides the
soul with joy and enlightenment. He also sees in the democratization of
culture the possibility of a new industry being born:

> In its entire range from alphabet to gym work, to chamber
> music, art exhibits, and murals on hospital walls, this program
> is the advance agent of a potential industry; one which will be a
> large-scale employer and will cater to the demands of workers
> to service the needs of literally millions of new consumers. Few
> things could add such a permanent volume of employment as
> would a program of educating the public to use the services and
> participate in the pleasure of the culture we possess."[19]

Making culture available to everyone, subsidizing performances and
artists, bringing art to the people who could not have afforded it or
were not living next to it was a way of democratizing culture. It also
was a way of embedding the arts into, rather than apart from, the
capitalistic world of American business. Culture, as Hopkins saw it,
could become a potential industry, one that would undertake to educate
the masses, thereby making them enlightened consumers of the arts.

But what sort of art would best educate and what would the education
consist of? Mostly, supporters of the WPA Arts Projects spoke in vague
ways of art's civilizing influence or art's capacity to make better citizens,
better and happier Americans, fulfilled rather than quietly desperate.
Lewis Mumford wrote to the president in 1936 protesting what he
feared might be the termination of the Federal Arts Projects. He assured
Roosevelt that they were anything but revolutionary in the dangerous
sense but, rather, invigorating; they cultivated new audiences, new regions, new morals for the nation. They are "a great civilizing influence,
capable of solving, as no commercially supported arts can solve, the
problem of how to use our collective wealth and our individual leisure
with dignity and sanity and permanent delight."[20] Like Hopkins, Mumford yoked art's civilizing influence with its ability to circulate profit –
monetary and moral. The Arts Projects were hardly threatening given
Mumford's definition but can be seen as part of the New Deal's desire

to placate revolutionary impulses by giving people an outlet or voice to their complaints.

The government could free the artist to produce without the restricting influence of either business or the rich patron, at the same time that it would enable many more people to consume the artist's product. This sounds theoretically possible, but in practice there were conflicts. The two-fold purpose of the Arts Projects – to embody the "higher values of our civilization," as one WPA official put it (higher than the business of the struggle for survival) and to extend culture to everyone – could very easily come into conflict when, for instance, the higher values don't seem either dignified or sane or delightful to the collective people.[21] Restricted from competing in the marketplace, protected from the marketplace, the Federal Arts Projects could afford to experiment with new forms. But at the same time they were enjoined to make art for the people, and produce popular works. New forms did not always prove to be a hit with the American people. This conflict undermined the identity of a "people's" theatre. When artists did create an appetite for what was new, business could manage their popular creations, ensuring the widest possible audience, and at that point there might not be an incentive to protect the noncommercial artistic space the FAP provided. Finally, as a patron of the arts, the government seemed to expect, at times, that artists would not take critical political positions or that their positions could be contained, neutralized, reconciled. And yet by giving voice to certain peoples, the government was unavoidably unleashing a new sense of politics, a new role for culture to play in politics. When artists were critical of the very government who gave it existence, the government almost reflexively moved to censor those voices.

III

Through the Federal Arts Projects, Hopkins hoped to create new cultural desires, to see if Americans would equate artwork with bridge work, to find out whether art created apart from commerce would still appeal to the people. He wasn't too clear about the particulars, about just who would be included and how. But he did know who he wanted to take on the task of leading the FTP. He turned to an old college friend of his, Hallie Flanagan, someone very much like himself: someone from a small town who had discovered the world, who combined the progressive's moral passion for uplift with a willingness to experiment and, in addition, who was masterful at organizing people. Both graduates of Grinnell College, Hopkins and Flanagan had been shaped by the same progressive beliefs: that public service was a duty and privilege, that the arts could help fight poverty and despair.[22]

By all accounts, Flanagan fundamentally shaped the FTP in her image. The director of the New York City FTP, Philip Barber, claims that "none of it would have existed, the intellectual quality, the standards that were present in many of the productions. It would not have been without Hallie. It came out of her intense faith and belief."[23] An idealist, an enthusiast, disciplined and winning, she inspired students, professors, and presidents with confidence and confidence in her. Born in 1889, her father, a salesman, moved the family around the Midwest before finally taking them to Grinnell, Iowa, around 1900. Attending Grinnell College, she was a leader, popular, surrounded by admirers. And she clearly missed the activity once she married a college classmate. But when her husband died, leaving her with two young children after only a few years of marriage, she returned to Grinnell, first to teach high school and then to teach theatre at the college. After this, she would make a series of choices between career and family, always choosing the first over the second. Accepted for the famous 47 Workshop taught by George Pierce Baker at Harvard, she moved back East to take advantage of the opportunity. He taught her, she said, everything she knew about theatre.[24] Her career as an experimental director was off to a good start when she accepted an offer to teach and run the college theatre at Vassar. She was one of the first women to win a Guggenheim Scholarship, which she used to visit European theatres. The influence of European directors and especially the theatre in Russia, which combined great artistic and social vision, would always shape her work.

Just as she was an inspiring teacher, so would she be an inspiring leader of a government program. Small but determined and usually able to get her way, at Vassar she was the center of a cult of students. She wore hats and a red cape from Russia; her students wore jeans. One remembered, "When Hallie would talk to us in the greenroom, I think we would all have gone out to slay dragons for her. Fatigue left and excitement took over."[25] Early on, she noted that people liked being needed, and she knew how to make people feel important; she also confided her own needs, showing an emotional vulnerability that appealed to men and women. Some people noted that she used her femininity to great effect. Paul Green, the southern playwright, said she was "the cutest person you ever saw. When Hallie walked into a room wearing one of her jaunty little hats, the men all looked."[26] As a female director in a theatrical world dominated by men, she always nurtured friendships with men in power. At Grinnell, Vassar, and at the WPA, she was supported by bosses because she did good work and because she always sought their advice. And during her stint at the FTP, at least until 1937, she had access to Hopkins and used it whenever she needed to get things done. Susceptible herself to flattery, she also knew how to give it out. But she always created a sense of a team, supporting those who worked for her and expecting in return admiration and loyalty from them. At the FTP, she hired many former Vassar students – all women, of course – to direct, design, and manage various parts of the bureaucracy.

Hopkins turned to Flanagan then, partly because he knew her and trusted the Grinnell connection, but partly also because she worked completely outside commercial theatre. Individual producers and Actors' Equity had already made various requests of the federal government for support. Hopkins could see that choosing one producer rather than another or making concessions to a union might threaten a national work project for the theatre. He avoided all of this when he turned to someone who was not beholden to Broadway in any way.[27] It is a key to all the FTP tried to do that its vision and mission were largely determined by people like Flanagan who had come not from Broadway but through noncommercial theatre – from the little theatre and university theatre movements. Gilmor Brown of the Pasadena Community Playhouse, Thomas Wood Stevens, who set up the first undergraduate drama program at Carnegie, Mr. and Mrs. James at the University of Washington, E. C. Mabie at the University of Iowa, and Frederick Koch from the University of North Carolina all became advisers and administrators during the FTP's reign. Flanagan's career, from Grinnell, through Baker's 47 Workshop, to Vassar, quite clearly was marked by the development of an experimental, noncommercial theatre movement.

It is crucial to understand the kinds of theatre Flanagan wanted to support so as to see how the Negro units would conform or break with the tenets of the sort of noncommercial theatre in which she was schooled. And it is also important to see just where the theatre stood with audiences in order to assess the possibility of making it a part of "everyday" culture. Historians agree that in the 1830s and 1840s, theatrical spaces brought together different classes under the same roof; various kinds of theatrical entertainment took place during the same evening, from Shakespearean speeches to popular songs, and that audiences actively participated in directing actors on stage, demanding encores when they particularly liked something or booing actors off stage when they didn't. Lawrence Levine argues that because various peoples – prostitutes, artisanal republicans, middle and upper classes – watched the same show, they must have shared similar attitudes toward culture. Robert Allen disagrees and stresses the conflicts between the classes who, he points out, sat in different places in the theatre – the pit, the gallery, the boxes. Just because the theatre once served as a place for various parts of the public to attend did not necessarily mean that they mingled or viewed the entertainment with the same expectations. A prostitute in the gallery engaging in business had, certainly, different interests from the businessman speaking to other men in the boxes, and they might have had dissimilar interpretations of what was presented on stage. I agree with Allen that shared space does not necessarily mean these people shared similar attitudes or cultural needs. Still, the drift of theatre history from the nineteenth to the twentieth century has been from that of different classes of peoples watching a wide variety of entertainment in a theatre to segregating audiences in different theatres so that they can watch different sorts of entertainment and engage in different sorts of behavior. The middle-class, commercial theatre was one of many institutions that played a part in regulating the manners of the "lower classes" by excluding them to other sorts of places of entertainment and by insisting on certain forms of behavior when they came.[28]

As in Britain, in nineteenth-century America, stars, rather than plays, fueled theatrical engagements. Audiences were willing to pay well to see great actors, and so stars began to put their own companies together and take them on the road. By 1870, resident stock companies in cities had given way to traveling companies, organized in New York around a name actor, which were then sent on the road. Cheap railroad transportation and syndicates that centralized control of most of the theatres in the country made the traveling company the most efficient way to bring the theatre to a large audience. But as railroad and other costs went up – for material, wages, and unions – traveling companies cut back on their circuits, eliminating more and more of the "one-night stands," and many theatregoers began to lament the increasing scarcity of theatre and also to complain about the second-rate productions coming their way.[29]

Just at this time, around 1910, various forms of noncommercial theatre sprang up around the country. By noncommercial, I use Jack Poggi's definition to cover the wide range of alternatives to the prevailing forms of commercial theatre that existed, centralized and radiating from New York. These were noncommercial not because some of the theatres did not want to make money (indeed, some of them were very interested in profit), but because they were organized differently from the commercial theatre. These theatres were independent of the major syndicate control that booked all the major theatres in the country; they remained small, usually located outside the central theatrical district of cities and towns where rents were too high, and they could not afford to spend much money on production. Many different kinds of theatres come under the umbrella of this alternative noncommercial movement: little theatres, community theatres, university theatres, art theatres, and the resurgence of stock companies in small cities. The variety, quantity, and geographical range of these theatres expanded greatly during the twenties and thirties.

Not all of the little theatres were interested in new plays, much less "art" plays or the classics, but some were. Influenced by and taking part in a widespread cultural movement embracing formal experimentation and sometimes political dissent, some of the noncommercial theatres were determined to engage modern playwrights and new techniques. Visits from the Abbey Theatre of Dublin and the Moscow Art Theatre inspired Maurice Browne, who founded the Chicago Little Theatre in 1913, and the Provincetown Players, who banded together in 1915. At the same time, a parallel movement began in colleges and universities, where there were efforts made to teach the theatre practically as well as academically. Baker started his 47 Workshop in 1912; by 1925, drama departments began to appear in many schools. Flanagan's impulse to create new sorts of theatre, to revitalize the classics, to experiment with acting techniques, and to pay attention to local concerns can be traced to this noncommercial movement in theatre and would make her championship of the Negro units seem natural.

Putting professional actors to work, however, was the basic aim agreed to by Congress. By 1935, commercial theatre had been devastated by the Depression, by the competition of cheap entertainment like the movies, and by rising costs. In the 1931–2 season, every Shubert Theatre in Chicago was dark during one week in March; 213 out of 253 companies playing in or near New York City had closed by the middle of May. Much of the professional actor population was out of work, some on relief, most unemployed.[30] The theatre could not compete with mass-produced forms of entertainment like the movies. Costs of materials used in productions between 1913 and 1928 rose 200 percent, and wages also increased as much as 522 percent. But ticket prices weren't raised for over twenty years because producers worried that higher prices would alienate more of their audience. There were more flops, fewer hits, and fewer moderate successes as people became less willing to take a chance on a play that would cost them six times as much as a ticket to a movie. The camera was simply more efficient in providing mass entertainment at a low price. Once the talkies arrived in 1930, the theatre was doomed as an everyday form of leisure (even without the Depression to contend with).[31] People did not abandon live theatre altogether, especially in bigger cities. But they increasingly thought of a night at the theatre as an extraordinary event, while a movie could be an everyday occurrence. Once "the road" disintegrated, audiences across the country were less likely to see the same show, and so theatre became mainly a local affair, either in noncommercial theatres or concentrated in New York and a few other cities. Noncommercial theatres of all sorts expanded during the early part of the twentieth century, just as commercial theatre played to an increasingly small part of the American population.

Flanagan wanted to restore twentieth-century theatre to its popular nineteenth-century status. She wanted it to become part of an everyday cultural experience, a necessity, for everyone. Her competition, inexpensive movies, might be given a run for their money since her theatre was going to be subsidized; her tickets would be as cheap as a movie or free. She could also sponsor productions that were different from the movies. Productions couldn't compete with the spectacle of the movies, but they could make people think. The FTP could produce classics and modern plays, literary dramas and experimental plays; it could feature Negro and Yiddish performers, all of which Hollywood did not do. She could see whether these different kinds of productions would excite the tastes of the public. She also wanted the theatre to be responsive to particular groups of people, to be a place where different people with different interests might come together, to sit next to each other, talk to each other, and become active participants in culture. Here she was going against the grain of normative audience behavior: to sit back and be passively entertained. And there was no established precedent in theatrical history that would make it seem natural for different peoples to respond to each other in the theatre or through a theatrical production. The FTP would test the possibilities of a national American culture.

Many of the academics who would later advise Flanagan were interested in establishing a national theatre made up of a confederation of noncommercial theatres. In 1933, Koch and Mabie, along with George Pierce Baker, went to a national theatre conference, but nothing substantive came of this meeting. Once Hopkins persuaded Flanagan to direct the FTP, she put into action a plan she had concocted with Elmer Rice, a playwright and producer in New York, and Mabie of Iowa, of a national theatre composed of many regional theatres, with centers in New York, Chicago, Los Angeles, possibly Boston, and New Orleans. They hoped that, although coordinated on a national basis, each center would produce plays their particular community wanted, ideally everything from Shakespeare to modern American works.[32]

Flanagan knew she must use the FTP as a place to relieve the unem-

ployed artist, but she also meant to try to create a great theatre organization. She did not take as her model the Abbey or the Moscow Art
theatres. They were single theatres designed to unify countries. In the
United States, she would be committed to a federal project not a national one. She explained the difference this way: national meant something unified, an "attempt to have one theatre expressive of one national
point of view," while federal meant bringing together "for purposes of
mutual benefit."[33] Although Flanagan stressed federalism, the rhetoric
of nationalism continued to play a role at the FTP. The people – rich
and poor, black and white, men and women, southerners and northern-
ers – were all universally Americans. The thirties were, as historians
have noted, a "new era of nationalism," and so the Arts Projects exploited the popularity of the idea of a national people. Contemporary
historians, artists, and politicians were equally interested in describing
the sense of a nation in terms of its culture: "what it means to *be* a
culture, or the search to *become* a kind of culture," and what binds a
people together rather than what makes them different from one another.[34] As Alfred Haworth Jones writes: "Thus, the nationalism of the
decade stimulated an emphasis upon the uniqueness of American ideas
and values, not the purity of any single racial or cultural stock. . . . The
leveling influence of the Depression encouraged an emphasis upon the
classless, inclusive character of the national experience."[35] As expressions of a leveling nationalism, the Negro units seemed problematic,
unless they were to prove how American the Negro was after all; as an
example of federalism, the Negro units could address differences to
everyone's "mutual benefit."

Whether the FTP would be federal or national in spirit, stressing
distinctive or universal American characteristics, the FTP was conceived
as an experimental effort to "do good" – cultural good. As Howard
Miller suggests, there was a "strain of social work" due to the times:
"We had, behind the whole movement, all the time we were in it . . .
this strain of social work that ran through the whole project. This was
because people were hungry and this is probably what gave it so much
strength."[36] When Hallie Flanagan heard Roosevelt's famous speech –
"I see one-third of a nation ill-housed, ill-clad, ill-nourished" – she was
ready to take her direction from what she called its "militant ring."[37]
But partly too, Flanagan's progressive education and career in noncommercial university theatre had prepared her long before the Depression to include all that was modern and experimental in practicing her
craft, to emphasize local control of production, and to think of the
theatre as a means to forge a newer, more critical, political, and more
inclusive culture.

IV

Most of all, Flanagan was committed to making a democratic culture accessible and relevant. Rejecting art for art's sake, Flanagan thought theatre vital only if it reflected and became a part of people's daily lives. FTP rhetoric refused to distinguish between "culture" and "life." A question like " 'What has the Federal Theatre done for Art?' " phrases the relationship in exactly the wrong way for Flanagan. She responds:

> This question will not stand analysis, for nobody can do anything for art. You do things for yourself or for other people but not for art. Art is created by and exists for people. It cannot be imagined either on the giving or receiving end except in relation to people. . . . The answer is that the Federal Theatre has done as much, and no more for art than it has been able to do for life – the life of its own workers, and its own audiences. The thousand people returned to private industry through Federal Theatre are a part of that equation; the general health, happiness and useful employment of every person on our payroll; the enjoyment of audiences in the city parks; the many young American dramatists given their first opportunity. Asking what the Federal Theatre has done for art as if it were something apart from life gives art a small and precious connotation. There is no place today for small and precious art.[38]

As she argues in her book about the history of the FTP, *Arena,* the theatre cannot be thought of as a luxury: "It is a necessity because in order to make democracy work the people must increasingly participate; they can't participate unless they understand; and the theatre is one of the great mediums of understanding."[39] Over and over again, Flanagan insists that the people who work for the FTP must be aware of what is happening in the world, "socially and politically, aware of the new frontier in America, a frontier not narrowly political or sectional, but universal, a frontier along which tremendous battles are being fought against ignorance, disease, unemployment, poverty and injustice."[40] As a form of participatory politics, culture generates understanding, and so culture must be embedded in everyday life. The new theatre would be a place devoted to bringing the people together to think about their lives critically. Flanagan's rhetoric draws on what seemed to her American principles: faith that the present has to be confronted, not with tradition but innovation, and the belief in democratic participation, in the common man and woman making decisions for themselves.[41]

She wanted to make "Arts for the millions" and saw this as an "ideological imperative."[42] Announcing that the Federal Theatre was born not "from an art theory but from an economic fact," and as a "functional" theatre of the times, she wrote, "We all want to find out whether this limitation is a liability or an asset."[43] Given her experimental and college theatre background, she had no problem forsaking the costly budgets of Broadway for simple sets, a light or two, a good script, and interesting actors. All of the rhetoric about modernism and relevance is a battle cry she sounded before the Depression and after; it was a cry of the experimentalist. From the beginning, she aimed to make the FTP part of the modern world: "We need a theatre adapted to new times and new conditions; a theatre which recognizes the presence of its sister arts, and of the movies and the radio, its neighbors and competitors, a theatre vividly conscious of the rich heritage of its past but which builds towards the future with new faith and imagination."[44] Impatient with theatre that clung to the past, she wanted new plays about new topics:

> Architects today shatter facades and let the steel show, musicians shatter melody and experiment with dissonance, painters turn away from sentimentality to an objective or psychological view of nature or the economic scene – but the theatre still clings to melody, to the facade, to sentimentality. . . .
>
> We must see the relationship between the man at work on Boulder Dam and the Greek chorus, we must study Pavlov as well as Pavlowa, Einstein as well as Eisenstein, must derive not only from ancient Bagdad but from modern Ethiopia. In short, the American theatre must wake up and grow up – wake up to an age of expanding social consciousness, an age in which men are whispering through space, soaring to the stars, and flinging miles of steel and glass into the air. If the plays do not exist we shall have to write them. We shall have to work more closely with our dramatists. We cannot be too proud to study our medium.[45]

Flanagan wanted plays to be written for particular peoples and particular audiences. In this respect, she drew on the tradition of community theatre. "I should like to know how many of our playwrights have gone, notebook in hand, and studied performance and rehearsal of any definite group, and the reaction of various audiences to that group, and then gone back and started to write a play for that playing group and for that audience?"[46] She would agree with the critic who wrote, "It is of no value whatever to stimulate theatre-going unless, once inside our doors, our audiences see something which has some vital connection with their own lives and their immediate problems."[47] Along with cultivating new material and new playwrights, Flanagan stressed the importance of audience participation:

> It is the strength and not the weakness of the Federal Theatre that it is impregnated with facts of life commonly outside the consciousness of the theatre worker. This consciousness that we are part of the economic life of America, that we are one with the worker on the stage and in the audience is the very core of the Federal Theatre.[48]

She believed that this new audience coming into the theatre for the first time could stimulate a new theatre to heights of greatness: "In this audience, if we have the patience to study it, lies our potential strength. The theatre has never been greater than its audience."[49] The theatre, once the most common form of entertainment for the masses, had been superseded by movies and radio. In order to win back that audience, the theatre must give them something "which they cannot get in any other form of entertainment; and give it at a price which they can afford to pay."[50]

Taking the theatre to Buffalo and Omaha was paramount to Flanagan and Hopkins, both for ideological and political reasons. Flanagan, who took pride in heading the "people's theatre," was determined to get the theatre to people who hadn't been so privileged before. Hopkins also supported the structure of a regional federal theatre, but the logistics of creating it within the WPA were enormous. Unlike other WPA projects, which had to rely on matching local support, from 1935 to 1937 the FTP hadn't had to ingratiate itself with local officials, precisely because they didn't depend on their money. By 1937, they would have to pay more attention to politics because when federal money was cut, the FTP would fold unless it could count on state or city funds. Why should a congressman support the FTP if his constituency hadn't benefited from the project? Would someone from Nebraska vote so that funds could continue to entertain the folks in New York? Highly unlikely. From 1937 on, given cuts in her budget, Flanagan was faced with closing regional theatres whose work she didn't admire or whose audiences were small. At the same time, Hopkins wanted to try to establish more support for the FTP by bringing theatre productions to the twenty-nine states without a project.[51]

Flanagan came up with a plan to take companies from New York, Chicago, and Los Angeles on tour, but this plan never got off the ground. A WPA rule forbade workers from crossing state lines. WPA administrators balked at having plays seemingly thrust upon them from Washington (or worse, New York). Too many approvals were needed from state, national, and local administrators before a touring company would be permitted in a particular state. Officials in Washington thought touring was too expensive, and besides, there was the problem of crossing state lines. When Hopkins turned his attention to presidential politics, his subordinates were much less likely to go out on a limb for Flanagan and instead tried to conciliate WPA officials. Finally, Flanagan had to give up her plan to regionalize fully the FTP. This meant that ultimately, because of the reductions of appropriations throughout the FTP's tenure and because of the administrative obstacles to touring, by 1939 Flanagan was left with an FTP still highly concentrated in three big cities: New York, Chicago, and Los Angeles. This would leave her without the deep support vital to the FTP's survival. From the beginning, Flanagan had struggled to broaden the base for a national theatre, but even without the Depression, the theatre found it difficult to sustain itself outside of New York. Institutional restraints undercut the sort of regionalization she had initially hoped would lead to a more democratically representative theatre. Cultural tastes also must have been operating, as there was no ground swell of support from the people (outside of the theatre world or Hollywood) who might have made a difference to representatives in Congress when they debated the FTP's future. The theatre had not reversed its decline into entertainment for extraordinary, rather than ordinary, occasions.

Flanagan's ideological rhetoric, her democratic zeal to promote culture of the people, by the people, for the people, remained consistent throughout the run of the FTP. But there were contradictions inherent in her own formulas. Sometimes Flanagan expressed solidarity with the people, sometimes she celebrated them, and sometimes she criticized them. On the one hand, Flanagan found herself taking pride in heading what was called the "people's theatre." The editor of *Federal Theatre,* Pierre de Rohan, writes: "We did not call it that because only the people can make the name appropriate. But where and as the people make it appropriate, we welcome it as describing what the Federal Theatre should be."[52] But on the other, she could be critical of the people: "The pious hope that the Federal Theatre will reach the point where it pleases all of the people all of the time is doomed to disappointment. If that time should come the news of its demise would be too unimportant to make an obituary column."[53]

The FTP's task to democratize culture was made difficult partly because not everybody believed in the same kind of art theatre Flanagan wanted to promote for the democracy. While Flanagan and some of her directors hoped to create an art theatre different from what they felt was a tired and dull professional theatre, those who came from that professional theatre had no desire to change it. Jane De Hart Mathews has argued that when all was said and done, the "real arbiters of taste were a New Deal cultural elite," who leaned toward modern, experimental art and whose tastes did not always coincide with the masses, nor even with many of the professionals who worked on the FTP.[54] Some of these actors resisted the retraining necessary to produce more experimental plays, and Flanagan constantly complained about the old-fashioned, stock plays that FTP units continually produced; for by and large, the professional actors who were to be the mainstay of the FTP had not been involved in community theatres or in the little theatres. Yet these were the people Flanagan was supposed to hire.[55] The first goal of the FTP, to give relief to professionals in the theatre, came into conflict with its second goal, to make new kinds of theatre that would respond to the problems of the present.

Perhaps too, Flanagan succumbed to a sentimentalization of the "folk" and assumed that her idea of the people was universally accepted by all the people, thereby misrepresenting what some Americans may have wanted.[56] But when she said that the FTP "stood from first to last" against reaction, against prejudice, against racial, religious, and political intolerance, such sentiments constituted her belief from beginning to end. In practice, however, certain kinds of intolerance and prejudices, "old habits," pressed back. Flanagan never conceded or never saw the ways her own liberal biases for the people conflicted with other tastes, other desires.

Although Flanagan invoked democratic principles of representation – of the people, by the people – she also often found herself at odds as a representative of the people with her boss – the democratic government, also supposedly a representative of the people. Which was more truly representative or who represented more of the people? Employed by a democratic government, she sometimes found herself in an adversarial role toward it: "Giving apoplexy to people who consider it radical for a government-sponsored theatre to produce plays on subjects vitally concerning the governed is one function of the theatre. . . . The Federal Theatre must continue to be, among other things, a thorn in the flesh of the body politic."[57] When it came to making artistic decisions on political matters, Flanagan always asserted the right of her fellow artists to make the final aesthetic choice. But she couldn't always protect the principle in practice.

Hopkins had declared in a speech announcing Flanagan's appointment that the Federal Theatre would be free and uncensored: "I am asked whether a theatre subsidized by the government can be kept free from censorship, and I say, yes, it is going to be kept free from censorship. What we want is a free, adult, uncensored theatre."[58] But from the beginning, neither he nor Flanagan could deliver. There were all sorts of ways in which theatre was censored. Early on there was a crisis that showed how interested the government could be in the FTP. A living newspaper called *Ethiopia* was set to open in New York City. Made up of excerpts from public documents, speeches of Haile Selassie and Mussolini, to protest the lack of American resolve to halt Italian aggression, the government feared that such a play could embarrass them and at the worst, jeopardize international relations. They demanded that the play not open or, as a compromise, be rewritten so that no international figures could be quoted.[59] Elmer Rice, the director of the New York Project, resigned, and it seems Flanagan also thought long and hard about whether she ought to do the same. That she chose not to signaled her commitment to the ends she had in mind and a greater capacity to bend the means of getting there.[60] Certainly the government never worked quite so innocently of political pressures and never so evenhandedly in relation to individuals or the people. Both Hopkins and Flanagan would come to see very quickly how restricted they were in attempting to negotiate the censorious and conflicting various public interests.

By 1938, there was a real shift in the sort of compromises Flanagan made. Her belief in principles still operated, but even she, so optimistic, so full of energy and commitment, was beaten down by the cuts in the program and the attacks by the Left from within and by the Right from without. Unions protested cuts and called strikes; conservatives protested the critical spirit of living newspapers. Both Flanagan and Hopkins felt that in order to protect the FTP, they had to placate the Right. Appointments in New York City began to be made to conservative theatre producers. She no longer wrote optimistic letters home reporting on events, documenting history; she was no longer first and foremost creating a project, she was "just trying to keep it from going under."[61] Though her public rhetoric contained the same mix of spirited support of the arts as a necessity in democratic culture, her private sentiments were much more defensive and embittered. She wrote to the editor of the FTP newsletter, "I think you and I have an unfortunate tendency to romanticize the workers" and called them "tiresome radicals."[62]

The conflicts between relief and professional theatre, between an "art" theatre and a popular one, and between the FTP's most liberal expectations and conservative constituency could not be resolved. Out of joint

with the increasingly conservative times, its cultural politics were perceived to be too radical, too New York, too Jewish, too communist,
too black. If Richard Pells's theory is right, that in every arena conservatism wins out after 1937, inhibiting criticism common in the early part
of the thirties and making serious experimentation next to impossible,
then Flanagan's concentration on the artistic innovation, experimentation, and political critique might have come to seem too radical to be
countenanced.[63] Just as historians were turning to the past to find examples of stability and direction, paying "meticulous attention to authenticity," Flanagan seemed to exhort her people to think only of the present
and the future.[64] It is striking that while much of the work on the
Federal Writers' Project and Art Project and even the Music Project was
historical – guidebooks, paintings of crafts, documentation of exslaves,
collections of folk songs – this cannot be said of the FTP. While Lincoln
plays and local pageants were staged, by and large, Flanagan's rhetorical
spirit sounds out of step with the increasingly celebratory and conservative times.

The officials of the WPA couldn't be happy with the publicity the
FTP continued to attract: especially the charges of being infiltrated with
Communists, of producing radical shows. But most of them didn't take
the "Communist threat" very seriously. Miller says of Flanagan and
himself that "the great Communist conspiracy as we know it . . . hadn't
developed at least in minds like mine. . . . We weren't trained for this.
We were show people. In those days we were lambs in the woods."[65]
Communists clearly orchestrated some of the protests and influenced
some of the choices of plays, especially in New York. Given the many
little leftist theatres that existed before the FTP in the thirties, it was
inevitable that some Communists and fellow travelers were hired by the
FTP. They were responsible for some of the most vibrant theatrical
experiments. But by and large, Flanagan and her trusted advisers focused on aesthetic lapses in taste not political deviancy. Ironically, when
Congress attacked the FTP for harboring Communists, Flanagan had to
defend the very people she found "tiresome" and who had caused her so
much grief.

When Congress as a whole came around to investigate the Arts Projects, the FTP stood out as the most controversial and the best way to
embarrass Roosevelt. Although it was attacked as ill-run and inefficient,
in the end it was its cultural politics that made the FTP the first of
the Arts Projects to be terminated.[66] Congress took aim at the Negro
units, questioning the very identity of the Negro units and the FTP, targeting them both as un-American. When the Dies Committee on Un-
American Activities convened, much of their time was taken up with

reports from disgruntled exemployees of the FTP detailing the radical mores found on the project. The sort of un-American pursuits investigated were, for instance, interracial dating. One newspaper account of the testimony runs:

> Miss Sally Saunders, a Vienna born actress on the New York Project and in the cast of "Sing for Your Supper," testified that she received a request from a Negro man on the Project who was unknown to her for "a date," and when she protested to Harold Hecht, producer of the revue, he expressed surprise and remonstrated with her, saying that the Negro "has just as much right to life, liberty and the pursuit of happiness as you have."

The integrated cast of *Sing for Your Supper* was also viewed as un-American, as were plays like *Haiti* and *Prologue to Glory*, both leaning to "radical propaganda."[67] Many of the plays also seemed to the congressmen to promote class hatred. In attacking the FTP in 1939, the Dies Committee was not targeting, as Loren Kruger points out, the *theatre* as such, but "the Federal Theatre's refusal to be merely theatre."[68]

The lawyer for the FTP, Irwin Rhodes, argued that one of the reasons Congress so disliked the Federal Theatre was because "half the appropriation roughly was going to New York City. And they didn't blame it on blacks; they blamed it on Jews and radicals."[69] Howard Miller, one of Flanagan's closest assistants, also blamed New York; its contentious unions and strikes brought too much notoriety to the FTP.[70] Philip Barber, who took over as director of the New York City Project when Elmer Rice quit and was himself replaced by a more conservative director, concurs:

> I'll tell you, it was part and parcel of the current attack by Ford on New York City. It's the same envy, the same suspicion. So in that sense Hallie was completely right in trying to keep the impression that the Project was the whole country and not New York. But the point is that, except on publicity, nothing that was done around the country ever kind of made a spark. Nothing took fire, nobody got excited about it whereas anything we did in New York almost that was halfway good, boom, it was like a skyrocket going off.[71]

With such a condescending attitude toward the rest of the country, no wonder congressional representatives from districts outside New York City were not so eager to support the FTP. The perception from Congress was that a mixture of radicals, Jews and blacks, and condescending, culturally elitist New York artists ruled the FTP. Congress had relatively little trouble cutting this marginalized government program.

Leonard De Paur, a musician who worked on the Harlem Negro unit, felt such reasons are only rationalizations for something out of everyone's control. In his view, the FTP simply rolled in and out with the tide of all artistic movements:

> It's possible that maybe Federal Theatre was just too full of rotten timbers and the residue of too much mismanagement, too much faulty philosophy to ever amount to anything. Maybe it was time to die. I have a somewhat fatalistic attitude about artistic things anyhow. I've always felt that they have a life span that's perhaps preordained. And when they reach the end of it, they die.[72]

As a movement that trained and sustained African Americans and others, the FTP served as a channel by which people could be carried along to other tributaries, other rivers. But as a movement that had grand designs on changing the fundamental relationship between politics and art in America, that wanted to make theatre a necessary cultural form, that wanted to form and shape the tastes of the American public, it did not change the habits of the masses; the people were never convinced that theatre was a *necessary* part of lives, like bread or the radio.

Like the New Deal itself, Flanagan paid attention to people who hadn't been included before. The soup she offered was real, though it may not have always been hot and may not have nourished everyone. But there were contradictions in her idea of progressive culture and in the institutions she inherited. The government apparatus was unwieldy at best, and at worst a positive interference, censoring shows. And finally, the theatre itself no longer seemed to be a vehicle for popular and mass entertainment, even at a price people could afford. In 1940, Brooks Atkinson wrote an article for the *New York Times Magazine* calling for a national theatre. Modeled something like the FTP, it would have local centers run by private management that would send five or six touring companies to two or three hundred American cities. But he realized that the public might not be ready for such a project. "Culture is not yet so deeply embedded in our national life. To us culture is still a pastime for women, children and the rich. . . . Our national life is elementary. It is still immersed in meaningless materialism." He cites Congress's "appalling ignorance about the theatre in general," and congressmen's "primitive culture" that "regard[s] the theatre as a leg-show" as part of the reason why it shut down the FTP. How to change this ignorance? Writing in the same language of the New Dealers Hopkins and Flanagan, he ends:

> Many people now believe that the time has come to abandon the old laissez-faire attitude toward culture and do something toward strengthening it on a national scale. We are constantly more and more in need of an enlightened population. A democratic national theatre, administered independently of politics for all the people, would help breed one, and help us understand each other and live together in peace and loyalty.[73]

Of course, this very argument had just been resoundingly rejected by a Congress and a public not interested in or not ready for such a project. How American to think that politics can be separated from culture; the ability to think that it can is surely part of the ongoing problem in which culture does not seem "embedded" in everyday life. But also how American and how innocent to think that enlightenment might come through culture, high culture, theatrical culture.

V

Flanagan was a great champion of the Negro units, but her involvement with the black noncommercial theatre or black university theatre was nonexistent. Her concern with racial issues was also mostly theoretical and largely untested until she worked at the FTP. But then, that was not unusual; she would not have come into contact with blacks in commercial theatre because she had never been involved in professional theatre and the schools she studied and taught at were virtually entirely white. Professionally or socially, she had little experience with blacks.

Forty years after graduating from college, her most vivid memory of the role she played as a popular student centered around a racial event. A planning committee had been elected to organize a freshman class party, and their first piece of business was to decide which boys should accompany which girls:

> When we came to one boy's name, the chairman said importantly, "Now this is a problem. The dean of women called me in and told me that maybe he could either go by himself, or with a group. Because he's a negro, the only one in college." There was a silence, then a clatter – "how terrible, what shall we do?" I remember getting suddenly very angry and ashamed. I said it was all silly and that I would like to go to the party with him.

(Of course this may have been just showing off or dramatizing it, but I think the main thing was a revulsion of feeling against injustice.) The committee was horrified, the boys said my parents would object. One boy said, "I would never go out with a girl who had gone out with a nigger." I said that no one could sit on our porch and call anyone that. The meeting broke up in a fight. . . . The affair came to little because the boy withdrew from college.[74]

This incident, so sickening, so disheartening, exposes the hateful sorts of segregation that the lone black student encountered at this "progressive" school around 1910. If there had been just one more black person, of whatever sex, no doubt the school would have made it clear that these two would have gone to the dance together. Otherwise, his choices were to attend the dance alone or in a group, but not as an equal partner of another white girl. Revolted by a sense of injustice, that someone would be treated differently because of his race, and, in her own words, perhaps dramatizing the injustice by inserting herself as champion, Flanagan offered to go to the dance with him, though, since the student left school before the dance, she never got the chance to right an injustice and play out the drama. While at Grinnell, she chose a strategy that minimized difference; she would go to the dance with this particular boy so that he would have a partner like everyone else. At the FTP, the Negro units would be an attempt to recognize injustice, but to do so not by minimizing differences, but by calling attention to them.

Whether the Negro units should try to include themselves in an American theatre or develop an exclusive and distinctive theatre was a question implicitly answered by the segregated units. They had been created out of the same interest in supporting diversity, different regions, different ethnic groups, different language groups, different artistic tastes. But no other group, Yiddish or French, for instance, ever had designs for a separate national theatre. The Negro units seemed to be qualitatively different. For those blacks who had lobbied long and hard for a theatre about, by, for, and near their own people, the creation of separate Negro units fulfilled at least part of their wishes. Some expected that from this beginning a national black theatre might spring. Flanagan herself wrote early on "that the chief value of a negro theatre unit is the stressing of racial material."[75] But just how and in which ways this should be stressed was a matter of great controversy.

The development of the Negro units put to the test many of the ideological commitments of the FTP and exposed the contradictions inherent in some of them. Flanagan had meant to give different audiences what they wanted, classical plays or vaudeville entertainment, the circus or experimental fare. The Negro units easily found a niche in this noncommercial, little theatre philosophy: they were local, they might develop new playwrights to write about current events, and there was a potential audience – black and white – who, in the past, had attended the theatre and might do so again if given "at a price which they could afford to pay." The best and the worst publicity belonged to the FTP's Negro units. Less affected by regional cuts because the strongest Negro units existed in cities that had a theatrical base before the Depression – New York, Chicago, and Los Angeles – the greatest hits of the FTP and the most visible cultural struggles to create a new, modern, and distinctively ethnic and national theatre occurred just here. When Flanagan came along with the order to give space to voices who hadn't been heard, to nourish old talent in new showcases, she wanted the voices to sound a particular way. As we will see, just about everyone – black and white – had a clear idea about what "the Negro" should sound like. And when the people became too tiresomely radical or the Negro writer too violently passionate, Flanagan reached her limit and pulled the curtain down.

The question of whether the institution truly represented the people's wishes, in particular, the Negro people, continued to crop up throughout the FTP's tenure. Most of the Negro units were not directed by blacks, which called into question in what way this could be properly called a theatre of, by, and for the Negro. Throughout the history of the FTP, blacks strove to get more black directors hired and to participate in national theatre planning. When in the fall of 1936 a group urged that a Negro coordinator be hired, the National Play Bureau responded that such an appointment would be a duplication of services. But, of course, a black coordinator was necessary precisely because no one seemed to be speaking for black interests.[76] Although a regulation was passed in June 1937 that "there be racial representation in all national planning," in fact this never occurred. A survey of readers' reports for some black plays shows misunderstandings and insensitivity. When Flanagan turned down efforts to produce a black living newspaper because she thought some of it too inflammatory and lacking in drama (itself a contradiction), one must ask which *part* of the black and white community she was worried about burning.

In any case, it became clear that the Negro people themselves were a diverse bunch and that even if the FTP had appointed one black representative to plan a national strategy, not every African American would have been represented satisfactorily. What played in New York might not go over in Peoria, and even within one city, one group might argue with another about what was deemed appropriate Negro theatre. There was an ongoing debate over what plays should be produced: folk drama exploring rural roots and culture; urban and social realistic dramas depicting contemporary dilemmas for blacks; the musical entertainment so popular with black and white audiences; white drama adapted (or not) for black troupes. The debate about appropriate plays and the difficulties of developing new playwrights in such a short time was accompanied by the difficulties in developing a Negro audience who would support the theatre.

The Negro units became not so much an artistic movement as a fulcrum around which swirled ideas about what a proper and authentic and New Negro artistic movement should look like and how American or how African the Negro theatre should be. Such debates had been going on in the black community for twenty years before the FTP got started, and little black theatres had also been struggling to survive through the teens and twenties. I turn now to those conversations. The differences and similarities in thinking about a national theatre and a race theatre will become clearer after surveying the debates about culture and politics that took place in black journals through the teens and twenties: for African American intellectuals, politics could *not* be separated from their hopes for culture and, in particular in the twenties and thirties, theatrical culture.

2

Critical Directions: Toward a National Negro Theatre

I am writing this article at Stratford-on-Avon. I know that when stripped to the last desperate defense of himself, the Englishman with warrant will boast of Shakespeare, and that this modest Memorial Theatre is at one and the same time a Gibraltar of national pride and self-respect and a Mecca of human civilization and culture. Music in which we have so trusted may sing itself around the world, but it does not carry ideas, the vehicle of human understanding and respect; it may pierce the heart, but does not penetrate the mind. But here in the glass of this incomparable art there is, for ourselves and for the world, that which shall reveal us beyond all propaganda on the one side, and libel on the other, more subtly and deeply than self-praise and to the confusion of subsidized self-caricature and ridicule. — Alain Locke[1]

Between about 1910 to 1940, black critics debated whether there existed (or should exist) a separate black culture and, if so, whether it could be nurtured and what relationship it should have to the white dominant culture; many of these critics turned to the theatre as a place to reshape the relationship between white and black America. The commercial theatre had defined and confined blacks to certain cultural roles, and those critics who wanted to create new types of Negroes fastened onto the noncommercial little theatre movement as one way to produce this alternative culture. A new national theatre for Negroes, like the Abbey Theatre in Ireland or the Moscow Art Theatre, could be like an ambassador to the world, a liaison between the races, an educating and uplifting institution. The desire for a separate theatre makes sense given the restricted roles for blacks in commercial theatre. But it would be difficult to create an alternative theatre, when the African American had so centrally defined and been in turn defined by popular entertainment. It might also be difficult to draw a sizable black audience to uplifting dramas if the uplift wasn't packaged in a popular form. Although there

49

was plenty of criticism about inauthentic theatrical stereotypes by critics and playwrights, they couldn't find an acceptable alternative that appealed to a large audience. The atres specializing in contemporary social dramas appealed to too narrow an audience, while the vastly popular theatre that could be seen at the Apollo Theatre didn't seem to encompass the kind of self-conscious social critique that some black playwrights and critics wanted. Finally, it might be naive to think that there would be only one alternative "New Negro" to theatricalize.

I

As Hazel Carby argues, the twenties "must be viewed as a period of ideological, political, and cultural contestation between an emergent black bourgeoisie and an emerging urban black working class."[2] Critics debated how Negroes should define themselves, their voices, aspirations, soul, and spirit, and struggled to rename and revise a history that had largely been imposed on their people, to refashion a culture and call it true, new, and authentic. Certain polarities get played out over and over: between what is representative and what is artistic; between education and entertainment; between decadence and morality. And certain problems of definition arise and recur. What is the relationship between a national culture and a minority, in this case, a racial culture? How much emphasis should these critics put on the African or American part of their people's identity? Does the dominant culture wholly determine the other in creating, for instance, the old type of Negro, from which these critics want to escape? How and to what extent does African American culture define American culture? Would commercial interests homogenize, subsume, or simply ignore individual black voices?

Certainly for those black intellectuals writing in the first part of this century, the debate over what sort of art best represents blacks is as vigorously joined as debates over political representation. Rarely is it possible to separate the two concerns because so often in African American history, the skills of reading and writing assured the right of representation. When slave narratives work as passports proclaiming a slave worthy of citizenship and slave songs, transformed and preserved by the Fisk Jubilee Choir, become an audible sign of the characteristics of an oppressed people, the power of art to define humanity, to bestow citizenship, to refashion history is a great power indeed. Black cultural critics took positions on one side or the other of the art-is-or-is-not-political debate. From a particular black perspective, a certain strain of New Deal cultural discourse that held that art can and must be separated from politics came to seem not only naively innocent but dangerously shortsighted in denying the political effects of culture. From another perspective, some black critics believed art best served political ends by refusing to take politics into account. Here is where the cultural debates are enjoined.

Numerous critics have pointed out the political importance of literacy for African slaves: to be able to read and write "proved" to the white world that they were not savages or "primitive" but human, worthy of all the rights of those in power.[3] James Weldon Johnson, poet and ambassador, said at a famous dinner in Harlem that "no race can ever become great that has not produced a literature. . . . It is through the arts that we may find the easiest approach to the solution of some of the most vital phases of our problem as a particular group in this country. It is the path of least friction. It is the plane on which all men are more willing to meet and stand with us." Charles Johnson shared these sentiments, believing that "literature has always been a great liaison between races." Alain Locke also thought that the arts existed in order to improve black people's lives: "The especially cultural recognition they win should in turn prove the key to that revaluation of the Negro which must precede or accompany any considerable further betterment of race relationships."[4] Through the organized attempts to establish African American artistic movements in the twenties and thirties, critics believed they were proving the greatness of the race that would have to be acknowledged by anyone who appreciated the greatness of art. No small ambition, these critics meant through their criticism to effect fundamental political and cultural differences that would reshape the dynamics of white and black America.

The critical debate over racial and cultural definitions was largely to be found in three journals: the *Crisis,* sponsored by the National Association for the Advancement of Colored People beginning November 1, 1910, edited by W. E. B. Du Bois until he resigned from the organization in 1934; the *Messenger,* founded by A. Philip Randolph and Chandler Owen, with some backing from the headwaiters union in New York and the Brotherhood of Sleeping Car Porters, published between 1917 and 1928, featuring columnists George Schuyler and Theophilus Lewis; and *Opportunity,* of the Urban League, edited by Charles Johnson from 1923 to 1928, and throughout the twenties and thirties the outlet for Alain Locke's cultural criticism. These three journals, all operating out of New York, are key sources for recording black intellectual positions toward social events between 1910 and 1940.[5] This period covers a great deal of eventful black history: the emergence of the antilynching campaign; the debate over black participation in World War I; Marcus

Garvey's black nationalism, which spawned the biggest black mass movement in the history of the United States; the infamous race riots of Chicago and East St. Louis; the famous artistic outburst known as the Harlem Renaissance; and finally the Federal Arts Projects, which invited black representation. During this thirty-year stretch, the pages of these three journals offered an outpouring of aesthetic criticism written by African Americans. Not until the black arts movement of the sixties was the intensity of this earlier period matched, and not until the late seventies and eighties do we see something approximating the range and breadth of the criticism published between 1910 and 1940. Over this thirty-year period occurs a deep, lively, sustained debate, one that was largely overlooked by white critics and artists but was enormously influential for black writers and artists.[6]

The black critical renaissance of the early twentieth century depended on a series of well-documented historical events. Without the migration of blacks to northern cities from the turn of the century, and in particular the Great Migration during World War I when a million and a half rural blacks left the South, neither the politics nor the concern with aesthetic questions of the "New Negroes" at the NAACP, the Urban League, and the radical Socialists could have flourished. When Booker T. Washington died in 1915, the scramble to replace Washington's leadership led to lively arguments in existing journals.[7] In the years just before and after the war, new opportunities opened up for blacks, especially economic prospects. The Chicago *Defender,* one of the most popular black newspapers, spent much of its space advertising the benefits of life in the North, urging blacks to pick up and leave the South for the freer, liberating northern climate. Writers and publishers, critics and race leaders settled in cities that attracted many black southerners who might be expected to spend their wages on popular urban entertainment. The educated black leaders would tell them how to spend their money to their best advantage, how to be both politically and culturally correct.[8]

These critics defined themselves in opposition to the complacent, stereotyped shuffling minstrel or Uncle Tom, the stuff of white lies. They were the true and authentic Negroes: proud, conscious of their rights, unwilling to take abuse, ready to articulate and demand their due, part of what Locke called the "New Negro," the title he gave to the collection of writing he edited in 1925. The ongoing attempts to define the "new" in the pages of these journals was in itself a move of empowerment. To name yourself, to take control – this is, after all, a recognizable feature of slave narratives in which the slaves throw off their manacles and proclaim themselves free.

In identifying and defining the "New Negro," each critic differentiated between what they considered the authentic and inauthentic Negro, though they did so in very different voices. Du Bois wrote like a good Victorian – thundering, biblical, prophetic, passionate; Johnson, trained as a sociologist, highly rational, eschewed the flowery excesses of Du Bois's old-fashioned rhetoric; Locke wielded metaphors like the enormously erudite professor he was; Theophilus Lewis and George Schuyler made incisive (sometimes insider) jokes, satirizing folly, using the vernacular as much as possible. The political, the professorial, the aesthetic, the populist, the elitist were all styles a critic could use in the hopes of attracting the widest audience. As they adopted and adapted voices, these particular black intellectuals attempted to redefine their people and their history.

The extended period of the critical renaissance, those years between 1910 and 1940, is marked not just by the production of art but by the active attempt by critics, artists, and consumers to form categories of good art and bad art; that is, this thirty-year period was a period of canon formation. The critic's style, unlike the artist's improvisations, riffs, or experimentation, rests on the persuasive articulation and codification of the reasons for accepting this work and not that one. These critics saw themselves as leaders, guides, interpreters, educating the white audience, thus creating a market for African American art and African American artists, as well as instilling pride in their own people. Some saw these two tasks as intertwined, others chose to emphasize the importance of addressing primarily a black audience. Although they applauded the abundance of art produced during this period and encouraged its production at every turn, they were also aware of the uncritical, that is to say, invariably appreciative coverage that most "race" art seemed to receive in African American newspapers. In the three journals, they meant to distinguish good from bad aesthetic work in order to affect the kinds of art artists would create. These were critics who did more than celebrate. They discriminated, making readers see what kinds of choices are possible for artists and for viewers and what some of the cultural meanings of those choices are. The choices had everything to do with identity. The discussion of aesthetic questions was never divorced from their relationship to the polis.

II

While no group in America has been so invidiously represented onstage and so relentlessly prevented from working backstage or enjoying the vantage of the orchestra as African Americans, neither has any other ethnic group in America been so centrally staged. Largely excluded from the American theatre as playwrights, directors, and designers, blacks had been represented onstage by whites in blackface before the Civil War and then by whites and blacks in blackface after the war in minstrel shows. In minstrelsy and then in the late nineteenth and early twentieth centuries with vaudeville and musicals, the songs, music, and dances identified as "black" have provided some of the most popular kinds of American entertainment. Recent scholars have acknowledged how deeply indebted popular American culture is to black performers, and they have also agreed that much of popular culture has been constrained by racist assumptions and stereotypes. It is precisely because black entertainment was so deeply embedded in American culture, indeed, came to define what was unique about American culture, and also so deeply inscribed by racism that black intellectuals were drawn to it as a place of potentially great transformative power.

Given the racist constraints and the central role of the theatre in American culture, the black intelligentsia's focus in the 1920s and 1930s on the theatre as the place to create a new cultural type and a national identity seems both problematic and understandable. One might argue that black critics, those talented tenth who did so much to foster the creative burst of energy by their people just before and after World War I – W. E. B. Du Bois, Charles Johnson, Theophilus Lewis, George Schuyler, Alain Locke – were, if not exactly innocent, then certainly optimistic about the possibilities of establishing a separate, national Negro theatre.

Ethnic theatre in America, which flourished in the late nineteenth and early twentieth centuries, had operated for most groups not only as a way of identifying with a particular subculture, but also as a process of Americanization.[9] For African Americans, an ethnic theatre of "their own" would be incredibly difficult to start up and maintain against the commercial and popular forces lined up ready and able to take it over. As Nathan Huggins argues, while other ethnic groups came to the United States speaking a different language, sharing a common history, and without a tradition within the United States to compete against, African Americans had already been "alienated within the American experience; alienation presumes no alternative culture."[10] Surely there was a difference between the Yiddish theatre, which, at least for a time, was safe from co-opting mainstream commercial forces because it was predicated on a language other than English, and a "black" theatre, which had never been designed for black people, but was peopled by whites and (even) blacks in blackface. For black intellectuals in the early part of the twentieth century (and for scholars throughout the century), the question is whether this kind of alienating cultural experience for blacks makes impossible an alternative culture. Could an authentic black theatre only exist apart from the popular and racist theatrical history, or was there something in that popular culture, racist though it was, that could be used again, authenticated, made to be genuine and genuinely unique? Would it be possible to use forms contaminated by racism to transform racism? Black intellectuals were divided on this question. Some believed that popular culture was thoroughly debased and that only a segregated theatre devoted to racial pride and race history, a theatre of uplift and moral seriousness, could create a weighty alternative; others thought that forms of dancing, singing, and music found in minstrelsy could be rescued from racist content and incorporated into a folk tradition worthy of a Negro national theatre.

To understand the great hopes these critics placed in the institution of a free, adult, uncensored, and (for some of them) separate theatre, one must understand the peculiar ways in which African Americans were both central and marginalized in American theatre. And to understand that is to understand also what kinds of drama were possible, what sorts of institutions there were to fight for and against. From the inception of African American history, the culture of African American entertainment could be interpreted and used for completely opposite purposes, as sign of enslavement and docility and as signal of humanity and rebellion. The masters see one thing, the slaves see another, and later readers, depending on who they are, see something else. A double consciousness – in which the truer self hides behind the veil, learns to deliver what the audience of masters expects (entertainment and laughs) and at the same time treats the players and the audience to another text and other purposes – becomes the defining feature of African American cultural history.[11]

African American theatre might be said to have begun on the slave ships that brought the first Africans to the Americas. The "performances" were compulsory, indeed a sign that freedom had been taken from them. Slave masters forced slaves to dance and sing on the passage as a way of making them seem cheerful and therefore controllable:

> The captors were always comforted when Africans displayed a cheerful or playful attitude and comported themselves in musical fashion. When the slaves were "a good natured lot," as one captain wrote, it meant that Africans were faithful to their customs, that hostility and the possibility of uprisings were diminished, and that more bodies might survive the excruciating midpassage.[12]

Forced to sing as a sign of their happiness and docility, their performances profited the masters. Perhaps too in watching the dancing and
listening to the songs, the masters' consciences were eased, or perhaps
they simply enjoyed the "show." What terrible irony it seems now to
think how being faithful to one's customs, singing a native song, can
become the very means by which one is alienated from oneself, turned
into property. But of course, singing may also have allowed the spirits
of the slaves to survive. It seems just as reasonable to suppose that the
imprisoned were singing as a sign of their humanity, even a sign of their
rebellion.[13] By reenvisioning the meaning and purpose of the songs,
they can reclaim and reappropriate themselves as "their own," not
someone else's property.

Although some of the earliest American plays included black parts,
they were almost always played in blackface by white actors, and the
parts were always comic ones. There were some antislavery plays written in the nineteenth century, and at least six companies toured the
country from midcentury through 1900 performing adaptations of
Stowe's novel *Uncle Tom's Cabin.* Here too, many of the black roles
were acted by whites in blackface. The one short-lived but heralded
exception to blackface performance before the Civil War was the theatre
known as the African Grove in New York City. Not much is known
about this theatre of the early 1820s. It seems to have grown out of an
independently black-owned ice cream establishment in which singers
would circulate and actors would declaim set pieces. A theatre opened
in lower Manhattan; blacks actors played to mixed audiences various
sorts of theatrical fare, some Shakespeare, some realistic dramas, and
popular songs. Newspaper reviews indicate the interest, condescension,
and hostility whites expressed at seeing black performers play roles
deemed inappropriate because they did not conform to stereotypes.
After much harassment, the theatre shut down, and Ira Aldridge, the
black actor who had performed in *Othello* and *Richard III,* moved to
England where he would successfully tour Europe in other Shakespearean productions.[14]

Shakespeare did not conform to white expectations of appropriate
material for black performers. Before the Civil War, few blacks stood
on the stage at all. The minstrel show, the most popular drama just
before the Civil War, was performed by whites in blackface. At the
height of minstrelsy's popularity, just before and after the Civil War,
thirty full-time companies toured the country. After the war, some
minstrel companies were black. In this original American art form, a
chorus and two end men sang songs and told jokes creating the black

man as an American icon of theatricality. (It wasn't until black burlesque troupes at the end of the nineteenth century began to tour that black women were included on stage.) Some critics argued that minstrelsy reinforced the worst sort of racist stereotypes, while others believed that blacks were bestowed with a wider range of attributes than other ethnic types. Nevertheless, the wider range of types – the sentimental and grotesque, witty and buffoon, pretentious and simple, pathetic and farcical – were all comic and racist.[15] James Weldon Johnson and W. E. B. Du Bois believed that the Stephen Foster songs "Old Black Joe" and "Old Folks at Home" were derived from Negro music and were, consequently, the "only real American music" and that minstrelsy "originated on the plantation and constituted the 'only completely original contribution' of America to the theater." But if originally derived, minstrelsy was not subsequently owned by black people. Frederick Douglass thundered that white blackface actors were "the filthy scum of white society, who have stolen from us a complexion denied to them by nature, in which to make money, and pander to the corrupt taste of their white fellow citizens."[16] Critics also argued over whether there is anything "genuinely" black about the form. When whites are said to be "imitating" blacks, were they merely creating a white image of black behavior? When blacks began to take over the parts, were they able covertly to critique the "genuineness" of the roles they were forced to play to white and black audiences? Who owned minstrelsy and whom did it serve?[17] It served different peoples in different ways at different times, a form that was undeniably racist and yet capable of being subverted, and certainly enjoyed, by all sorts.

Bert Williams and George Walker are probably the best known of the black minstrels from the late nineteenth and early twentieth centuries. They billed themselves as Two Real Coons, and played for white and black audiences. They introduced a plot to the minstrel structure and pioneered the musical comedy form. They performed, as did whites, in blackface, painting their faces even blacker. Critics then and now continue to debate about the success of the duo's revisionary tactics: how truly revisionary could they be given the history of the racist form? By calling attention to their "reality" in the billing Two Real Coons, perhaps Williams and Walker signified that they were more than aware of the inauthenticity of white men playing blackface, and even more pointedly, the title may have signified that Williams and Walker were aware of the inauthenticity of their roles. By making up "black," they signaled a theatricality all their own. Others have argued that the basic patterns of racist stereotypes embedded in the form of the minstrel show could never be eradicated by a change of costume or a few added lines. Certainly, the minstrel form would always be restrictive, its roots racist, and black performers would want to play different parts.

The proliferation of other forms of theatrical entertainment at the turn of the century – burlesque, variety, vaudeville – did not lessen the restricted stereotypes open to black performers.[18] No love scenes were possible, and nothing depicting middle- or upper-class social values was allowed. Against this backdrop of restrictions, the possibility of a black theatre that would be more inclusive drew black critics. Many theatres for blacks were started during this period with different ideas about what true representation would mean. The Gilpin Players in Cleveland, founded by white liberals, was an interracial group from the beginning. The Pekin Theatre in Chicago and the Lafayette Theatre in Harlem, both "me-too" organizations, proved that black actors could act the plays they weren't allowed to be in on Broadway.[19] Anita Bush, a dancer and actress who had toured with Williams and Walker, formed a company in 1915 at the Lincoln and then the Lafayette Theatre in Harlem. The Lafayette Players lasted until 1932 performing popular plays from Broadway retooled for a black audience.[20] The Pekin was also located in the black community and presented new plays every two weeks to mostly black audiences. The Pekin was so successful that white managers in Chicago began opening theatres catering to blacks.[21]

For a short time between 1900 and 1910, black ownership of independent theatres increased and the first black syndicates were formed. Black shows, some thirty in all, were produced in black neighborhoods and on Broadway between 1890 and 1915. But the window of opportunity was short lived. The same forces that caused white theatre to suffer also hurt independent black theatres: higher transportation costs, low cost movies and the added burden of racism, the lack of financial sponsorship for black shows, second-class bookings due to racism of owners and managers combined with the death of many of the first-class black performers caused independent black theatres to suffer more.[22] Between 1910 and 1917, no black performers except Bert Williams performed on Broadway.

By the early twentieth century, then, there were three kinds of black entertainment. Variety and vaudeville acts and minstrelsy still proved the mainstay for all black actors. But these were slowly dying out, to be replaced by movies as the most popular form of entertainment, and thus black performers were especially hard hit by this change in popular forms. Still, the minstrel show persisted well into the century, even into the FTP's Negro units. The FTP produced *Marionette Vaudeville* with stringed puppets dancing to minstrel tunes. Helen Bannerman's *Little*

Black Sambo adapted by Shirley Graham in Chicago for the Negro unit also was given by puppets with black faces and "thick red lips." In addition, the FTP sent around the country material called *56 Minstrels,* which could be used by schoolchildren, Boy Scouts, and clubs; it included: "The Coon-Town Thirteen Club," "The Darktown Follies," "Watermelon Minstrel," and "Plantation Days with the Snowflake Family," with "instructions indicating whether blackface or white face was to apply." [23] Quite clearly, some people working within Negro units had no qualms about producing such entertainment. The Negro unit in Chicago would perform realistic plays about black life and minstrel shows for children.

After 1917, serious attempts to write dramas about blacks, mostly by whites, led to some Broadway parts for actors in Edward Sheldon's *Nigger,* Ridgely Torrence's three one-acts, southern writer Paul Green's plays, and Eugene O'Neill's *Emperor Jones* and *All God's Chillun Got Wings.* One of the distinctive cultural features of the twenties and thirties is this outpouring of white-authored books depicting black subjects: from Edna Ferber's novel *Showboat,* to DuBose Heyward's novel and George Gershwin's opera based on it, *Porgy and Bess.* [24] Although critics celebrated the abilities of the black actors who starred in these shows, these opportunities to play on Broadway siphoned off the best talent from the black community where presumably the alternative national Negro theatre was supposed to take hold. White producers could offer bigger salaries and a chance for fame that could not be matched in the black community. As Charles Gilpin and Paul Robeson made names for themselves in Eugene O'Neill's successful plays and Florence Mills became the toast of Broadway in *Shuffle Along,* it seemed more and more hopeless to think of luring them back to Harlem to appear in plays written for a black audience, in community theatres. A few stars would cross over from Harlem to Broadway, but they would be exceptional. Community theatres, university theatres, small amateur drama groups, and professional black companies made up the third sort of theatre possible for blacks during this period. These black noncommercial theatres made up the smallest venue for black performers. Although the producers often had to struggle to find an audience, they had an intensely theoretical belief that through the theatre an alternative culture could be created for all of their people. [25]

III

I turn now to the critics and their criticism in order to give a more thorough account of their predicament: how to create a space under the then current economic, political, and cultural conditions for an alternative theatre that would not be so alternative as to reenact a marginalization; how to attract a critical mass, but not so massive an audience that they would create a theatre that could be exploited by others, and like so much of African American culture turned over, taken over, made to cross over and so lose control of an "authentic" point of view. The attempt to articulate authenticity around the idea of a national theatre often seemed to entail refusing to acknowledge the diversity of philosophies, the differences within black culture. This problem also, however, affected the white liberals on the government art projects as much as it did the black and white critics of African American culture.

As a means of educating and instilling race pride, one critic wrote in *Opportunity:*

> That the theater should always, and seriously, be considered as an educational institution side by side with the school is evident for one reason if for no other, and that is that the theater has the ear of more reasoning people, more adults, than any other institution, not excepting the church.[26]

Neither music nor literature seemed to offer the same promise. A theatre could be generated at a local level, fairly cheaply, unlike film, which had so quickly come to depend on large amounts of capital. Music, too, seemed to have been taken over by companies who would market only what people thought would sell. The small theatre might be able to withstand the pressures of commercial success if kept in the community as a distinct entity, retained for the populace, on the one hand, but not snatched up and made too popular, on the other.

The examples of such enterprises as the Abbey Theatre in Ireland and the Moscow Art Theatre in Russia had struck Flanagan as revolutionary. She wrote about new acting styles, new sorts of serious dramas. Black cultural critics also viewed these theatres as revolutionary, but they concentrated on their potential to revolutionize a people's identity, on the theatres as national theatres. When in the early twenties the Moscow Art Theater Company came to the United States, Raymond O'Neil, the director of the Ethiopian Players in Chicago, saw immediately a resemblance between "the Negro and the Russian." Like the Russian, the Negro "is gifted with a sensuous nature. He loves life and he lives life with the sensuous and the emotional parts of him constantly exposed to it." In contrast, the unemotional Anglo-Saxon "lives without a music of his own . . . with a literature just emerging from the nursery, and with a stage reflecting a life as hollow and painful as a drilled-out aching tooth." He takes note that the Russians have tried to guard their arts from Westernization, and so too should the Negro

> guard his from one hundred per cent Americanization. Particularly must he be on his guard against the white friends of his art who will urge its development in the direction of their prejudiced imagination. A very great advantage which Negro art has enjoyed has been white contempt or indifference towards it, qualities which are rapidly changing now to interest and to eventually commercial and intellectual exploitation.[27]

Most black and white critics throughout this period agreed that commercial and intellectual exploitation damaged the purity and authenticity of the Negro voice.

The Moscow and Irish theatres provided instances that not only expressed, but seemed to bring about, national independence. In 1936, Anne Cooke, the director of dramatics at Spelman College, went to the Third Moscow Theatre Festival, and upon her return she wrote:

> The strength of the Russian theatre rests largely in the fact that it has a great national ideal which gives unity and direction to its activity. The Russians believe in something. . . .
>
> Looking toward a Negro theatre, it seems to me incontrovertible that the future Negro theatre will be as amorphous as that of the past until we as a theatre group establish a point of view, develop a philosophy of the theatre arts in which we heartily believe and to which we can consecrate ourselves. We must find both an idea and an ideal without which there can be no permanence nor significance to our work. We are a theatre group without any single, far-reaching philosophy.[28]

Cooke wanted black theatre to have what she believed necessary and wanting, a sense of direction, "a point of view," a philosophy. A Negro theatre should first and foremost right the wrongs of past theatrical views of the Negro and replace old stereotypes with new types. The example of Ireland, a small country building a national drama that produced playwrights and actors respected the world over, should and could be duplicated by a new Negro theatre. Sterling Brown, a colleague of Locke's at Howard and an editor for Negro affairs on the Federal Writers' Project, describes how the Irish theatre resisted common stereotypes by refusing to stage plays with old comic roles:

> Their works were misunderstood by the people whose true character they wanted to show, and whose latent geniuses they

wished to arouse and sustain. Riots were frequent when in contradistinction to the stereotype of the vaudeville stage they refused to set up plaster-of-paris saints. . . . But they had their own quiet heroism; they persevered; and today the players they trained, the plays they wrote, make up a cultural embassy from the Irish Free State to the world. Indirectly, for they believed that the creation of a literature was their calling more than the creation of propaganda, they advanced Ireland politically; certain it is that culturally their movement went step by step with Ireland's advance to independence.[29]

The banishing of stereotype results in truer art, better culture, and indirectly, political justice. But Brown carefully points out that the theatre's first allegiance is to art not politics. Different critics will address just this question: whether art and politics, literature and propaganda, are mutually exclusive and contradictory things or whether they must be yoked together.

Both W. E. B. Du Bois and Alain Locke wrote about and worked for this alternative national Negro theatre. Du Bois believed in the importance of maintaining a segregated theatre that would emphasize racial pride in African and African American history. And he believed that serious drama was the best means to educate black audiences and provide moral uplift.[30] Throughout Du Bois's experience in the theatre, two sorts of tensions are manifested: between art and "propaganda," and between the intellectual's desire for uplift and a popular audience's disdain for the forms uplift takes. Serious drama may have been a means to educate, but it had to attract an audience to begin to do its work, and this was a chronic problem for many of the middle-class black (and white) theatres.

One of the beliefs of almost every black intellectual was that certain kinds of art could create political change. The debate in the twenties centered on what sorts of art could best serve a political purpose. A conflict that afflicted the entire FTP, it particularly divided the Negro units among social activists who highlighted prejudices and abuse, among those who were offended or feared others might be offended by a portrait of a New Negro, and those who believed that art could do a better political job by being artful rather than propagandistic. For African Americans, any critical discussion of the place of the arts confronted the relationship between them and the dominant culture, and merged into questions of nationality and style.

As early as 1905, Du Bois had tried to use journalism to teach and uplift a very specific and select audience. His "high class journal" should "circulate among the Intelligent Negroes," since the black press of the time, the weekly papers, and the monthlies do not "fill the great need I have outlined. . . . The Negro race in America today is in a critical condition. Only united, concentrated effort will keep us from being crushed. This union must come as a matter of education and long continued effort." A journal of the sort he envisioned would provide this education for his people; it would "interpret the news of the world to them, and inspire them toward definite ideas."[31] The two journals Du Bois edited, *Moon Illustrated Weekly,* from December 1905 to the summer of 1906, and *Horizon: A Journal of the Color Line: A Periodical of Purpose and Prehension Devoted to the Interests of the Darker Races,* from January 1907 to May 1910 in Washington, D.C., included marriage announcements and other local news that one presumes would have interested "Intelligent Negroes" hungry for society news. But they also contained analyses of literature and culture: "What Negro American literature needs now is careful dogged workmanship among the educated classes."[32] Du Bois's cultural pronouncements consistently sound like this from 1910 to 1940: true culture means high culture, defined as that which must exist beyond the constrictions of the marketplace. Great art, crafted and accomplished, can only be appreciated by an educated audience, in Du Bois's mind made up of the very small number of educated black elite and the educated white population who, impressed by "beauty," would open their minds to the possibility of beautiful art created by black artists.

But beautiful art could never be divorced from politics in any of Du Bois's thinking. Forever an unabashed propagandist, Du Bois was resolutely unafraid to prescribe for his people politically and culturally.[33] In his generally positive review of Locke's collection *The New Negro* (1925), Du Bois took issue with Locke's emphasis on style:

> Mr. Locke has newly been seized with the idea that Beauty rather than Propaganda should be the object of Negro literature and art. His book proves the falseness of this thesis. This is a book filled and bursting with propaganda but it is propaganda for the most part beautifully and painstakingly done; and it is a grave question if ever in this world in any renaissance there can be a search for disembodied beauty which is not really a passionate effort to do something tangible, accompanied and illumined and made holy by the vision of eternal beauty.[34]

Insisting that art becomes only more beautiful when anchored to the tangible, Du Bois warns that if Locke's "art for art's sake" thesis

> is insisted on too much it is going to turn the Negro renaissance into decadence. It is the fight for Life and Liberty that is giving

birth to Negro literature and art today and when, turning from this fight or ignoring it, the young Negro tries to do pretty things or things that catch the passing fancy of the really unimportant critics and publishers about him, he will find that he has killed the soul of Beauty in his Art. (141)

Nine months later, Du Bois reprinted in the *Crisis* an address he delivered at the Chicago Conference of the NAACP, entitled "Criteria of Negro Art."[35] One of his most incisive pieces of writing on the subject of art, it spells out what he means by insisting that all great art must also be propaganda. Here, he tempered his criticism of Locke. He understood that black artists, to the detriment of their art, have been restricted by a white audience that only wants to hear certain plots about certain kinds of characters; either white audiences want to see the degradation that they would not stand for in portrayals of white people, or they want to see comic Topsys and pathetic Uncle Toms. He also concurred with Locke that black critics have restricted black artists by asking them to put their best foot forward:

> We are bound by all sorts of customs that have come down as second-hand soul clothes of white patrons. We are ashamed of sex and we lower our eyes when people will talk of it. Our religion holds us in superstition. Our worst side has been so shamelessly emphasized that we are denying we have or ever had a worst side. In all sorts of ways we are hemmed in and our new young artists have got to fight their way to freedom. (297)

Like Locke, Du Bois had always known that art can be a universalizing, humanizing passport: "The point today is that until the art of the black folk compels recognition they will not be rated as human" (297).[36]

But Du Bois differs from Locke because he never believed that art, much less critical appreciation of art, would bring about the political changes he hoped for. If scholarships are withheld on the basis of race, no artist of color can hope to create great things. So political struggle must be waged to make a world in which artists can practice freely without prejudice and constraints. In the most often quoted passage of this talk, Du Bois makes utterly clear his decision to back the propagandist:

> Thus all Art is propaganda and ever must be, despite the wailing of the purists. I stand in utter shamelessness and say that whatever art I have for writing has been used always for propaganda for gaining the right of black folk to love and enjoy. I do not care a damn for any art that is not used for propaganda. But I

do care when propaganda is confined to one side while the other is stripped and silent. (296)

Without the right to enjoy life, no one would be able to enjoy art. For Du Bois, art always serves that great purpose, "the right of black folk to love and enjoy," which nicely articulates political rights in the critical language of aesthetics. Indeed, Du Bois does not care to see art "stripped and silent," a figure, after all, that harkens back to the helpless slave, while propaganda struts around fully clothed. Both art and propaganda should be free and fully clothed. Indeed, when art chose freely to take its clothes off Du Bois was made uneasy. Such a use of freedom struck his rather old-fashioned aesthetic tastes as tasteless. Du Bois's critical choices often are made on the basis of whether a work of art is "properly" clothed in genteel, Victorian, middle-class fashion. Decadence becomes shorthand for the ways in which certain kinds of representation, usually depictions of lower-class life and usually the site of a popular performance, are criticized as inauthentic representations of the black race and bad propaganda. Du Bois's journals never reached beyond the small audience of elite readers who appreciated his brand of beauty mixed with propaganda. But he still longed to reach a national audience. Du Bois turned to the theatre because it might provide him with a larger, even mass, audience. One of his first attempts to use theatre to further his political and cultural agenda took place in 1913, when he wrote, directed, and produced a pageant called *The Star of Ethiopia*.

Historical pageants were extremely popular in the United States around 1910. They appeared at a moment when "civic officials were casting about for new forms through which to develop public consciousness of a 'collective' history and culture in their towns." By invoking a common past, honoring successive immigrant groups, and watching them join together, the pageants enacted the breakdown of "social and cultural barriers between local residents" and thus created a "coherent public out of a hodgepodge of classes, interests, and immigrant groups."[37] Significantly, Asians and African Americans remained emphatically outside the melting pot ideology of pageants; if blacks were depicted at all, they only appeared as comic buffoons or, in an idealized way, thoroughly contented with plantation life in the Old South. When George Pierce Baker directed a pageant in New Hampshire, he had Old Black Baker (no relation) drink some whiskey, see a Devil, and run hysterically from the scene (132). Blacks could only be synthesized as they had always been on the popular stage, as comic foils, not as equal citizens.

Thus, when Du Bois decided to organize a pageant, he took on a form whose very basis was to emphasize national commonality but which had deliberately excluded all representations of blacks as American equals. In general, pageants were supposed to create a national fervor and patriotism among Americans; Du Bois wanted to create a fervent racial nationalism for his own people. His pageant would celebrate race pride, which would separate African contributions from American ones and African American ones within this country. His pageant marks the limits of the melting pot thesis as he chronicles a race's continuing separate history. He rejected the melting pot ethos of American pageantry, but he could also see the usefulness of the genre, as Baker did and Flanagan would in the FTP, as a way to educate, counter popular mass forms, give people a more direct role in representing their own history, celebrate past achievements, and suggest a glorious future.

Du Bois produced his pageant, *The Star of Ethiopia,* first in New York as part of a celebration of the Emancipation Exposition, and then in Washington and Philadelphia. With twelve hundred actors cataloguing the glories of the African race, the pageant chronicled "the tale of the Wisest and Gentlest of the Races of Men whose faces be Black" from Africa to America, from paganism to Christianity:

> And this shall be the message of this pageantry: Of the Black man's Gift of Iron to the world; of Ethiopia and her Glory; of the Valley of Humiliation through which God would she pass and of the Vision Everlasting when the Cross of Christ and the Star of Freedom set atop the Pillar of Eternal Light.

This celebration of African civilization and African moral superiority known as "Ethiopianism" always appealed to Du Bois.[38] A popular success in New York, the pageant seemed to him a perfect medium for educational uplift:

> Literally, thousands besieged our doors and the sight of the thing continually made the tears arise. After these audiences aggregating 14,000, I said: the Pageant is the thing. This is what the people want and long for. This is the gown and paraphernalia in which the message of education and reasonable race pride can deck itself.[39]

He decided two years later to produce it in Washington, D.C., with a cast of a thousand and then in Philadelphia:

> It seemed to me that it might be possible with such a demonstration to get people interested in this development of Negro

drama to teach on the one hand the colored people themselves the meaning of their history and their rich, emotional life through a new theatre, and on the other, to reveal the Negro to the white world as a human, feeling thing.

But there were problems. As he went on to produce these next two pageants, he lost money, in spite of good reviews. Du Bois blamed the lack of interest on the white public and specifically on the American Pageant Association's lack of support for his plans. But he also noted there had been personal attacks by blacks accusing him of greed and selfishness.[40] Both of these reactions, the lack of white support and personal backbiting among blacks, would continue to plague him. Like almost all black artists, Du Bois found himself having to please two audiences who might want very different things. The American Pageant Association was silent because he challenged their notion of common ground; they did not want to admit that there were some things that could not be melted, nor did they want to heat up the pot sufficiently to melt all peoples into Americans. And his great sense of purpose seemed to alienate the very people he wished to uplift.

In any case, the historical pageant movement did not last much after World War I as a popular form, among whites or blacks. Modern times did not seem aptly represented by stories of historical continuity. Pageants would become wholly nostalgic exercises, quaint, and briefly rise up again in the thirties when the national mood became, in the last part of the Depression, desperately interested in "folk" history. Though Du Bois's attempts to start a pageant movement for blacks led to only a few other productions in Washington for black students and two masques in Cincinnati, he didn't give up on the idea that the theatre could teach his people to have pride in their history and at the same time humanize blacks in the eyes of the white world.

Over ten years later Du Bois organized KRIGWA, the Crisis Guild of Writers and Artists, a little community theatre in Harlem. In 1926, Du Bois sent out a call hoping to lure black artists back to Harlem to create a theatre exclusively *for* blacks:

> The plays of a real Negro theatre must be: I. *About us*. That is, they must have plots which reveal Negro life as it is. II. *By us*. That is, they must be written by Negro authors who understand from birth and continual association just what it means to be a Negro today. III. *For us*. That is, the theater must cater primarily to Negro audiences and be supported and sustained by their entertainment and approval. IV. *Near us*. The theater

must be in a Negro neighborhood near the mass of ordinary Negro people.[41]

Du Bois's separatist manifesto relies on a fairly straightforward assumption about realism. If an artist creates what he or she knows, then it will be authentic. The short history of KRIGWA reflects its tenuous base of support in the community it hoped to serve. A national theatre of, by, and for blacks could not be sustained without an audience of blacks in their community. But how to get them there was a problem all black critics and artists faced. The reasons for low attendance given at various times – the lure of Broadway for the greatest actors leaving only amateurs to act in the community, white producers producing shows blacks refused to see, the lack of money available for community shows, the lack of training and opportunity necessary for people to pursue technical skills – were all true. KRIGWA could not pay company members even when there was a successful production because that money had to go into the cost of the show. This lack of pay seems to have discouraged enough actors to quit after three years. Then there was the endemic problem of the lack of good scripts.[42] These were all obstacles, and yet they did not fully account for the nonemergence of a committed community audience for "uplifting" theatre.

Part of the problem was that many black intellectuals found themselves estranged from a mass black audience as well as from the popular forms of art that they denounced as denigrating. The most politically radical black critics, Du Bois and the socialists Philip Randolph and Chandler Owen, tended to have the most conservative artistic tastes. In this respect they shared with the mainstream Left in the United States high-culture sensibilities. Champions of the masses, they nevertheless found themselves at odds with mass culture, which they saw as tainted by commercialism.[43]

As a Socialist, Randolph believed that the best way to improve the urban black's working-class life was to strengthen the labor union movement, rather than begging for civil rights from Democrats or Republicans. Like other influential black critics of the period, Randolph and Owen, who had met in 1915, turned to journalism as a worthy tool for disseminating ideas. In 1917, they began to edit the *Messenger: A Journal of Scientific Radicalism*.[44] Although neither thought as systematically about the value of art as did Du Bois or Locke, much of the journal consisted of reviews and editorials about what constituted politically progressive art. In a typical editorial in the *Messenger* from the early twenties, one half of a column is devoted to an appreciation of Helen E. Hagan, a young, black pianist who had graduated from the Yale University School of Music and had gone on to study classical music in Paris. Readers, "our white and colored friends," are urged to hear her at a concert in New York:

> In this gifted young woman may be seen a model of what we would present as representative of Negro art rather than the clownism and buffoonery of Negro buck and wing dancers, ragtime piano plunkers, black-faced comedians and questionable jubilee singers. . . .
>
> We urge that the white people who have been to see "Shuffle Along," "Put and Take" and Bert Williams' "Chinaman Not Shimmying Off Tea" – to put off going to this trash one evening, take a night at the feet of a real Negro artist, and then 'shuffle along' back home with something uplifting from the Negro's soul. These plays like "Shuffle Along" ought to be spurned by the Negro. They are hardly above the "Clansman." They stress every bad quality of the Negro, namely shiftlessness, laziness, vote stealing, vote selling, criminality and immorality. Happily, however, there is another side – the side which geniuses like Helen Hagan keep bright with the highest touches of art – that clear liquid melody and music which throws a beautiful and irresistible charm over human life.[45]

Ragtime piano plunkers are equated with buffoonery, while classical music is depicted as beautiful and irresistible. "Real Negro artists" play the type of music that uplifts the soul, while black and white exploiters (not artists) create shows that cater to easy listening as well as racist stereotypes. Music without words seems to float above the ugliness of, at least, certain forms of debased representation, while popular lyrics describe the ugliness of everyday life – vote stealing and vote selling. Another editorial in the *Messenger* characterized opera as "culture, poetry, and art; the blues represented only what was loud, boisterous, cheap, tawdry, [and] unmusical. . . . A race that hums operas will stay ahead of a race that simply hums the 'blues.' "[46] The value of certain kinds of art are made quite clearly; to identify with opera instead of the popular blues will allow a race to "stay ahead." To be able to choose to identify with one form rather than another allows any race to move ahead or stay behind.

Randolph and Owen had no patience with attempts to figure out what is special about a particular race. Their eyes were on the worker. In cultural criticism, they always tried to uplift tastes, to guide their audience from low to high culture, attacking low culture for its degrading portrait of the Negro and foregoing any critique of high culture's potential for equally degrading racism. Randolph had no sympathy for strains of black nationalism or artistic Ethiopianism. Du Bois's hope to create a theatre "about, by, for, and near" Negroes would not have appealed to Randolph either. Black separatism of any sort conflicted with a socialism committed to endorsing solidarity among all workers. But such cultural ideals came at a cost. These editorials show the distance between the leaders who wished to convert the masses and the masses themselves. Randolph admitted that the magazine " 'went over the heads of the masses of the people.' " Leigh Whipper, a black actor, said, "It was a fine publication, but the community was not up to it." Another writer for the journal recounts that "the general population of Harlem did not pay much attention to it."[47]

By 1923, when Owen left to go to work in Chicago and Randolph had become a union organizer, the *Messenger* shifted from the scientific radicalism of its first six years to a more sedate journal, one that now called itself "the world's greatest Negro monthly." Randolph began to put his energies into organizing the Brotherhood of Sleeping Car Porters and stopped writing the fiery political editorials of his earlier years. He turned the magazine over to three writers who had significant interests in the artistic Harlem Renaissance: George Schuyler, Theophilus Lewis, the drama critic at the magazine, and Wallace Thurman, a young novelist and critic who would co-write with William Jourdan Rapp a play called *Harlem* and write a novel, *Infants of the Spring,* that satirized the "niggeratti" of the Renaissance. Between 1923 and 1925, Schuyler and Lewis wrote a column called "Shafts and Darts," a satiric look at events occurring in the black world. Although the *Messenger* never had the monetary resources of the *Crisis* or *Opportunity,* with these three resourceful writer-critics, the magazine, for a few short years, published some of the best-known figures of the Harlem Renaissance.

Theophilus Lewis's articles in the *Messenger* chronicle the ups and downs of uptown and downtown African American theatre. Lewis was not formally educated like Du Bois, Randolph, and Owen, and he enjoyed the theatre, all kinds of theatre, in a way that also distanced him from their more pious "high culture" sentiments. He was ready to encourage almost all forms the theatre took in Harlem. Lewis immediately noticed and praised the first season of Du Bois's KRIGWA theatre. Unlike the National Ethiopian Art Theatre, another small theatre group, which spent two years training their young actors how to enunciate "duty" but failed in their attempts to change the way the actors spoke, Du Bois dispensed with training and began immediately to put on plays.[48] Lewis approved. However, by December 1926, Lewis called the

KRIGWA season something like "slow motion pictures." Postponing opening after opening, their audience had begun to lose interest:

> When it comes to this little theatre business it seems that I belong to that class of individuals Barnum had in mind when he said there was one born every minute. Every time a new group appears and announces its intention of establishing a real race theatre I swallow their blah hook, line and sinker and immediately begin to dream dreams of a Harlem neighborhood playhouse rivaling the achievements of the one in Grand Street. I suppose it's just another case of being parent to hope. My ardent wish to see the Negro theatre become something vital and lovely instead of the glamorous brothel it is now makes me susceptible to the smooth talk of anybody who expresses a desire to work toward that end. I have had kind words and big hopes for every little theatre group which has appeared in Harlem, but so far not one of them has given me an even break by accomplishing anything. . . . The idea that a stable and effective theatre can be founded on social standing or the prestige of one man is all wet.[49]

Lewis made fun of the moralism of the Harlem Community Theatre Organization. Article III of the constitution proclaimed that only a "person of good moral character" need apply; Lewis responded: "That lets me out. I am notoriously immoral and do not regret it; damned and glad of it, so to speak."[50] Lewis speaks in the voice of jazz: antigenteel, not provincial, a New Yorker! He also satirized the elitism of Locke's cloistered view of collegiate theatre. Of Locke's promotion of college productions through the Inter-Collegiate Association, Lewis wrote: " 'Inter-Collegiate' seems to indicate that the group flying that banner intends to confine its membership to a close corporation of college folks; that is, to pedantic people whose intelligence is so unapparent that they must submit documentary evidence to prove its existence."[51] University theatre productions seemed stiff, exclusive, and boring. Lewis acknowledged more forthrightly than either Locke or Du Bois the resistance audiences had to the high-toned theatrical fare designed for their cultural education.

This split between popular and elite culture would extend throughout the twenties and thirties in Harlem. While noncommercial alternative theatres struggled to find audiences, popular commercial theatres attracted large and loyal crowds. The Apollo Theatre, which opened in 1935, had initially been billed as a high-class theatre. It quickly turned out to be the most popular theatre in Harlem, in direct competition with the FTP. With a mixture of all-girl revues, chorus girls, and elaborate production numbers, including appearances by the Scottsboro Boys and the Hot Mikado troupe, mixed together on the same bills, the mostly black audience of this white-owned theatre made its likes and dislikes known immediately. Descriptions of the audiences of this theatre sound like those from the early part of the nineteenth century. Vocal and eager participants, they were as much a part of the performance as the stage show: "Performers have always spoken of the unusual rapport between Apollo audiences and them. . . . In many an Apollo engagement, members of the audience would rise and seemingly float down to the edge of the stage, demonstrating by their eager presence the respect, delight, affection, and kinship they felt for the artist in the spotlight."[52] The entertainment was not morally uplifting except insofar as people were uplifted in their chairs, electrified by the great dancing and bawdy comedy, uplifted because they were proud by what seemed to be "theirs"; just as they embraced the Scottsboro Boys as heroes, so they would cheer Billie Holiday as one of their own great singers. The audience of the Apollo seemed empowered to participate, to find its standards of taste represented on stage.

Lewis noted other examples of popular forms of entertainment. Indeed, no other reviewer for these three journals quite gets into the appreciative swing of things as Lewis does in his writing for the *Messenger*. He admires popular singing and dancing even when it comes into conflict with his more politically advanced ideals. The Lafayette Theatre, he writes, offers a variety of drama:

> It is my present belief that Coleman Brothers are running the best *à la carte* theatre in the country. . . .
> Vaudeville one week, drama the next, musical comedy the next and "Art" stuff the next; with movies, revues, burlesques and old line melodramas not neglected. And some of the stuff is good. In fact almost all of it is toothsome to a rabelaisian. If there are any two theatres in the country catering to such a variety of tastes I want to know where they are.[53]

The chorus line at the Lafayette Theatre never hired women who were dark skinned, a practice Lewis found contemptible; nevertheless he appreciated their looks. The Lincoln Theatre's chorus line, also light skinned but much more lively than the Lafayette women, *really* pleased him: "I'd like to see Girlie at the Lincoln, where she could put on the real works" (145). Popular theatre may not build cultural pride, but it does satisfy certain desires that Lewis does not entirely scorn. Sometimes he very clearly distances himself from the audiences who frequent the Lincoln Theatre in Harlem:

> The Lincoln Theatre is a cheap movie-vaudeville house. Its audiences consist of the kind of people who kick the varnish off the furniture, plaster chewing gum on the seats and throw peanut shells in the aisles. The imperfectly disinfected odors of the lavatories somehow contrive to seep out into the auditorium to mingle with the scent of cologne and sachet powder and the body smells of people who sweat freely and frequently and bathe now and then.[54]

And yet he understands the reasons why these people go there because he too finds himself entertained by what they see:

> The world is still gaudy enough for rich men and preachers, of course, for those fortunate fellows are always assured of an adequate supply of private women. But for the luckless ledger clerk or chauffeur, whose one woman soon wears away her schoolgirl complexion with cooking and sweeping, if he is legally mated with her, or becomes wan and wrinkled from earning her own living and using contraceptives, if he is only courting her, life is a pretty drab proposition. It is to this repressed and sex-starved citizen that the modern musical show brings a royal bounty of color, hilarity and vicarious sin. It not only brightens up the dull grey monotony of his present existence but it also enables him to drink deeper of the joys of impure love than he could ever do in the past. . . .
>
> As I said in the beginning I look upon these musical shows and call them good. It is the business of the theater to satisfy spiritual craving. Whether the craving is refined or ethical is beside the point, so long as it's human. Since these shows satisfy a very definite and intense desire they are sound theatre.[55]

It is striking to note how explicitly male Lewis's theatregoer is here and how explicitly his desire for pleasure and spiritual craving is to be found in watching "girlie" shows. When Lewis describes a black male audience watching black women, the particular mixture of power and pleasure derived from the spectacle carries a different meaning than if a mixed black and white or entirely white audience were watching black women perform. The way in which black and white women in popular theatre, burlesque, and vaudeville become the objects of male desire makes some of the black bourgeois male critics squeamish. Lewis, on the other hand, is willing to acknowledge that a "sound theatre" must pay attention to the desires of at least one sex.

The little theatre movement had been sustained by a very small white, liberal, urban, educated audience. Would blacks interested in the theatre be able to count on a similar audience for support? Lewis argued that "the success or failure of the Negro theater depends on an accurate analysis of its potential audience."[56]

> It ought to be obvious from the outset that they cannot sell their commodity to the community as a whole. A part of the public will be found to be opposed to the theater on principle while another section is satisfied with the offerings of the local vaudeville house, and a third contingent is disinterested in the theater as a vehicle of entertainment. . . .
>
> The first appeal of the little theaters should be made to those members of the community who are so dissatisfied with the commercial theater that they are willing to contribute toward subsidizing a movement to bring the stage up to the level of the community's culture and spiritual life.[57]

When in 1924 the National Ethiopian Art Theatre planned to build a school and then a theatre to be located in the theatrical district of New York, Lewis argued the following in the pages of the *Messenger:*

> If the organization's aim really is to foster colored community theatres, as its constitution declares, then these theatres should be in the districts where the colored people live. . . . Another advantage of having the theatre in Harlem is that it could be partly if not wholly supported by a subscription audience. It would have to be a *little* theatre, however, for the kind of plays The National Ethiopian Art Theatre is likely to present will not have a very wide appeal.[58]

At most "the actual audience immediately available for the Negro dramatic theater will hardly exceed five thousand," which would make the budget necessarily small. A week's run could exhaust the potential audience.[59]

Lewis understood that the white owners of the principal theatres in Harlem were uninterested in serious drama, much less in the experimental works he hoped to sponsor:

> They have no knowledge of the true nature of the theater, and even if we concede their willingness to adjust the stage they control to the finer feelings of the public they serve their limita-

tions stand between their good intentions and success. Out of touch with the refinement of their own race, they cannot be expected to meet with much success when they attempt to gauge the more delicate sentiments of a people whose ways are strange to them.

While some black owners may be more sympathetic to the aspirations of their race, they make even less of a profit and are so even less willing to take risks. "Foreign financial" control and the repressed life these oppressed people are forced to lead combine to create the taste for music, comedy, and legs. Until more owners are black, Lewis argues, there will be no clear incentive to try to create a change.[60]

The sophisticated and educated community he felt himself a part of would not be satisfied with the necessarily amateurish little theatre productions of KRIGWA or with beginning playwrights and actors not up to Broadway standards, while the people who frequented the Lincoln Theatre needed the glitz of melodrama and musical comedy to lure them to the theatre. So Lewis advocated that little theatres begin with popular genres, with farce and melodrama written by black playwrights in order to please the public: "Once the audience has been won, higher forms of drama can be judiciously inserted in the repertory as a means of educating the audience."[61] If there was any hope of doing such a thing, critics would have to stop thinking of a monolithic black audience and would have to be prepared to think more positively and strategically, as Lewis did, about the virtues of popular theatre. In his criticism of the theatre, Lewis addressed what very few critics faced: that a black audience was divided by their differing cultural expectations. Most of the black audience, regardless of class, like most of the white audience, was interested only in entertainment provided by mass culture.[62] But in the end, Lewis believed, like Du Bois, that only "higher" drama could educate the race. Farce and melodrama were a tease, a prelude to more serious plays. Similar ambivalence and condescension can be found in the attitudes of directors and writers of the Negro units as each tried to figure out what the proper relationship should be between artist and audience.

IV

Du Bois, Randolph, and Owen had ultimately antipopular cultural designs. They may disagree over the advisability of a separate African-American culture, but on balance, they would subordinate artistic concerns to propagandistic ones. Lewis, who was more sensitive to the differing expectations and desires of black audiences, opened up the possibility for a multivarious culture, though he too believed only certain forms properly educate. Alain Locke and Charles Johnson, who also hoped that a New Negro culture would effect change, were more open to variations within it than Du Bois, Randolph, or Owen. Rather than celebrate a static sense of racial and national history as did Du Bois in his pageant, or insist on the importance of maintaining high cultural standards, and elite rather than popular allegiances, Locke and Johnson historicized the concept of race and by doing so enabled, at least theoretically, new cultural roles and types to be created. Neither chose to ignore racial differences, but they both saw differences as always in the process of changing. Race was not the site of an authentic self because what people consider authentic itself undergoes change over time.

In trying to jar loose old ways of thinking about Negro characteristics, Locke and Johnson rejected some of the more rigid categories of race, nationality, and cultural hierarchy and, in doing so, pointed the way to a more inclusive and ever changing American national culture. Racial difference and specific racial contributions would be their starting point, but they were eager to show the ways in which these differences changed the whole. The African "primitive" can become high modern art, and jazz becomes the sign of a historical age. Locke and Johnson's critical formulations provide more supple ways to interpret culture of different peoples and alternatives to the singular patriotic nationalism of George Pierce Baker or W. E. B. Du Bois.

Much of Locke's criticism in the twenties attempts to show the pressures that are brought to bear on black artists, but one can also see some of the same pressures on Locke, the critic, as he swings between a set of criticial standards that he believes are scientific, "technical," and "universal" and those that are rooted in racialism. In the introductory essay to *The New Negro,* he writes:

> The Old Negro, we must remember, was a creature of moral debate and historical controversy. His has been a stock figure perpetuated as an historical fiction partly in innocent sentimentalism, partly in deliberate reactionism. The Negro himself has contributed his share to this through a sort of protective social mimicry forced upon him by the adverse circumstances of dependence. So for generations in the mind of America, the Negro has been more of a formula than a human being – a something to be argued about, condemned or defended, to be "kept down," or "in his place," or "helped up," to be worried with or worried over, harassed or patronized, a social bogey or a social burden. The thinking Negro even has been induced to

share this same general attitude, to focus his attention on controversial issues, to see himself in the distorted perspective of a social problem. His shadow, so to speak, has been more real to him than his personality. Through having had to appeal from the unjust stereotypes of his oppressors and traducers to those of his liberators, friends and benefactors he has had to subscribe to the traditional positions from which his case has been viewed. Little true social or self-understanding has or could come from such a situation.[63]

Locke welcomed what he called a "scientific" interest in the Negro because he believed the scientific would dispel a "distorted perspective" that forced the Negro to see himself only as a "social problem." He believed that a true self existed and could be known. Science, objectivity, statistics, realism could delineate the truth: "For this he must know himself and be known for precisely what he is, and for that reason he welcomes the new scientific rather than the old sentimental interest" (8). Locke, who certainly knew all the ways art could be misinterpreted, argued that a trained critic could interpret neutrally, truthfully, scientifically and that the "scientifically absolute principles of art appreciation" would lay to rest certain pernicious beliefs.[64] He intended to counter stereotypes with individual cases to help define (or even create) an artistic movement.

Throughout the twenties and thirties, Locke pays attention to and insists on the relationship between white American history and black America. In his introduction to *The New Negro,* he comments that whites as well as blacks moved from rural America to the cities during the first part of the twentieth century and that both groups were forced to adjust to new surroundings: "The problems of adjustment are new, practical, local and not peculiarly racial. Rather they are an integral part of the large industrial and social problems of our present-day democracy."[65] He conflates black demands with American ones:

> The Negro mind reaches out as yet to nothing but American wants, American ideas. . . . So the choice is not between one way for the Negro and another way for the rest, but between American institutions frustrated on the one hand and American ideals progressively fulfilled and realized on the other. (12)

When Locke tries to define the newness of the New Negro, especially in his essay "Negro Youth Speaks," the type he describes is an antitype, verging on the paradoxical; the new young black artists he celebrates are culturally mature precisely because they no longer feel the need to *be* representative:

> The interval between has been an awkward age, where from the
> anxious desire and attempt to be representative much that was
> really unrepresentative has come; we have lately had an art that
> was stiltedly self-conscious, and racially rhetorical rather than
> racially expressive. Our poets have now stopped speaking for
> the Negro – they speak as Negroes. . . . There has come the
> happy release from self-consciousness, rhetoric, bombast, and
> the hampering habit of setting artistic values with primary re-
> gard for moral effect – all those pathetic over-compensations of
> a group inferiority complex which our social dilemmas inflicted
> upon several unhappy generations. . . . Where formerly they
> spoke to others and tried to interpret, they now speak to their
> own and try to express. They have stopped posing, being nearer
> the attainment of poise. (48)

This key passage sets Locke apart from the past. *His* generation refuses
to be afflicted by a group inferiority complex. *His* generation will be
free to set artistic values without regard for moral effect. When Locke
writes that the older generation of Negro writers were forced to express
themselves in "cautious moralism and guarded idealizations," he understands that prevailing attitudes – Puritanism and racial prejudice – made
this reaction necessary. "They felt art must fight social battles and
compensate social wrongs; 'Be representative': put the better foot foremost, was the underlying mood" (50). Part of Locke's newness resides
in rejecting the linkage between art and moralism, art and social justice.

Locke's critical emphasis on discriminating between aesthetic styles
could be and was construed as a turn away from considering the "moral
effect[s]" of art. Du Bois charges Locke with decadence precisely because he believes Locke separates art from politics. And much about
Locke's rhetoric around 1925 supports this view. In the same year *The
New Negro* appeared (1925), Locke wrote a short essay, "To Certain of
Our Philistines," in which he decries the way many "philistines" look to

> art to compensate the attitudes of prejudice, rather than merely,
> as is proper, to ignore them. And so, unfortunately for art, the
> struggle for social justice has put a premium upon a playing-up
> to Caucasian type-ideals, and created too prevalently a half-
> caste psychology that distorts all true artistic values with the
> irrelevant social values of "representative" and "unrepresenta-
> tive," "favorable" and "unfavorable" – and threatens a truly
> racial art with the psychological bleach of "lily-whitism."[66]

Locke argues that the struggle for social justice has made artists create
characters who conform to certain types, Caucasian types. In rejecting

as a foremost influence the politics of struggle, an artist may be freed to create countertypes. But Locke never strays far from his own proper, even moral sense of what a countertype should be. Charges of decadence could hardly be leveled at the ending of his essay when he notes with pleasure a Winold Reiss drawing entitled "Two Public School Teachers." He praises it because it reflects a

> professional ideal, that peculiar seriousness, that race redemption spirit, that professional earnestness, and even sense of burden which I would be glad to think representative of both my profession and especially its racial aspects in spite of the fact that I am only too well aware of the invasion of our ranks in some few centers by the parasitic, society loving "flapper." (156)

In another paragraph he argues for a "vital" and "contemporary" cultural expression of the Negro:

> This isn't the creed of being new-fangled for the sake of being so – let others who have more cause to be decadent and blase than we, be eccentric and bizarre for the sheer need of new sensations and renewed vigor. But for another more vital and imperative reason the artistic expression of Negro life must break through the stereotypes and flout the conventions – in order that it may be truly expressive at all – and not a timid, conventional, imitative acceptance of the repression that have been heaped upon us by both social persecution and by previous artistic misrepresentation. (156)

Locke never ignores the conditions surrounding black artists who find themselves in a racist culture fighting confining stereotypes. But in the twenties, he hoped that style itself, modernism, would provide a formal way to break with racist conventions.

Locke is always suspicious about art wholly defined in racial terms because he reacts, as does Du Bois, against derogatory and confining racial artistic standards. Black singers might find themselves able to sing only spirituals because that is deemed "natural" to them and opera is not. Locke will always argue against the confines of the "natural."[67] He does not reject the particular arts or talents of a specific race, but *only* to give expression to race art reflects a provincialism that identifies the black citizen and artist as second class, not worldly. Locke wants to ensure international and historical recognition for African American artistic *genius,* a category that transcends the provincial limits of racial or nationalistic art.

Locke can be accused of accepting the categories of the mainstream

when he writes that a career made of singing spirituals would be medio-
cre because provincial, while great artists would be known by their
success at "higher" techniques, in this case, classical music. But Locke
embraces universalism because it provides the artists of color the chances
to escape being known only for their culture. In his interpretation of
"universal" great art, there must be room for any great artist, regardless
of race. Locke believes that since Roland Hayes exhibits great technique,
he does more for the civil rights of his race than if he merely sings the
great spirituals of his people. Singing great spirituals and singing them
authentically is just what the white audience expects of him. But when
he sings European classical music, he makes it, in fact, his or everyone's – and thus truly universal.

 Though he is suspicious about racial categories, Locke doesn't dismiss
them altogether. Racial categories too must be adapted and changed
over time, through the practice of different cultural styles. Locke recognizes the importance of an African past, just as Du Bois did in his
pageant, but Locke is more interested in the *way* the African past has
been reinterpreted by modernists. In reinventing the category of the
primitive, modernists have spawned a cultural revolution that affects
not only Africans but the Western world as well. When European art
forms and expression seem exhausted, a wasteland of empty forms,
work on African art – its forms, designs, and colors – come to seem
"cunningly sophisticated." Negro art "is no longer taken as the expression of a uniformly primitive and prematurely arrested stage of culture."
Now "primitive" is a technical term only, not a damning cultural desig-
nation.[68] Although Locke pays homage to African roots and the "peculiar emotional intensity" that links Africans with African Americans, he
is really interested in the way the knowledge African American artists
gain of their ancestors' art might enable them to plan newer, "fresher,"
"bolder forms of artistic expression" (138). The authentic Negro for
Locke is mindful of the past, but never imitative of it. Authenticity is
itself a category that changes, adapts, deforms. Always the modernist,
attentive to form, Locke wishes not to preserve spirituals in their original form but to adapt them to modern purposes: "We cannot accept the
attitude that would merely preserve this music, but must cultivate that
which would also develop it."[69] African things, and African American
arts, the sorrow songs, the folk stories, are all to be freshly minted in
new styles in order that they may remain vibrant. Locke invoked the
universal in order to escape the provincial, but a more powerful argument that he also invoked did away with this binary opposition. Recognizing that there are different traditions always in the process of being
modified would be for him one way out of a stultifying and rigid
cultural and political practice.

Charles Johnson was not a professional aesthetician like Locke or a polemicist like Du Bois, but a sociologist, trained to see the ways in which theories and opinions, rather than facts, determine the idea of authenticity in people's minds. While there might be something distinctive about African American culture, Johnson was mostly impatient with those who continued to debate national allegiances. He responded to Langston Hughes and George Schuyler, who had taken issue with each other on the authenticity of race art.[70] Johnson wrote that neither author defined his terms, so that "when one of them is talking about art form the other is discussing art content; one is thinking of the Negro bourgeois, the other of intellectual parvenus; one of art, the other of artists. . . . And both discuss art as if they were thinking of culture."[71] Johnson believes that the question "is still open as to whether or not there is or can be such a thing as distinctive Negro art. Certain it seems, if there could be, it would not remain distinctive for long. It is more important now that we develop artists and let the question of a distinctive art settle itself" (238). He continues, "What is most important is that these black artists should be free, not merely to express anything they feel, but to feel the pulsations and rhythms of their own life, philosophy be hanged" (239). Perhaps Johnson's reliance on the powers of artistic "freedom" too easily dismisses the political and social constraints on artists that Du Bois could not ignore. But Johnson wanted to make room for an idiosyncratic rhythm, the weary blues of a poem.

Johnson was more interested in showing the way theories about art, culture, and politics had constructed and restricted the conception of a "true" Negro:

> This body of beliefs compounded of this mixture of truth and fiction, self-interest and passion, forms the structure of public opinion on the question of the Negro. These beliefs unchallenged not only magnify themselves and breed others, but react upon the Negro group, distorting its conduct. This distortion provokes in turn a sterner application of these beliefs and so on indefinitely, and with each step the isolation increases, each group building up its own myths and stiffening its own group morale. If the myths can be dissolved, if indeed the beliefs, can be honest questions, many of our inhibitions to normal, rational and ethical conduct will be removed.[72]

Beliefs and opinions by the dominant group construct the myth of the Negro. When the myth begins to be internalized, both whites and blacks treat the myth as fact. As a sociologist, Johnson believed that he could counter the construction of beliefs with true facts, to revise the theory to better adhere to the facts as he saw them:

There are certain physical facts that do not change. It is not the purpose here to deny or make apologies for the existence of them, whatever they are. But with respect to these there is a disposition to assume that the theories about the facts are as unchanging as the facts themselves; to deny the fact when it contradicts the theory; and to see facts when they do not exist because the theory demands them. (201)

Johnson's sense of the shiftiness of categories aligns him with Locke as both do what they can to identify new questions, new identities. Locke used aesthetic styles to judge whether one work was better, more original, more modern than another; Johnson didn't care as much about policing a black artistic canon. He just wanted to ensure its continuing existence and to give black artists the opportunity to create new works, forcing the rest of America to devise new theories to fit them.

When Johnson did address the question of national identity – African hyphenate American – he rejected Du Bois's Ethiopianism race pride and Schuyler's belief that Negroes were simply Americans with black skin. Instead, he argued that mature African American artists can and should celebrate what is distinctive about their lives in their art, but they should also recognize the ways they have been influenced by the dominant culture and the way they have, in turn, influenced it. In two separate essays, written in 1925 for *Opportunity,* Johnson defines the "new awakening."[73] In the past, Negroes, like early American writers, imitated the manners and style of the dominant group. "A criticism of Negro efforts at artistic expression well merited has been that the members of this group with a background of deep toned and gorgeously colorful experience all their own, have, with the characteristic self consciousness of the parvenu, strained desperately to avoid or deny it" (131). In avoiding the specific strains of Negro life, "they have ignored perhaps the only vital differences that can give prestige, which is, incidentally, the very object of most of the effort" (131). To stress the vital differences means to pay attention to those things at home, the dialect, the spirituals, while avoiding either classical Western art *or* Africanisms, what Johnson calls "wholly irrelevant Egyptian altars" (131). Some amalgamation of cultures has taken place and should be recorded.

Johnson never gave up the idea that great art surpasses popular or classical distinctions. He purposely blurred the hierarchy between high and low culture, a hierarchy that Du Bois and Randolph were so committed to upholding. In the same essays in *Opportunity,* he defended jazz against black critics like Randolph and conservative white critics who denounced it as a "symptom of a national disintegration." He goes on: "When the subtle effects of this 'movement' first began to be felt, there was a horrified revolt of the intellectuals against it. No primitive rhythms for these aesthetes! It was their duty to Art to resist the magic and lure of the African's syncopations and cacophony" (132). But its popularity with black and white audiences testifies to its greatness, and it has become a symbol not just of Negro music, but "the American temperament . . . a sign and symbol of the American pace – of its moving spirit" (132). For great art, "like true goodness flames, and is unmistakable; that it must leap sheer from the depths of feeling and be at its best understandable even to children. The great crowd is thus in good company in its appreciation of these magic tunes" (132). How different Johnson's premises are from the decadent charge leveled against popular art. Popular art is not seen as vulgar and minor, but as a sign of greatness and universality. The small elite group of intellectual critics don't get to define great art; the masses do. More importantly, he argues that in the case of jazz, an art created by a minority has exhibited enough power and popularity to appropriate the terms by which the majority culture defines itself: the twenties were known as the Jazz Age, then and now. In a breathtaking but characteristic Johnsonian move, he declares that black art has done more than merely bequeath blacks with full civil rights, it has defined the discourse by which whites as well as blacks see themselves as Americans. For Johnson, who rejected Du Bois's cultural separatism, jazz was to be celebrated because it had become as American as apple pie. As someone who did so much to advertise a cultural movement encompassing all of the arts, the Harlem Renaissance, Johnson was well aware that the movement might not sink roots into American culture, that it might only be taken up as a fad, in vogue because of white commercial interests. With jazz, however, the facts were apparent: black music had crossed over and defined a cultural national movement.

V

All of these critics, Du Bois, Randolph, Owen, Lewis, Locke, and Johnson, were keenly aware of the ways different voices could be used for and against them. Sometimes some of them praised high forms of art too uncritically and ignored the way such ideas as the universal co-opted the specific critical force of a particular, minority tradition. Although they recognized the risks in glorifying "authentic" folk ways when used to perpetuate stereotypes of shuffling, lazy, colorful Negroes, they also believed that folk culture could be the start of something new, something transformative and, at the same time, universal. Du Bois's Ethiopianism seemed mythical and silly to Randolph and Johnson. For Randolph, the New Negro takes his place alongside the white working classes, joining the struggle of laboring men and women. For Johnson, the New Negro was in the process of redefining the very definition of American culture with popular music.

All of the black critics shared common concerns even though they had very different ideas about how to represent their people. Each believed that discrimination and prejudice weakened the opportunities of artists and undermined the chance to create great art. Hence, civil rights could never be ignored; all argued that the arts could help to promote civil justice, although some believed more strongly than others in the efficacy of cultural ambassadors to promote the fortunes of the race. In constructing a type of New Negro, each critic thought he was creating the true Negro, whether American, African, or as an ever changing construct. Each conception of the New Negro contained some oppositional force, although it would be difficult to say that any made a clean, irrevocable break with the past to create a truly revolutionary figure. As they wrestled with categories, like the idea of universal standards, and the makeup of racial identity, they created different possibilities; they made it possible for someone to imagine more than one way of being. This, I think in the end, is the most important legacy of these critical debates. Locke would, in Houston Baker's terms, deform categories like the primitive and emphasize the evolution of all artistic and cultural forms like the spiritual and the blues. Johnson believed that theories were subject to historical change. But that is the most hopeful sign of all: a form such as jazz or the blues, a form once scorned as cheap and tawdry emerges as the most honored of cultural styles, defining a new national culture.

In African American cultural discourse, the ongoing redefinition of identity continues: is there a separate black culture or a hyphenated one? From Du Bois to the black power movement of the sixties to the films of Spike Lee and the Norton Anthology of African American literature of the nineties, cultural separatism has always been an attractive means of empowerment to cultural critics. Some, like Charles Johnson and Alain Locke, resolutely rejected such language because they feared that instead of acquiring power, cultural separatism would relegate them to a cultural ghetto. Neither Johnson nor Locke rejected black differences; they certainly saw them as a selling point, just not the only ones. And they believed the only market available was managed by whites.

Cornel West has reviewed the African American critical generation of the twenties and thirties and criticized it on two counts: first, critics often elided differences between black and white people on the basis of their belief in universalism, a false universalism, according to West, because all too often the things considered universal "belonged" to white culture, opera, for instance, and black forms like the spiritual were considered provincial. But this underestimates the fluidity and strategic quality of, for instance, Locke's and Johnson's ideas. Johnson believed that jazz could become as universal an art form as opera, and Locke thought that spirituals, like any other vital art, could change over time to become as modern as the present moment. West's second charge, that too often those critics ignored differences of class between black people, seems more serious and problematic. He recognized that their strategy of resistance to namelessness and invisibility was "moralistic in content and communal in character."[74] Such strategies tended to suppress differences within communities, thus sometimes inhibiting the freedom of expression and the development of different audiences for different sorts of art that these critics said they supported.

But the risk was, as so many black critics and artists understood, that a particular cultural expression might just be a fad, in vogue, and then quickly out of style. Popular forms change quickly; how could one ensure that black contributions to culture were firmly embedded in institutions that would nurture them with audiences committed to supporting them? As the country headed into the Depression and the thirties, critics responded to what they felt to be new times with new language. With Owen in Chicago and Randolph immersed in union activities, the management of the *Messenger* was left to others; Johnson quit *Opportunity* in 1928 to take a position at Fisk University; and Du Bois broke with the NAACP over its policy of integration, thus giving up the editorship of the *Crisis*. The Harlem Renaissance dispersed in the thirties. Chicago became a rival center for black arts, and the fear was, as Langston Hughes put it, that Harlem and, by extension, all black cultural expression was no longer in vogue.

Locke wouldn't write as much about primitivism in the thirties; his vocabulary shifted to social realism and folklore. More often in his writing, he embraces what seems to him "inevitable": proletarian art, social realism, folklore, Marxism. Even though publishing opportunities for black writing rapidly decreased during the Depression and black journals shifted from concentrating on the arts to history and sociology, the black critics who had believed that cultural expression could emancipate the race continued to believe it.[75] Locke certainly continued to practice his critical art: to inspire, cajole, define, and enable, to control and prescribe the ways in which an artist could free his people. What remains constant in Locke's critical pantheon is his abiding hatred of commercial influence over the arts and his belief that criticism has an integral role to play in the construction of art, culture, and civil rights.[76] Locke knew, of course, of the grave obstacles in the way of black artists who wanted to escape commercial slavery: the lure of mainstream success was great and the lack of alternative support debilitating. But as a cultural critic, Locke could do little about the commercial practices of a racist America, at least in frontal attacks. Instead, he pitched his argument to the black artist and the black audience who could resist the lure of popular culture.

Would a black theatre be able to cross over and embed itself in American culture as successfully as black music? The theatre seemed to have so many more stereotypes to fight. Could actors and playwrights break free of old roles? In an attempt to create new types and resist old ones, black critics turned to two alternative institutions: the little theatre in the community and the university theatre, both of which had proved hospitable to white artists interested in the experimental techniques and idealistic fervor found in the Russian theatre. Black critics never gave up thinking that the theatre might help generate a new identity and better roles for their people.

Locke insisted that the theatre must be noncommercial; it would have to be located either in little community theatres or in the university movement. The university movement coordinated by the Intercollegiate Association took off in the early twenties as one more attempt at organizing a black theatre. In 1922, Alain Locke wrote in the *Crisis:* "In the idea of its sponsors, the latter [a national Negro theatre] includes the former [race drama], but goes further and means more; it contemplates an endowed artistic center where all phases vital to the art of the theatre are cultivated and taught – acting, playwriting, scenic design and construction, scenic production and staging."[77] Howard University had instituted a drama group overseen by Professor Montgomery Gregory of the Drama Department called the Howard Players, and Locke described their work with a good deal of sympathy, arguing that the university setting allows both experimentation and continuity, with the same professors, directors, and a captive audience every year. For Locke, the university setting could provide just the protection from the marketplace for a Negro theatre to develop without worrying about finding a mass audience. Citing the work of university professors like Professor Baker of Harvard, whose 47 Workshop had sponsored many a fledgling playwright, and Professor Koch of the University of North Carolina, whose Carolina Players featured regional plays, Locke argued that colleges had become the place where people can learn how to write plays, and the university had become the place to sponsor a national drama.

The question remained throughout the twenties and thirties whether, in Locke's words, "internal support" from within the race could be generated, whether white publishers or white critics could help bring into the world an accurate, authentic new type of Negro, or whether some combination could work together to create an authentic culture. In the thirties, many radical groups involved in the theatre sprang up around the country and so, of course, did government support for the arts, in both cases support not tainted by commercial interests. The FTP seemed to present an unparalleled opportunity to those who wished to set a new course for American culture – free from commercial interests and yet eager to engage the largest possible audience. African American critics who had been advocating a race theatre would be able to see their theories tested. Locke wrote that the FTP offered a chance for "Negro art and artists" to develop a "sound group organization."[78] But just because the FTP wasn't a commercial enterprise didn't mean it was exempt from the struggles and contradictions involved in representing an authentic national people's theatre. The Negro units, like other parts of the FTP, would battle over whether the theatre should entertain or teach, and over what forms were properly and authentically Negro, testing what was genuinely different about the African American experience.

3

Producing New Dramas:
The Politics of Choice

– How do you account for the lack of a playwright who might write about
social issues? . . .
– They were writing about 'em, but nobody would produce them, you know.
There were some attempts at what is now Community Theatre, but they
weren't terribly successful because they weren't patronized. And there was
certainly no hope of money to produce them with in the sense that you can now
get your project funded Bed-Stuyvesant, build it into a renewal project or
something. There was just no way.   – Leonard De Paur[1]

Some playwrights and directors thought that the only way to
showcase social issues relating to African Americans was through dramatic realism. Consistently, workers' theatre in the thirties dramatized
the most pressing racial issues, in various agitprop performances about
the Scottsboro case, for instance, and in one of the most popular interracial dramas, *Stevedore,* written by George Sklar and Paul Peters and
produced by the Theatre Union, and then by the FTP. In 1935, Sklar
paid homage to working-class theatre that tried to present Negro "reality" on stage:

> In America, it's time we had a theatre with courage enough to
> present on the stage the life issues and realities which confront
> the twelve million Negroes in this country everywhere. We've
> never had such a theatre in America. Not until very recently,
> when the working-class theatre emerged and shot up into full
> flower, was there even the faintest glimmer of it.[2]

In 1927, Locke had contrasted the "drama of discussion and social
analysis and the drama of expression and artistic interpretation," and
had chosen the "folk play" as the form from which will grow "the real

future of Negro drama."[3] By 1935, he had to acknowledge that in spite of his lack of political sympathy with Communists, the Left had taken black subjects seriously in their dramas of discussion and social analysis:

> The radical theatre groups (dance groups too) are more and more incorporating Negro affiliated groups, I hear – Even Rose McClendon is supposed to be interested. They hope to interest the Negroes in communism, but if I know anything, it will be the art that they take to – and they will spit out the doctrine. . . . It's good to realize that (with the success of *Stevedore*) the movement may take Negro actors and Negro drama along with it to a place of greater truth and sincerity.[4]

For Locke, working-class theatre was only a tool to advance the "greater truth" of African American drama. He believed that Communist "doctrine" could and should be easily separated from "art," though it is hard to know where one starts and the other stops in any one particular production.

Certainly some productions of the FTP's Negro units, including *Stevedore, Turpentine, Sweet Land, Hymn to the Rising Sun,* and *Big White Fog* were examples of dramatic realism, inspired by an urgent sense of social issues and a desire to criticize the status quo. And they did upset different members of the FTP and its audience. They offended both black and white constituencies, and yet they still managed to be produced. Some plays expressly written for the FTP with social issues at their core, *Liberty Deferred* and *Panyared,* however, were judged to be too inflammatory and were suppressed. Did these radical plays break the mold of black entertainment? How satisfying were they to audiences, how effective in representing social issues?

The static qualities of photographs don't give us much to go on. Was the staging static or the texts? The basic drama in all of these social issue plays lay in whether speeches, preaching, and exhortations would overcome silence enforced by all sorts of power, by whips, guns, and by the fear of stepping outside one's seemingly natural spot. Who would win and what were the best strategies? In the photograph of *Sweet Land* (Figure 1), people are sitting neatly in rows, listening to the black man speak. He looks like an outsider, dressed up or at least better dressed than the workers sitting before him. Will they believe him because he is different or because he is one of them? Will they rally around him to risk change and fight their oppressors? *Stevedore* (Figure 2) enacts a tense standoff. In the figure, the white policeman has his back to the audience, while we see the looks of utter distrust on the faces of the black men. Their faces are set, closed, wary, not beaten, but not ready to confront

Figure 1. LCFTP. New York City. "A fervent appeal, *Sweet Land*."

Figure 2. LCFTP. Seattle, WA, June 1936. "Tense standoff, *Stevedore*."

Figure 3. LCFTP. New York City. "Convicts and power, *Hymn to the Rising Sun*."

head on, at least not yet. In *Hymn to the Rising Sun* (Figure 3), we can see a scene that might have been at least one of the reasons the Negro unit in Chicago protested against performing this play. To act the part of the convict face down or those cringing from the whip, to be the abused and silenced was not at all what they had in mind as an exercise in either entertainment or social uplift. The sets of *Big White Fog* (Figures 4, 5, and 6) were said to be so real that one felt as though one were walking into someone's living room. At the beginning of the play, the black family is well heeled, well dressed; the home looks homey. But in the course of the play, we have the father giving money to the outlandishly dressed Garveyites. Losing to them and to the Great Depression, the family is on the verge finally of losing their home. In the last scene, the living room is empty of furniture, but full of people. One black man, partially obscured, lies dead on the couch, and a single black policeman stands in front of a mixed crowd looking on. The order is unbalanced. Who will give in first? Will things revert to normal, will the oppressed still be oppressed, or will some other combination, of black and white working people, make a stand and a change?

Figure 4. LCFTP. Chicago, IL, April 6, 1938. "At home, *Big White Fog*."

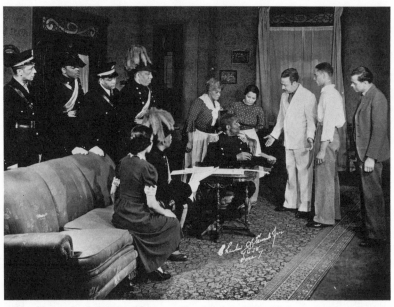

Figure 5. LCFTP. Chicago, IL, April 6, 1938. "Money to the Garvey-ites, *Big White Fog*."

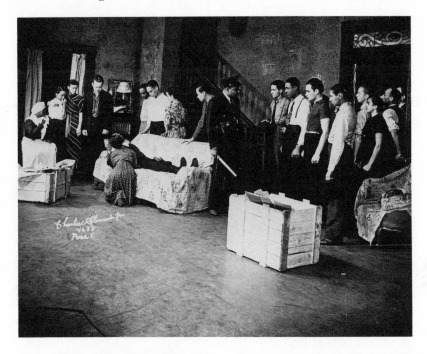

Figure 6. LCFTP. Chicago, IL, April 6, 1938. "Last act – a new beginning, *Big White Fog*."

When did an outsider seem most compelling, and when did groups find strength through listening to their own? When did actors fall back on familiar ways of entertaining, and when did some sort of interracial alliance liberate and create new ways of being? The drama behind the dramas, how particular plays were chosen to be produced and others rejected, mirrors the drama on stage between those who risked speaking up in a different voice and those who felt the cost was too high.

I

In choosing directors of the Negro units and in choosing particular plays, we can see how the ideal of a people's theatre was put to the test. Harlem, the showcase of major black theatrical talent, would speak with many voices about who would be best to direct the Negro unit. Indeed, this was of no small importance since, during the Depression, the FTP became the largest employer of blacks in Harlem.[5] In detailing the discussion of who should direct the Harlem Negro unit, we can see what was at stake: not only what sorts of plays would be produced and who might in turn direct them, but who would be employed and whose ideals would be voiced. The many examples of censorship reflect the tensions between whites and blacks and within the black community and white community. By following the production controversies about a new play, *Big White Fog,* written by Theodore Ward for the Chicago Negro unit, we can see in microcosm the competing ideals and impediments of a people's theatre, how various desires of intellectuals and writers came into conflict with actors and audiences.

Hopkins had made a case to Congress and the rest of the American people that writers, painters, musicians, and actors should be allowed to do the work they were trained to do, and further that the art they made should be enjoyed by all Americans, that art *must* be part of the daily lives of any great nation. Black leaders like Du Bois, Locke, and Johnson as well as many others agreed that great black artists could prove the worthiness of their race. A lot was asked of the theatre: to provide cultural appreciation and insight into African Americans, to uplift a community and also integrate it into the main currents of American life. More than the other arts, theatre depended on bringing together different kinds of workers with very different skills – directors, actors, writers, designers, producers – people often with very different sorts of training and understanding of the work they did. How to harness diversity of experience and ideas and make people work together was the main task of all the directors on the Negro units of the FTP.

Of course, it would be ridiculous knowing something of the debates in the black community over representation to expect that a single point of view, an overriding philosophy could be agreed upon. Although most people involved (though significantly not all) agreed that the traditional African American theatrical stereotype – the comic, bumbling, shuffling, or tragic, primitive, sensual character – had to be replaced, not everyone had the same idea of what the replacement should look like. Disagreements and struggle over who was to represent whom and how marked the history of the Negro units, and no more vividly, loudly, and vociferously was the right of representation argued than in Harlem, the home of a long and rich artistic African American tradition.

Expectations were high in Harlem when the Lafayette Theatre re-opened under FTP auspices. An essay written by a performer in the Negro unit listed some of the work he believed this particular theatre could do:

> 1. raising to the level of cultural appreciation and preserving the Negro's contribution to American folk lore;

2. offering both black and white Americans the opportunities for getting a more accurate insight into the psychological or thinking processes which are responsible for many of the customs, mores and traditions which have resulted from the influence of Negro life in America;
3. offering a basis of personality integration for the average Negro who views his racial characteristics as handicaps and unfortunate personal characteristics chiefly because of the result of commercial exploitation of his folkways by whites;
4. offering a basis of community integration and appreciation of the Negro's contributions to American culture as legitimate;
5. bridging an economic and social adjustment which our country has been undergoing at a critical pace within the last few years.

The FTP is more than simple work relief: it is a kind of cultural consciousness raising for blacks and whites. It instills pride in Negro culture and, with new plays, revises American history. By fostering new plays and new stories, the theatre will show "that black as well as white hands tore away the underbrush and helped to raise the gigantic industrial structures. The theatre can be a means of welding this branch of misunderstanding and help to unify America." In rescuing blacks from the hopelessness of poverty and unemployment, the FTP's Negro units will save "the spark of Americanism which economic and traditional adversities threatened to smother. . . . Federal Theatre is an institution – an institution designed to keep America, America, and, if possible, to make it more American!"[6] There are at least two missions mentioned here, not necessarily in conflict, but not necessarily the same: to raise the level of awareness of African Americans in African American influences on American culture and to raise the level of awareness in whites of the same thing. On the one hand, the ideal is to integrate difference into the American mosaic by acknowledging racial contributions and, on the other, an insistence on the genuine difference of "Negro" folklore and the race's different and unique history within America. To integrate differences and at the same time proudly celebrate American differences contribute to some of the tensions of the FTP's Negro units. At some point and for some people, the language of difference becomes an impediment to integration, while to others the language of integration censors and covers up distinctions.

The choice of the directors of the flagship Negro unit, the Lafayette Theatre in Harlem, illuminates the difficulties and compromises in finding single philosophies, as do the choices of plays over the next four years. Nowhere was the struggle for control over the FTP's direction more fierce than in the Negro units of Harlem. With the Depression hitting blacks hardest and Harlem itself the scene of riots in 1935, with rents double what they would have been elsewhere and businesses in the community still unwilling to hire blacks, people eagerly sought employment in the FTP. But who would direct the Lafayette Negro unit?[7] John Houseman recounts in his memoirs three factions competing for power: a group of black actors who had been performing at the Lafayette Theatre for decades felt that the director should come from their ranks; some of the talented tenth, middle-class Negro intellectuals in Harlem thought a white person should be appointed, with Negro advisers from their ranks, because they did not respect the work of black community theatre; and professional black actors like Rose McClendon were torn between their desire to choose a black director and the feeling that only a white man would elicit the kind of respect needed outside Harlem if the Negro units were to succeed.

Rose McClendon, the most esteemed black actress of the time, asked that John Houseman run the Negro unit in Harlem because of his experience as a director. According to Flanagan, McClendon reasoned that most blacks were performers and hadn't enough training or experience in directing and designing to be effective. Whether she herself believed there were no qualified blacks or whether she believed that whites believed there were no qualified blacks is unclear.[8] Others have noted that white directors were necessary because a black director could not be sure he or she would be allowed on an elevator in a downtown New York building to attend an organizational meeting.[9] Carlton Moss, who became one of Houseman's black aides and who was to take over as one of the directors after Houseman left, said:

> In my opinion, McClendon suggested Houseman because the separation between the black and white community was such, and this was in the total life, that to guarantee that the community would get half of the half a loaf, you have to have somebody who the community felt could go downtown and not be thrown off the elevator or not be insulted before he got into the building. And this person should have demonstrated by something that he could be trusted.[10]

It would seem that no one in the upper echelons of the FTP (all of whom were white) believed that a black person had the necessary clout and respect to run a Negro unit; and since the black community itself was unsure on this point, codirection seemed a viable compromise.

McClendon's role in advising that separate units be created for blacks, her previous work in community theatre emphasizing topical dramas, her ability to secure key actors and directors including Carlton Moss and Harry Edward, who would take over from Houseman and McClendon in a short time, made her an important, though historically unappreciated, part of the FTP. Illness cut her work short, and by 1936 Houseman continued on alone.[11]

Houseman might have been perceived more trustworthy to the black community because he had directed a black cast in *Four Saints in Three Acts* and because he was not American-born. Moss continues:

> He was an adult when he came to the United States, and there was an assumption, and it's not necessary to go into whether it's real or not, but there was an assumption that having been raised outside the United States, that he would not have the manifestations of racism that conceivably most people who come up in the United States could have or might have or do have. . . . Now this is true that Houseman had the personality and has the personality of getting things done. He is a fantastic administrator, a developer, a manipulator.[12]

With McClendon sick at the time and only operating as a figurehead, Houseman and his team of white men, including Orson Welles, and his two black aides, Edward Perry, the stage manager of *Four Saints,* and Carlton Moss, a former drama counselor, took on the direction· of the Harlem Negro unit at the Lafayette Theatre. This was a compromise appointment. The Negro unit was separately configured and yet, of course, not entirely autonomous, with the director from outside the community running interference downtown as well as uptown. Still, the importance of creating separate racial units, of insisting that racial equality would be achieved only through autonomous, separated units, was key to Flanagan's thinking as well as to someone like Rose McClendon.

Houseman immediately confronted his first problem, a problem that afflicted all of the directors of Negro units: "I had encountered our first predictable hazard – the absence of performable Negro scripts."[13] The Communists said no "hankerchief-heading" – no minstrel comedies; the Urban League wanted nothing to do with sex and squalor; the sophisticated Harlem theatre audience had already seen *Emperor Jones* downtown. Houseman decided to set up two companies, one devoted to contemporary plays, presumably focusing on "racial material," and the other classical. He chose the first play for the Lafayette by a process of elimination. The politics of the situation made it imperative that he choose a contemporary play but one that wouldn't offend the various factions. *Walk Together, Chillun* by Frank Wilson didn't outright offend anyone because it was hardly new or exciting. The second play, *Conjure Man Dies* by Rudolph Fisher, was more successful with Harlem audiences, who liked its mystery, its in-jokes, its topical plot. But Houseman was not primarily interested in building up a community audience for community interests. He had personal ambitions and wanted a hit, and it came not from explicit racial material but from a production of Shakespeare's *Macbeth*. Set in Haiti amid tropical palms and witches chanting a "native" language, Orson Welles, the director, adapted the English classic to a New World beat. A total of 109,435 people attended a run of fifty-nine performances after which the production moved downtown for two weeks and was finally sent on tour to play in seven major cities.[14]

The *Macbeth* production did what it was supposed to for Houseman and Welles. It made them marketable. Houseman only supervised one more play after *Macbeth* for the Negro unit, a political play with plenty of racial material called *Turpentine,* about the conditions of black labor in the South. What Houseman really wanted was to produce more plays like *Macbeth* with Welles. When he asked to be released from Harlem, the FTP allowed him to start a new Federal Theatre unit, a classical theatre, in which he and Orson Welles could continue their theatrical experiments.

When Houseman left, he took with him his key white assistants and told the blacks, in effect, "Now it's time you take it all over and you run it."[15] But who was "you"? Flanagan announced that, on the recommendation of Philip Barber, three directors should take Houseman's place: Gus Smith, a committed leftist who had cowritten *Turpentine,* would be managing producer; Harry Edward, a West Indian intellectual, would be in charge of administrative service; and Carlton Moss would be head of publicity.[16] Leonard De Paur, music director on the project, believed that "an internal political battle of some magnitude" was in progress and that no one person could have satisfied all factions:

> Gus and a woman named Frances Smith – no relation – were very strong people and coming from a certain segment of the black theatre, had a certain constituency of people who had had similar experiences.
>
> Carlton, the educated, accomplished professional, was well regarded in certain quarters. Carlton, I think, fancied himself something of a politician but he wasn't quite.
>
> Harry was perhaps the ablest of them all but Harry just never

understood these blacks. Harry was a West Indian of superior attainments, intellectual, educational, and an excellent man. But he was as remote from the Gus Smith type of individual as I am from a Martian.

And so it would have been, I think, disastrous had either of those three been given the directorship. As it evolved, it worked out fairly satisfactorily with Gus Smith as a kind of figurehead director, supported well and being smart enough. As I say, he had a very keen mother wit or intuition. He took good advice from Harry Edward because he realized that Harry had the book learning. . . .

I mean, I could have seen Harry and Hallie being a powerful combination, had they traveled in concert, you know. . . . She could have used somebody like him, and he would have been attracted to her. Because she had all this imagination and drive and an honest-to-God, almost Populist's desire to see this kind of theatre happen. And Harry approved of this, you know. He reminded me of Jefferson in the sense that he was a philosophical Populist but a real patrician down deep, you know. There was an ambiguity about it. Yes, that should happen for all those people; yes, the masses should have this. But let him rub shoulders with them and he would cringe. It's a strange thing, and I suppose we've all got some of that. It's an extreme middle-class attitude and nothing is more middle-class than a middle-class British-oriented black and Harry came out of this. Anybody with three initials in the middle of his name: Harry S. V. Edward. Not Edwards, but Edward. Don't put an "s" on that. He's gone now, but he would turn over in his grave if you put an "s" on it.[17]

Everyone recognized that the three represented different factions. Smith's radical politics and Edward's "foreign" status made them easy targets, and Moss's alliance with Houseman may have discredited him as well. Smith's group was resented by those who felt passed over. An unsigned letter written to Philip Barber in 1937 lists the complaints of one older female singer against the "clique" of Gus Smith, Frances Smith, Charles Tayler, and several white members of the unit. She complained about the dues required by the CPC Union (City Projects Council, a left-wing organization). If you refused to pay, she claimed, you would not be cast in shows or you would be sent to other projects. Then she charged that the people in power are neither true theatre people nor true Americans: "I am making an appeal to you to send some

White person up to this project 806, and get conditions straightened out.
. . . if it were left to me I would deport every West Indian in America,
they are forever criticizing the American Government, and the President
of the United States."[18]

Being "poor" and "hungry" and committed to social change doesn't
necessarily mean that, as some nostalgic-minded people suggest about
the thirties, everyone got along.[19] With the community itself split over
who was American and who wasn't, the three directors couldn't devise a
single direction for the Harlem Negro unit. At best they compromised,
producing some racial plays like *Sweet Land,* about a World War I
veteran returning to the South, and "classical" plays like the four one
acts of the sea by O'Neill and Shaw's *Androcles and the Lion.* Just as
Houseman balanced classical with contemporary plays, in order to satisfy various audiences, so too did the black directors find it necessary to
please their diverse audience.

II

Many black intellectuals had long hoped to found a national
black theatre, one that could create new dramas for the American people. Within the four short years of the FTP, the Negro units would
provide a space, one that was always circumscribed by congressional
cuts and theatrical prejudices, by racism, and by the politics of artistic
choices. Both the hierarchy of the FTP and the black artistic community
agreed that it would be important to generate new plays and new
playwrights, especially ethnic plays by ethnic writers. How to foster
plays and writers, how to teach the craft, and what sorts of plays to
support were some of the pragmatic questions worked out in the FTP.
Workshops were begun and new plays read; some were censored and
others produced. New plays by young black playwrights were written
for the FTP, but not all were produced because they were considered
too crude, too dangerous, or too offensive. The tense negotiations over
whether a young black playwright in Chicago, Theodore Ward, would
be able to persuade the FTP to produce his new work, *Big White Fog,*
demonstrate that although new dramas were written during the tenure
of the FTP, old ones continued playing.

Controversies split the Left and the Right, the black and the white
communities over whether, for instance, the plays of a white southern
liberal playwright, Paul Green, were appropriate material on political or
aesthetic grounds for a Negro unit. The case of Green's plays inspired a
great deal of discussion over what was authentic or inauthentic in them
with wildly different opinions about how progressive or regressive,

outdated or all too current they were. A student of Frederick Koch at
the University of North Carolina and part of the Carolina Players,
Green wrote a series of "folk dramas" in the twenties about southern
blacks. Locke thought Green was "steadily moving us toward a tragic
Negro drama with light and power and universality."[20] Another critic,
Montgomery Gregory, liked Green's *The No 'Count Boy* because it was
"an excellent demonstration of a charming play wrought from the
homely materials of the southern Negro. Here is fidelity to the actual
life of these people, yet an artist, not a reporter, has painted the picture."[21] But others disparaged Green precisely because they found his
portrait of southern black life *in*authentic. Writing for *New Theatre,*
Eugene Gordon claims that the workers weren't fooled by Green's or
O'Neill's dramas:

> Negro workers who know the "stark realism" of, say,
> O'Neill's, Green's and Heywood's plays look upon it not as the
> kind of realism the black man actually encounters, but as just
> another and a more "civilized" method of attack. It is only the
> upper class Negroes who accept the false fatalism of *All God's
> Chillun Got Wings, Roll, Sweet Chariot,* and *The Emperor Jones* as
> true to Negro life.[22]

Alliances that crossed class lines occurred among critics who attacked
Green's authenticity. Both Du Bois and Theophilus Lewis, the theatre
critic for the *Messenger,* disliked Green because his tragedies seemed to
leave no room for change, for uplift, for a new story to be written. Du
Bois's review of Green's 1927 play, *In Abraham's Bosom,* attacks it because it is a tragedy. Du Bois writes that Green "feels with his black
folk," yet

> he and his producers between them have presented the same
> defeatist genre of Negro art which is so common and at the
> present apparently inescapable. It arises from the fact that the
> more honestly and sincerely a white artist looks at the situation
> of the Negro in America the less is he able to consider it in any
> way bearable and therefore his stories and plays must end in
> lynching, suicide or degeneracy.

On the one hand, the defeatist genre arises because from the sympathetic
outsider white point of view, the black man and woman's lot in America
seems insupportably tragic. And on the other hand, when an artist,
Du Bois claims, attempts to show how a black hero may rise above
circumstances, the producer blocks it because the audience (the white
audience) won't like anything that contradicts their sense of "reality":

"It can't be done; the audience won't stand it." If the comic Sambo reassures white audiences that the black man is happy, then the tragic Abraham reassures because he plays out the only other acceptable role. Du Bois ends his review by asking for parts for blacks that end occasionally in "plain and unquestionable triumphs."[23]

When Theophilus Lewis reviews *In Abraham's Bosom*, he simply states that the play does not accurately depict Negro life. A playwright

> can get away with murder if he is shrewd enough to call his play a treatment of Negro life. Once the leading character is identified as a mulatto the Park Row boys throw Aristotle, Hazlitt, Lessing and the rest out of the window. . . . Lack of space prevents me from pointing out other numerous instances where Massa Green has mistaken the obvious for the actual and other places where he has attempted to palm off mere irrational behavior for authentic Negro character.[24]

In another piece, Lewis writes on what he calls the Paul Green "menace"; he sees him as a blocking figure, "an evil geni threatening the development of Negro drama":

> Now the general run of white people are absolutely ignorant of Negro life and white critics appear to cherish wild and antinomian ideas about it. This ignorance on the part of both critics and public enables an incompetent playwright to get away with murder by the simple expedient of calling his gaucheries "Negro" plays, provided he writes about sordidness in a sentimental way and winds up his stories with a sad ending.[25]

Tragic flaws should be found *in* the tragic character as well as in fate, but in Green, the "calamities which occur . . . happen independently of the beliefs and conduct of the character. Hence the play as a whole is artificial, illogical and unconvincing" (18). The Green menace perpetrated yet one more stereotype of the Negro, the tragic Negro, only this time conceived by a southern white liberal.

Given the divided opinion of black critics, it isn't surprising that white playreaders on the FTP were equally divided about whether Green was appropriate material for the Negro units. One playreader judged *In Abraham's Bosom* a "fearfully realistic presentation of the Negro problem," while another called it outdated and rejected the play for the FTP:

> This is definitely not a play for the project. Among other things, the scene in which Goldie and Abraham go off to lie in the bushes and the other negroes discuss their being "like

Hawgs" and get so sensuous a thrill out of it vicariously that they break into a primitive dance, punctuated by odd giggles – well, it is interesting to a different audience, but it might be censored by those ready enough at best to criticise the project. Moreover, the conditions of negro education which existed in 1885, the time of the play, have been largely overcome and the prejudice on which the play is based is certainly mostly dissipated. – Even ten years ago when the play was written, the subject matter was frankly dated though the treatment was modern, and the only audience interested was that which enjoyed the technical power of the author, or that which enjoyed the emotional orgy. Granted this, why bring up to a mixed audience, not always composed of the most controlled elements, the bitterness and vicious enmity between the blacks and whites which existed fifty years ago and why deliberately do a play which works so powerfully on the emotions of race antagonism? Our audiences are inclined to take plays personally – to heart – not as finely wrought curios to be viewed with a mental perspective and an historical interest. If there are any reactionary sparks, they should not be lit in the mass mind.[26]

This is a mixed message at best. The play is dangerous but out of date, yet the audience may not read it as history but as a realistic portrait of the present. It is powerful enough to incite race antagonism even though the reviewer claims that racial prejudice has "mostly dissipated." Making the decision to produce the play more problematic seems to be the fact that the audience will be racially mixed and that they will come with very different perspectives. Blacks who are bitter and whites who are racist may sit within the same theatre and touch off "reactionary sparks." But does the reviewer mean reactionary as in "having a reaction" or in political "regression"? Who would be reacting to what? Although not clearly spelled out, it seems that the fear the reviewer speaks to is simply that of having different reactions to the play expressed in the same space; some blacks presumably would be embarrassed by the scene in which Goldie and Abraham "go off to lie in the bushes," and some whites might consider this "interesting." What is insulting to some entertains others. Richard Wright and Theodore Ward championed Green's plays as dangerous and incendiary, while Lewis and Du Bois criticized Green's plays as tragically quiescent, dulling the mind of the audience. This particular playreader expressed in a muddled way how audiences could and would have mixed reactions to the play. No agreement on the correct political reading of Paul Green's plays seemed to be possible. Was fatalism quiescent or a critique of society? It depends, in part, on who was speaking.

Most of the people connected with Negro theatre through the twenties and thirties and in the FTP produced Green and other white playwrights because that was what was at hand, but they hoped that black playwrights would come forward to tell the story of their people. Critics blamed white producers, commercial pressure, and an unsympathetic audience for the lack of black playwrights. Theophilus Lewis argued that a national Negro theatre needed plays by black playwrights. Without Shakespeare, Ira Aldridge would have never been famous, likewise Gilpin and Robeson without O'Neill. There are plenty of great black actors but

> drama, to employ a theatrical metaphor, is the very bones and nerves of a national theatre; acting is only the grease paint on its cheeks.
>
> It ought to be obvious that a national theatre that tries to advance by developing its acting at the expense of its drama is marching on quicksands. Acting, however great, is compounded of stuff even more flimsy than human life. If the actor follows the call of the flesh, as most actors do, dipsomania or Dr. Bright's disease or some other murderous malady is almost certain to cut him down in the prime of his years. Even if he leads an abstemious life, as hardly any actor does, he will eventually be deprived of his power by the palsy of old age. And the most he can bequeath to his heirs and assigns of the theatre is a bit of worthy tradition. On the other hand, great drama is as enduring as the civilization that produces it.[27]

Like Locke, Lewis believed in an artistic hierarchy in which words held highest place. Sterling Brown thought that after the successes of O'Neill and Green on Broadway, plays on serious black topics had the potential to be a critical success if they were well crafted. But craft is neither natural nor easy to come by:

> A man may have ability at characterization, at dialogue, a wide knowledge of life, a deep and sincere humanity and still be a dramatic flop. There is so much of technique to be learned; so arduous an apprenticeship to go through. Obviously a first hand knowledge of the stage is essential – often an absolute prerequisite. To this of course must be added a knowledge of the underlying laws of dramatic construction.[28]

But when blacks were routinely prohibited from buying tickets to mainstream theatres, the means of apprenticeship to the theatre was sharply circumscribed.

The FTP looked like it might be one institution that would be able to provide the necessary instruction about dramatic construction while paying a living wage to those who were to be instructed. In Harlem, George Zorn organized the Negro Dramatists Laboratory, lasting from November 1936 through February 1937. One hundred aspiring playwrights came to an initial meeting; during the first month, about fifty people attended night classes. They heard lectures on playcraft, on "middle class comedy," and on collective playwrighting; people came from the Federal Theatre to tell them what sort of plays had already been produced, how authors secured copyright, the technique of O'Neill, and the art of scenic design. In the second month, people began to submit their own plots, and then they attempted to write a play separately and collectively. About twenty-five people remained at the end of the course. In his final report, Zorn wrote, "The problem now before us is virtually the same as before we started, the need of better written plays by Negroes for Negroes but the limitations of the Laboratory were such that it was impossible for us at that time to get adequate authors on playwrighting."[29] Four months, or even four years, was not enough time to develop the "discipline" and the craft necessary to produce a cadre of playwrights. Carlton Moss underscores the necessity of proper "motivation":

> Well, this [playwrighting seminars] was, let's put it this way, a neglected area. Because we didn't have the forces to do this and also, when you say "forces," this is difficult to create. You have to have motivated people if you are going to talk about writing. You know that. You just can't go home one night and say, "I'm going to write." This requires tremendous discipline. So we didn't have that. We didn't have it, so what we largely did was had a place to give employment to people who needed employment and to give entertainment that had a higher level than the standard stuff in the community and hope, and we did develop one or two individuals who went beyond that. Now you have 600 people, 500 people in the theatre and if one comes out fairly successful, that's not a bad average.[30]

Writers like Langston Hughes who already had a reputation didn't immediately gravitate to the FTP. Leonard De Paur says such established writers gave varying reasons:

> In the first place, I don't think they were fully convinced that
> because the Federal Theatre was a government agency, they
> were gonna be allowed to do anything decent, you know. There
> was this lack of confidence, and I think we would have had to
> produce a couple of successful *Turpentines* and things of that
> sort before they would have overcome their doubts.[31]

They were right to be cautious, for their idea of what was "decent"
might conflict with either community or bureaucratic standards.

Hopkins had said the FTP was to be free, adult, and uncensored. The
first two goals were relatively easy to ensure, but the latter was not.
Flanagan herself admitted in her book about the FTP that a government
theatre "necessarily" found itself in the business of censorship:

> As directors of a government theatre, all of us on the policy
> board, and that included all regional directors, were necessarily
> censors. That is, we had to bar out material which seemed
> inappropriate or dangerous for a public theatre to do. We did
> this constantly on questions of public taste and policy. But in
> the matter of selection we were motivated by the general princi-
> ples of a theatre as vigorous and varied as possible, a theatre
> belonging to no one region or political party but to the country
> as a whole.[32]

What one part of the public may consider inappropriate or dangerous
may seem tasteful and necessary to another, but clearly the FTP had to
negotiate between public tastes and policies in planning their productions. Sometimes the hierarchy at the FTP wasn't willing to be as
vigorous as some thought they might be; often the FTP was thought to
be much too vigorous for its own good. Though everyone considered
the Negro units part of the "varied" nature of the theatre, there were
always limits as to what sort of variations would be allowed. The limits
changed from unit to unit and from production to production.

At least two new plays written for the FTP by black playwrights were
never given productions. The playwrights had been encouraged to take
up the subject of race and did so only to find FTP backing slip away.
Abram Hill and John Silvera collaborated to write *Liberty Deferred,* a
recounting of the history of African Americans in the United States.
Hill had graduated from Lincoln University in 1938. Upon arriving in
New York he had been assigned to the Negro Youth Division of the
FTP and then transferred to the playreading division where he says,
"My job was to read scripts and to recommend these scripts. . . . My
particular job was to scrutinize scripts with Negro characters or Negro

themes to see that these were true to honest portrayals of Negro life or whether they were the stereotyped kind of plays." While Hill read submitted work, his supervisor suggested he write a living newspaper on Negro history. The FTP had achieved fame and notoriety with other living newspapers about the courts, utility companies, housing, and syphilis, all current and controversial subjects. Piecing together reports and factual information, the living newspaper was supposed to present different sides of a problem. Flanagan particularly liked the form because it fulfilled most of the FTP's requirements: it provided parts for many actors; its reliance on newspapers and current events meant that even the most amateur playwright could get a grip on a subject; multiple writers could be used for research; and finally the living newspaper, because it addressed topical subjects, challenged an audience to think about present problems. A living newspaper about race seemed daring but within the scope of the FTP's sense of purpose.

Hill remembers getting a "tremendous amount of encouragement out of Mrs. Flanagan and one or two others in the higher echelons of the organization." But he believed that although *Liberty Deferred* came close to production, the "agitation from Washington eventually killed the Federal Theatre" and the play also.[33] There are signs that Emmet Lavery, the director of the National Service Bureau who had initially defended the project, withdrew support from it, perhaps swayed by the fierce congressional investigations. In a letter to the Negro Arts Committee, which had demanded to know why *Liberty Deferred* hadn't been produced, Lavery wrote that while he once had "great hopes for the play," he did not feel that it turned out to be what he had expected.[34] Lavery had encouraged the authors to think there might be a production by allowing publicity to be released about their project. Perhaps he lost confidence not in the play but in the play's possible effect on an audience.

The script begins with Mary Lou and Jimmy, two young whites, talking about going to Harlem to see "how our darkies live."[35] As they sit down in a nightclub, a series of scenes take place in front of them, caricatures of the way most whites "insist upon seeing" the Negro: cotton pickers singing happy songs, vulgarly dressed Negroes playing craps, a traditional vaudeville act (4–5). As the lights go down, a young black couple are seen dancing, watching the whites watch the blacks. "Don't they see anything else?" Linda says, and Ted answers: "Nope. They have blinders attached to their eyes – blinders that are made out of stuff which is a combination of news-print, movie-film and essence-of-microphone, with just a dash of grease paint" (5–6). Hill and Silvera proceed through African American history, from slavery to a rousing finish during which at a meeting of the National Negro Congress, white and black workers join together crying, "We must fight! – and fight together – Liberty – give us real Liberty" (141).

It is instructive that Philip Barber, the director of all the New York City projects, could not remember the existence of *Liberty Deferred*. He claims further that the directors of the Negro unit never knew about it because although they brought him "script after script," they never brought him a living newspaper about black history. Playreaders, he believed, were "very, very critical of black attempts." What black scripts he did see were very "uneven, and very often in the script you'll see either 'Rough draft' and then exclamation point and that kind of thing. But they were trying to do things that somehow or other the ordinary playreader off the street would not be into."[36] Perhaps the play itself was too politically charged for the FTP, especially given the charges already being raised in Congress about its un-American status. Carlton Moss said, "It would have taken a Houseman to get it through."[37] In any event, *Liberty Deferred* was deferred indefinitely.

Hughes Allison must have been encouraged by the success of his play written for the FTP, *The Trial of Dr. Beck*, to continue writing plays about current race topics. *Dr. Beck* explored the effects of color prejudice within the black race through a contemporary mystery murder plot. Another script he wrote for the FTP, entitled *Panyared*, focused on what he called the "genesis" of African Americans:

> We, who have authored Negro plays in the past, no matter the type of play, have made one big mistake. We forgot *Genesis*. No matter the themes we handled or our methods of attacking them, we forgot that the public, no matter its attitude toward the Negro, did not have full knowledge of the Negro's *origin*. To my knowledge, not one of us has bothered to begin at the beginning of the story of the Negro in America and tell *that story*.[38]

Panyared, meaning "man seized" or "kidnapped," takes place from 1800 to the present. Divided into three acts, the first takes place in Africa showing how the main character, Bombo, is captured by African tribes and sold to white slavers; act II follows Bombo on board the ship taking him to America; and act III focuses on Bombo's experience on an American plantation, meeting with slaves who had been in America for two hundred years. Allison wanted to show the effects of the slave trade on Africans and Americans, as well as the positions of pro- and antislavery people.

Allison knew that his material would strike some as simply sensationalism. But he was careful to say his play was grounded in history and that he tempered the horrors as much as he felt he could. Still the play proved too objectionable for Hallie Flanagan. The plot seemed carefully worked out, but she called the language "impossible to swallow. Look at early scenes of Bombo and try to *imagine* a Negro saying: 'To find me uneasy about an enemy all of us have to face,' etc." Dramatically she thought it would be impossible to produce on stage the scene in which "the baby [is] being battered to death on the tree." Finally she believed that there were cultural limitations that would prevent the play from being produced: "By the third scene it is apparent to me that a play dealing so violently with miscegenation is not possible for us; certainly not for any except a most gifted cast, director and designer." Although her word does seem to be final, she thought that perhaps the play should be read by "several very good Negroes" to see what they thought about the play.[39] In this case, Lavery wrote back a three-page letter arguing strenuously in favor of producing the play and supporting a "fine talent." Had she even bothered to finish reading through to the end of the third act, he asked? The play, he argued, wasn't about violence and miscegenation but about the historical origins of slavery. Perhaps one of the regional directors might take it on. Surely some of the dramatic impossibilities she refers to could be smoothed over in rehearsal. Even the crude language of Bombo makes a dramatic point, reflecting the difference between the lofty cadences of the "African" language and the inferior patter of African American English. Lavery wrote that he didn't wish to show Flanagan's analysis to Allison. This play seemed so much better than the rest of the plays that passed across his desk, and he complained of how difficult it was to find the "right script" for Negro units.[40] Flanagan's notes about the dramatic quality of the play do seem much too harsh. It is the drama that she objects to: the fierceness, the violence. Beating a baby to death on stage – even a baby doll – would be too upsetting. Perhaps Flanagan was right that such a forthright examination of the violence of slavery would be unacceptable to the average audience, but she herself, hardly average, also seems to find the play to have gone too far, too violently far. In this instance, Flanagan sees herself at one with the average audience and casts herself as the representative of public taste.

Why did Lavery support this play and not Hill and Silvera's? In an interview with Leonard De Paur, Lorraine Brown suggests that the two decisions were connected:

Brown: I've got a theory which I won't bother you with on tape but I think they'd gotten perhaps into some trouble with a play called *Liberty Deferred,* which was a Living Newspaper by Abe Hill, John Silvera. And I think – it looks to me . . . I'll be glad to show you the letters. It looks to me like they got in difficulty with that so they decided to bring Hughes Allison along as a substitute. Because the laudatory letters from Lavery, for instance, about just pushing him up. He didn't write about anybody else in that way and Lavery has this great lapse of memory now. If you ask him, "How was it you praised so extravagantly *The Trial of Dr. Beck,* the *Panyared* play?" He can't remember. But it was all out of perspective, and it looks as if Hughes Allison came along. He was young and there's a foreword to *Panyared,* where he pours himself out about . . . his responsibilities as a young playwright and what a wonderful opportunity this is to have the chance to write this play and bring him along. And then, of course, after that – like you say, if he was before his time, he just became so embittered because he had nowhere to go. But it seems to me that this is the kind of thing, from what I know about Federal Theatre, that could happen. You could be somehow spotlighted for purposes that had very little to do –

De Paur: Had nothing to do with the value intrinsic–[41]

Allison left the theatre after the FTP shut down and never thought about trying his hand at writing again because he knew he would never find an outlet for his plays.[42] Certainly the FTP gave him mixed signals, valuing and then devaluing his efforts.

From the start, the FTP was committed to supporting new American playwrights and hoped that black playwrights would appear with producible plays.[43] But the scarcity of money and time along with the examples of censorship in the Negro units dissuaded all but the most determined. The split nature of the audience, black and white, further complicated the black playwright's task. Some banked on black folk plays, others on social realism, while many black actors, as well as white and black directors, just wanted to work and so were willing to act in and direct the plays, nearly all by white authors, that had been popular in the past and that they felt would still be popular in the present. Although the claim would be made repeatedly that blacks were developing their own theatre from their unique point of view, the records show that directors and playwrights had to take into account multiple points of view in order to produce a show. The Chicago Negro unit, like the Harlem unit, had its share of conflict and constraints.

III

Chicago's black community could rival the vitality of New York's. Chicago boasted an extremely active black community with hundreds of organizations to which people belonged on the South Side: one author estimated 167 churches, 47 college clubs, 97 fraternal orders, and over 18 local and national college fraternities and sororities in existence in 1927. Also, 257 different social clubs, 36 political organizations, 30 art and music associations along with over 50 representative women's clubs, business, charitable, and other social clubs were listed in Chicago black newspapers between 1927 and 1929.[44] Certainly black theatre was as varied and as promising in Chicago from the early part of the twentieth century through the thirties. Theatres and actors of all sorts existed. Tony Langston, a vaudevillian actor, was dramatic editor of the Chicago *Defender* for over fifteen years. Billy King produced black shows and wrote over a thousand plays and sketches. Other actors from Chicago included Billy Caldwell, who wrote "Miss Dinah Lee"; Evelyn Preer, who started her career in Chicago as a member of the Lafayette Players, worked as a film actress in black movies, and played opposite Lenore Ulric in David Belasco's play *Lulu Belle;* and Clarence Muse, a Lafayette player, film actor, song writer, and director of *Run, Little Chillun,* produced by the Negro unit in Los Angeles.[45]

Robert T. Motts founded the first black stock theatre in Chicago. A cafe owner, born in 1861 in Iowa, Motts had come to Chicago at the age of twenty. After traveling to Europe where he saw music halls, he wanted to start something similar in Chicago. In 1905, Motts opened the Pekin Theatre, seating twelve hundred; he charged a fairly high admission but ensured a frequent change of shows. Abbie Mitchell and Charles Gilpin played in productions along with eleven permanent members called the Pekin Players. But Motts began to run into competition from white-owned theatres. These theatres offered popular vaudeville programs rather than the more sophisticated comedies that played at the Pekin. By 1911, Mott's brand of entertainment couldn't compete with vaudeville.[46] With such a theatrical history and such a rich and varied social infrastructure, the Negro unit in Chicago would seem to be poised for success. Given the mix of strong community organizations, a professional group of actors from vaudeville, opera, and drama, and various political artist-activists, it is no wonder that the Chicago Negro unit had a particularly tempestuous history. Since its beginning, struggles occurred over who should direct the unit as well as individual shows, and also over what sort of shows should be produced.

In her memoir of the FTP, Flanagan described different projects in dramatic terms: "New York would have been staged as a living newspaper, Los Angeles as a musical comedy, the South as a folk play, and Chicago as melodrama."[47] Although she firmly believed in supporting new playwrights who wrote about people who would not be at home in drawing room comedies, she too, had limits. Allison's *Panyared* was dramatically unacceptable, in her opinion, its serious subject matter too unpalatably told for most audiences. But the comic plays that both the Negro unit in Chicago and Harlem started with also disappointed Flanagan and other progressives of the FTP. T. W. Stevens, the regional director, wrote to Flanagan:

> The Negro Theatre has been in "hot water" ever since it started because of the factional battles of the negro community. There is a very strong feeling there against anything in the way of a Negro Folk play. I have finally agreed to let them start with a script written by some negroes and containing a sort of Harlem Romeo and Juliet with the two houses represented by the South and West Indian negro aristocracy of Harlem. I hope a little later to be able to employ them on negro folk material of a more realistic type.[48]

Of course, one might ask why a feud between southern African Americans and African West Indians was *not* realistic, given the animosity expressed in Harlem against the West Indian Harry Edward, but then the whole notion of what was realistic or authentic was exactly that which was contested at every moment during the FTP. In any case, what Flanagan saw during a visit to the Chicago Negro unit disgusted her as well:

> The Negro Theatre got away to a good start because as we went in we were welcomed by the sign "Federal Negro Theatre, W.P.A." and adjoining it a huge legend "Republican Headquarters for _____ District". Even the Republicans would have liked our negroes playing with gusto a perfectly awful play called *Did Adam Sin*. I am not clear about Adam, but I certainly had a sense of guilt myself as I thought of spending taxpayers' money on this awful drivel. I am increasingly convinced that we must have a more autocratic choice of plays and certainly more rigid supervision.[49]

Flanagan's desire to uplift culture occasionally put her at odds with the "lowbrow" taste of some of the workers. "Rigid supervision" suggests the ways in which the people's "gusto" would be restrained.

After *Romey and Julie* and *Did Adam Sin?*, a white director, Marie Merrill, chose to direct an updated *Everyman* in Chicago, a production for which Richard Wright expressed nothing but contempt. On relief just at this time, Wright was transferred from the South Side Boys' Club to the Federal Writers' Project, where he was to work for the Chicago Negro unit as a publicity agent. His description of the battles he fought there, recounted in his autobiography *American Hunger,* indicates some of the strains that attended this unit:

> The Federal Negro Theatre . . . had run a series of ordinary plays, all of which had been revamped to "Negro style," with jungle scenes, spirituals, and all. For example, the skinny white woman who directed it, an elderly missionary type, would take a play whose characters were white, whose theme dealt with the Middle Ages, and recast it in terms of southern Negro life with overtones of African backgrounds. Contemporary plays dealing realistically with Negro life were spurned as being controversial. There were about forty Negro actors and actresses in the theater, lolling about, yearning, disgruntled, not knowing what to do with themselves.
>
> What a waste of talent, I thought. Here was an opportunity for the production of a worth-while Negro drama and no one was aware of it. I studied the situation, then laid the matter before white friends of mine who held influential positions in the Works Progress Administration. I asked them to replace the white woman – including her quaint aesthetic notions – with someone who knew the Negro and the theater. They promised me that they would act.[50]

They did. The FTP appointed as a director on the project Charles DeSheim, "a talented Jew," according to Wright, and he and Wright proposed an evening of three one-act plays, two by Will Jackson, *Burning the Mortgage* and *God's Mortgage,* and one by Paul Green, *A Hymn to the Rising Sun,* this last play about chain gangs in the South. Wright continues in his autobiography:

> I was happy. At last I was in a position to make suggestions and have them acted upon. I was convinced that we had a rare chance to build a genuine Negro theater. I convoked a meeting and introduced DeSheim to the Negro company, telling them

that he was a man who knew the theater, who would lead them toward serious dramatics. DeSheim made a speech wherein he said that he was not at the theater to direct it, but to help the Negroes to direct it. He spoke so simply and eloquently that they rose and applauded him.

I then proudly passed out copies of Paul Green's *Hymn to the Rising Sun* to all members of the company. DeSheim assigned reading parts. I sat down to enjoy adult Negro dramatics. But something went wrong. The Negroes stammered and faltered in their lines. Finally they stopped reading altogether. DeSheim looked frightened. One of the Negro actors rose.

"Mr. DeSheim," he began, "we think this play is indecent. We don't want to act in a play like this before the American public. I don't think any such conditions exist in the South. I lived in the South and I never saw any chain gangs. Mr. DeSheim, we want a play that will make the public love us."

I could not believe my ears. I had assumed that the heart of the Negro actor was pining for adult expression in the American theater, that he was ashamed of the stereotypes of clowns, mammies, razors, dice, watermelons, and cotton fields. . . . Now they were protesting against dramatic realism! I tried to defend the play and I was heckled down.

"What kind of play do you want?" DeSheim asked them.

They did not know. I went to the office and looked up their records and found that most of them had spent their lives playing cheap vaudeville. I had thought that they played vaudeville because the legitimate theater was barred to them, and now it turned out that they wanted none of the legitimate theater, that they were scared spitless at the prospects of appearing in a play that the public might not like, even though they did not understand that public and had no way of determining its likes or dislikes.

I felt – but only temporarily – that perhaps the whites were right, that Negroes were children and would never grow up. DeSheim informed the company that he would produce any play they liked, and they sat like frightened mice, possessing no words to make known their vague desires.

Soon after this, the actors drew up a petition to fire DeSheim, and as Wright tells the story, when he told DeSheim such a petition was circulating, the actors called Wright an Uncle Tom:

I tried to talk to them, but could not. That day a huge, fat, black woman, a blues singer, found an excuse to pass me as often as possible and she hissed under her breath in a menacing sing-song:

"Lawd, Ah sho hates a white man's nigger." (114–16)

Wright asked for a transfer and got it.

This story encapsulates all of the problems that plagued this "people's theatre." Wright's idea of a "genuine Negro theater" clearly conflicted with the actors' idea of genuine (or legitimate) work. Wright expected true theatre to antagonize an audience; the actors believed that their mission was to entertain them, make themselves beloved. Both Wright and the actors seemed to think the other an Uncle Tom, a "white man's nigger." Wright was called this for working with white men, for thrusting a white man's play on them, for espousing contempt for what the actors must have considered a black tradition of acting, and Wright, in turn, thought the actors were acting like children, wishing only to please, as well as being brainwashed and manipulated by those in power. Wright thought their vaudeville cheap and ignorant, amusement for the master, a tradition entirely tainted by white racist expectations and stereotypes. The actors dismissed Wright's (and Green's) version of realism – one actor because, he said, he had lived in the South and had never seen chain gangs. Wright and DeSheim said they wanted to help the people direct a theatre, but they were not prepared for opposition to their idea of a proper direction and, in the face of opposition, backed out. Neither side seemed convinced that the other knew what was genuine theatre or what the public genuinely wanted to see. The misperceptions of audience desire along with the open rivalries and crossed ambitions of members of the project point to a disquieting aspect of cultural construction: a people's desire for self-representation seems inevitably to involve a degree of exclusion (we are *this* way, not *that* way), stereotype, and mystification.

IV

It was just at this time that Theodore Ward, one of the very few black artists who was to have a socially realistic drama written and produced by the FTP, came on to the scene. He remembers that during the struggle over Green's play, he tried to help get it produced. He knew Wright from the South Side Writers' Club, and Wright had asked him to help DeSheim:

> I knew about DeSheim because I'd been many times over at the Repertory Group. I thought their whole outlook was a sound one. They were unprejudiced whites in the sense that, you know, the developing thing in the labor movement that the

Negro was absolutely necessary if the white workers was to be free, you know, and they had this sort of a perspective. As far as you could see, there was no prejudice to be discerned. I also knew that DeSheim was a product of the New York Group Theatre and the Group Theatre had been out here and they had offered classes, some of them were available. So I went to help DeSheim. Well, we didn't have any luck. We didn't have the luck because the leadership triumphed, probably in cahoots with some of the whites. I don't know but they didn't want Paul Green's *Hymn to the Rising Sun*.[51]

It is very plausible that the black actors' opposition to Green's play also had the backing of conservative whites at the FTP.

Though Wright, DeSheim, and Ward lost the fight over the Paul Green play, Ward recalls, "By that time I was on the project, so I couldn't transfer back to teaching speech and drama over at Lincoln Center. I decided to write another play, so I wrote my *Big White Fog*."[52] About the differences within the black community and the fog of prejudice that blinds everyone, the play elicited conflicting responses from the divided black and white community; some considered it too inflammatory, "inciting race hatred"; while others saw it as a serviceable documentary, a kind of "social worker's notebook" designed to stir reform.[53] Ward quite clearly found a solution to his people's problems in the rhetoric of working-class theatre: at the end of his play, the labor movement becomes the hero and hope for all working-class people. For Theodore Ward, as a beginning black playwright, the promise of interracial coalition the labor movement seemed to provide made the hopeful ending of his play possible.

By the time he arrived in Chicago, Theodore Ward had transformed himself from a poor country boy to an educated urban intellectual. At the age of thirteen he left Thibodaux, Louisiana, and traveled around the United States working as a bootblack and a hotel bellboy. In Salt Lake City, he entered the University of Utah; one of his articles won him a scholarship to the University of Wisconsin, where he worked at the radio station as a script writer and actor. After graduation, Ward moved to Chicago, became an instructor for the Lincoln Center Players in the black neighborhood of Chicago, met Richard Wright, and joined the group of aspiring black writers in the South Side Writers' Club.[54] Another white writer on the Chicago project, Arnold Sundgaard, remembers Ward as a gifted speaker, acting monologues from Roark Bradford's book on which the hit play *Green Pastures* was based. Both Ward and Wright depended on certain progressive interracial alliances to make their way. The fear that a black director would not be allowed in an elevator in a downtown building in New York informed relations in Chicago as well. Sundgaard relates this story about Ward and Wright: a Mrs. Henry H. Harrison

> used to tell Ted Ward about the great Negro performers like Bert Williams and the others who "knew their place." And we used to wince when she told these stories to Ted. One day I remember Ted saying, "Yes, one day I'm going to write about that kind of man." And I do remember another time when Richard Wright, who was not too long out of Mississippi then – there was an art exhibit at one of the galleries over on Michigan Avenue and Dick asked if I had seen it. I said, "No, but I'd like very much to." He said, "Would you mind if I went along?" And I said, "No, by all means." So I remember we went over to that art gallery on Michigan Avenue and I know that he went with me because he was afraid that he might be turned down at the door. . . . We were disturbed by it, but . . .[55]

Even the most optimistic of black playwrights, championing working-class coalitions, saw daily the corrosive limitations to his equality. Ward's bitterness at such conditions as well as his hope of eventual release can be found in *Big White Fog*.

Ward's journey from the South to the North mirrors those of thousands of blacks, and his first play chronicles what happens to their dreams once they hit the big northern city. As Ward circled the country by train, sometimes working, sometimes "hoboing," he read about "the new poets' so-called renaissance." He explains where he got the idea for *Big White Fog*:

> I was going to the Pacific Coast and we happened to reach the Great Horseshoe Bend on the Great Northern. It's magnificent. If you've never seen it, you don't know what a tremendous spectacle it is. The trains have to go this way and come this way and go around the mountain that way so as to cross the canyon. God knows how deep it was. Maybe it's a mile deep, I don't know. You see the fog is growing, you know, across us all the way up. And so I saw this and I was very struck by the magnificence of America and all of a sudden it occurred to me, "What the hell you lookin' at? This don't belong to you." (laugh) And that set me back and I began to dwell on the question of where do we stand in America. We're supposed to be here, we're supposed to be people, American citizens. Others

could pride themselves on that but I couldn't. I began necessarily going back over what did I know about what was to be done about us. What could we do? It occurred to me that we just didn't have any point of view. We didn't have it and what we did know was only the idea of the white folks. So we were surrounded by this big white fog. And once I had that image I guess I must have been satisfied so I don't remember even bothering to start thinking about that again.[56]

In the last scene of *Big White Fog,* a black man who has defied a notice of eviction is shot in the back by the sheriff, while white comrades gather to join hands with the black man's family. Frightened by this display, the sheriff halts the eviction for the moment and leaves, as the people who remain – white and black – pledge to dispel the fog of prejudice, the miasma composed both of white man's racism and black man's defeatism. It is a familiar ending not peculiar to the 1930s, although strongly associated with the Depression – the bonding of the powerless into a new coalition, in this plot, the black and white working class, a community that can wield power. But if this ending makes us long for such a moment of community, it can also make us wince at the seemingly naive idealism thus provoked. Experience tells us that moments of sympathy created by a spectator/reader's reaction to a performance/text often go no further than a private expression of sympathy and hope. Explicit reformist literature, such as Ward's *Big White Fog,* bears the burden of history more directly than "imaginative" texts, since art with designs to reform seems to demand that we measure whatever artistic merit it may have by investigating first its efficacy *as* reform.

Still, of all the socially realistic plays written for the FTP about the black condition, I think *Big White Fog* had the potential to be the most troubling to its Chicago audience. Unlike *Turpentine* or *Sweet Land,* two problem plays about black sharecroppers in the South, performed by the Harlem FTP Negro unit, *Big White Fog* takes up the condition of urban blacks in the North, the very people most likely to see this play. Ward carefully shows not only the cultural contradictions of American rhetoric, but also how these contradictions infect the complicated and contradictory desires of the urban black family. *Big White Fog*'s plot relentlessly uncovers the ways in which the attempt of the black working class to fashion itself into one middle-class type or another is impossible given America's racism and capitalist system. Working-class blacks' attempts to own a business or acquire an education are all thwarted by racism and by capitalism. Everyone in *Big White Fog* has a dream, and the play chronicles the excruciating business of watching dreams undercut, exposed as illusions. The fog of white prejudice not only frustrates the aspirations of this particular black family, but alters how the family members feel about each other and about themselves. The fog of capitalism pits people against each other instead of fostering community.

The play begins in 1922 when Vic moves his family from the South to Chicago because he hopes that in the northern city his family will find freedom. Vic has been educated as a scientific farmer, but he cannot buy land in the South. Unfortunately, Chicago does not open its arms to this man either, in spite of the promises that in the North the black man is free. All he can find is construction work. This proud man becomes persuaded by Marcus Garvey's argument that the black man will prosper only in Africa. In the meantime, his mother-in-law will not let him forget his failure and goads him, laughing at his belief in Garvey. She prides herself on her white blood and taunts her son-in-law: "No Dupree would-er thought 'bout marryin' sich a *black* crank in the first place."[57] The grandmother's self-esteem as a black woman has been bolstered by her belief in the power her white blood carries, while Vic's Garveyism allows him to damn her white blood as a sign of degradation.

His brother-in-law believes that the Garveyites are all "bunk" and that the only way to advance is to become a capitalist; he urges Vic to invest his money in real estate – kitchenettes – which they can rent to the flood of black people moving North. But Vic doesn't want to make money, at least not by capitalizing on poor blacks. He dreams of the dignity of black leadership and the power of education. But when Vic learns that his son, Les, who had been promised a scholarship to attend college, has been rejected because the authorities have found out that he is black, he donates all of his money to the Garveyites in his disgust and disappointment. Even when he learns that Garvey has been jailed, convicted, and finally deported, that Garvey's ships have sunk and his investments are worthless, Vic still holds to the nationalist dream because it is all he has.

The final act opens ten years after this disaster, in the midst of the Depression. Vic's brother-in-law is now a ruined businessman, and Vic and his family are about to be evicted. Vic's daughter offers herself to a white man in order to get enough money to save her parents from eviction. Vic's wife stops talking to him because she blames him for the disintegration of their family. But Les thinks he has a solution to their problems. He has been listening to friends who argue that "the only lasting solution for the problem of minority groups today is unity with the majority on a common ground. . . . It may sound remote. But what's there to prevent all the underprivileged from getting together on problems in which they have a common interest?" (301). With the sweeping naive goodwill typical of Popular Front rhetoric, the fact that prejudice might block the "common interest" of the people is swept away by thoughts like these: "I'm beginning to wonder if it isn't a matter of simply being just distrustful" (301).

Events happen quickly in the last five minutes: Vic decides to fight the eviction; the workers, white and black, arrive to help the family; off stage Vic blocks the sheriff from entering the house; and then the audience hears a shot. The sheriff has shot Vic in the back, and as Vic is brought back on stage we hear the comrades off stage swelling the ranks and the sheriff telling his men to back off. Vic is dying in despair, feeling that he lost this battle too, but his son points out to his father the crowd outside the house; a personal tragedy seems mitigated by the vision of a brotherhood and its power to stare down authority, at least momentarily. Ward organizes his drama around the breakdown of different black communities: political, economic, familial. Separately, these communities cannot be sustained as sites of resistance. Only when the largest community – comprised of all people, white and black – bonds together can a family or nation be healed.

Ward's belief in the power of community to overturn the existing powers was put to the test during the Chicago Negro unit's production of *Big White Fog*. In the play, an interracial coalition seems to provide hope for poor people and an alternative to sheriffs' guns. But in the course of the play's production, a divided white and black community made coalition seem close to impossible. The divided response to this work from both blacks and whites reveals that Ward's polemic against race hatred and his belief in class and interracial solidarity struck all kinds of nerves. The FTP staff themselves argued about what the work represented, where it should be produced, and even *if* it should be produced.

As a play written *by* a black man, *about* black people, *Big White Fog* fulfills Du Bois's manifesto. Du Bois would have said, *Big White Fog* should be produced "near us," in a black neighborhood, but Ward wanted the widest possible response: the Loop and an interracial audience. Given the play Ward wrote, this made sense. Ward rejected Du Bois's separatist manifesto of "about, by, for, and near." *Big White Fog* endorses a coalition not drawn exclusively from black leaders but from left-wing liberals and Communists, white and black. The question of where it should be produced and who it had been written for raised the question of who it was "good" for and what was "good." Aesthetic questions were inextricably intertwined with the political.

Harry Minturn, the acting director of the Chicago Project in 1937, was initially reluctant to book *Big White Fog* into a Loop theatre, but hoped that a place might be found for it on the South Side, in the black community. He sent a black director from the Negro unit to drum up support within the black community for such a neighborhood theatre.[58] Shirley Graham, who was to become better known after her FTP days as Shirley Graham Du Bois, the wife of W.E.B., was the black director Minturn sent out to scout for a black audience. Graham was forty years old when she accepted a job on the FTP. Having taught at various colleges, she was among a small band of trained black musicologists, earning an undergraduate and master's degree from Oberlin College. Her master's thesis was entitled "The Survival of Africanism in Modern Music." A one-act play she had written at Oberlin, *Tom-Tom,* had been produced as an expanded three-act opera in Cleveland, *Tom-Tom: An Epic of Music and the Negro.* Visiting a brother in Chicago, she heard that there might be a job for her on the Negro unit, interviewed with the regional director, George Kondolf, and accepted a job as a director in the Negro unit. Kathy A. Perkins argues that "like many Blacks of her generation, Graham was educated and socialized according to the philosophy of 'uplift' and Du Bois's concept of 'the talented tenth' – to aid Blacks in whatever way possible. Growing up in a racist society with a fierce sense of race pride, ambition, and dedication, Graham wanted to make a great artistic contribution to 'uplifting' her people."[59] Very few, if any, blacks served in supervisory positions in Chicago, and certainly Graham was highly trained, committed to black music, and all in all a great catch for the Negro unit.

Graham played a central role in the production of *Big White Fog,* mediating between Minturn's grudging support, Ward's progressive views, and portions of the black and white communities' nervous anticipation of a race riot. Her power stemmed from the fact that Minturn believed she had the ability to find out what "her" people wanted. Like the entire white bureaucratic elite of the FTP, Minturn thus operated according to the belief that black people all wanted the same thing: the task was to find out what it was. She was set up as the conduit of information, the sole representative of her people. Her role was to represent her people's needs and to reconcile their conflicting desires, if necessary, so that she could speak with one voice when she reported to the head of the project. Like Du Bois, she saw herself as one of the chosen, one of the black elite who could translate black people's wishes for whites.

She knew full well how divided the black community was, politically and culturally. But she too lumped the "Negroes" together. In a letter to a friend at the Washington Conservatory of Music, Graham writes in November 1937 to complain about the Chicago Negro unit: "Chicago is the hardest place in the world for an 'outsider' to attempt anything which involves a group of Negroes. I found that out much to my sorrow. . . . Frankly, the Negroes here care for only one thing – money. The city as a whole is utterly devoid of cultural interests." Graham finds that her commitment to uplift the cultural life of her people – to make them appreciate more than lowlife comedies or vaudeville – is frustrated by the crass concerns that pervade Chicago: "Standards are set by Joe Louis and Al Capone."[60] The Negroes of Chicago, Graham suggests, are as affected by the city's gangsterism, vulgarity, and melodrama as anyone else living in Chicago. As a trained musicologist and as a black woman interested in cultural uplift, she was finding herself at odds with popular entertainment. However, Graham carefully tempers the tone of frustration and contempt that clearly emerges in this private letter to her friend when she speaks or writes in her official capacity on the Negro unit.

Minturn directed Graham to find a theatre for the play in the black community. She knew from the moment she read *Big White Fog* that the black community in Chicago had not seen a play like this before. *Big White Fog* was "so very different."[61] She decided to hold a "preview" at the YWCA on the South Side, having Ted Ward read his play, with the white director, Kay Ewing, there to answer questions. She invited representatives from the NAACP and the Chicago Urban League, black and white dramatic groups, black churches, funeral associations, black music clubs, and selected fraternities – "groups which I had reason to believe would not be unfriendly." Minturn reported:

> *Big White Fog* was presented Wednesday night of this week (as a rehearsal only) to a selected, invited audience, mainly Negro, whom we hoped to interest in sponsoring this production in Chicago's South Side. International House has signed a contract to sponsor the play on February 17th and 18th; Northwestern University expressed interest; DuSable High School was interested. We have hardly had time yet to obtain a more general reaction to the play, and will try to give you more detailed information in next week's report.[62]

Up to this point, Graham says she supported the play; aside from "some tightening up and some minor changes . . . I thought it had definite theatre possibilities."

But that evening, based on the reaction of the audience, she changed her mind. In a letter she wrote to Minturn, she describes what happened at the run-through:

Nobody attacked the play that night. Everybody was courteous and everybody showed intelligent interest. A few questions were asked and then everybody dispersed *without doing anything.* But that night Miss Ewing made one remark which has since been repeated all over the South Side. From where I was sitting in the back of the room I caught that reaction and became aware of this unexpected danger. The remark simply was, "This play is so absolutely typical of the Negro family in Chicago." Miss Ewing said this in all sincerity and with the best intention in the world, but it has been resented and repeated a hundred times. People have said to me, "This play is *not* representative of us. We *do* have many successful business men in Chicago – our sons *do* get scholarships – we *do* support our own businesses – black *men* are respected not only in their own homes, but throughout the community – our respectable women do not keep all kind of rooming houses – and our girls *do not* have to sleep with white men to get fifty dollars."

When Graham reread the play with these thoughts in mind, she began to believe that it would offend almost the entire black community: the church leaders who were opposed to what they perceived to be a Communist ending; the people who saw the possibility of advancement through education and hard work; businessmen who believed in the opportunities of free enterprise; and the West Indians who were sensitive about their memories of Garvey. She wrote:

> Mr. Minturn, the problem of color *within* the Negro race is rather difficult for a white person to understand. No Negro can escape it. This play does tear open old sores and leaves them uncovered and bleeding. . . . Miss Ewing sincerely believes that the play will further the cause of an oppressed people, but I fear that its production at this time will do immeasureable harm to the very people it is attempting to help.

In the same letter she explains why, after reading the play again, she no longer thinks the play should be produced. Her initial enthusiasm had been based on reading *Big White Fog* as a "play" and as "theatre": "I am used to going to the theatre, perhaps I have fewer inhibitions than people whose lives have been more limited. But certainly my second reading did reveal dangers of which I had not thought before." These "fewer inhibitions" had allowed her to overlook the effect this play's critique of society would have on others deemed less sophisticated. People whose lives have "been more limited" – the condescension rings out here – might not be able to separate an aesthetic experience from a political one.

The ensuing struggle over the worthiness of *Big White Fog* would be framed in terms of realism and stereotype and authentic and inauthentic representation. Immediately, people contested Ward's plot as realism, a portrayal of life "as it is." Everyone began to see that to produce *Big White Fog* meant producing a certain version of history, certain cultural attitudes and biases. The drama now lay not in the words of the play but in the fears and outrage expressed by the people listening to that first reading. Who represents whom most authentically? As mediator between blacks and whites, Graham first carefully asserts her power to give an authoritative version of what is at stake for blacks. Whites, no matter how well meaning, just do not understand how certain sorts of representation affect blacks; as a black woman, she understands. She mentions the "problem of color" as depicted in the play, referring, no doubt, to the grandmother's scorn for her dark black son-in-law. Graham never says that Ward's presentation of the color problem is not realistic but that his play is insensitive to the feelings of his black audience; his portrait of black life hurts too much. She now begins to see how a production of the play could have political consequences by harming "the cause" of black pride and community solidarity.

The cause that Ewing, the director, and Hal Kopel, the set designer, were concerned with is unmistakable. They firmly believed not only in the realism of the play but in the good such a production would generate. Ewing and Kopel believed that in representing the Negro more "realistically" and in rejecting old stereotypes, they were helping an oppressed people to shake off the slurs of hatred thrust upon them by people in power as well as the internalization of hatred. Ewing testified that the set seemed to fit the circumstances so well that when the actors walked onto it "they settled down in it as if they'd always lived there." But the designer seems to have been confused about whether this family was primarily constituted by their difference from or similarity to white families of the same class:

> While the play is about the Mason family, one feels that it is really talking about the whole Negro race, and the setting, instead of trying to show an individualized Negro home, tried to give the essence of all Negro homes. This naturally raises the question, "How is a Negro home different from the homes of his white neighbors?", and the answer, in the designer's opinion, is that it is not different.[63]

Kopel wants it both ways: to distinguish blacks from whites by talking about the whole Negro race and yet at the same time to insist that one race is not *really* different from another. Accurate or stereotype, authentic or unrepresentative – these were the concepts at stake when the people of Chicago fought over the production of this play.

Minturn was undecided about what to do:

> The *Big White Fog* rehearsal for some Negro organizations last Wednesday night brought in, out of seven letters, about six protests against it. However, we are playing it on the 14th and 15th of February at the International House, which is an auditorium out at the University of Chicago. We have not decided about presenting it in one of the Loop houses, feeling it would be prudent to wait and see what happens.[64]

Graham collected responses from those who had attended the preview at the YWCA. Most of the responses were negative. The NAACP felt that the FTP wanted to rid themselves of the controversy by asking the black community to find a place for it on the South Side. They also objected to the play's "communist propaganda" which seemed to present "some of the worst phases of Negro life." The representative from the Illinois State Employment Office believed that they wouldn't be able to muster the necessary publicity without FTP support. Other responses, even favorable ones, expressed wariness as to how it would be received. Mrs. Bertha Lewis, chairman of the Dramatic Committee Northern District of Colored Women's Clubs, acknowledged that the " 'propaganda' had been skillfully handled . . . [but] I doubt if any regular white theater audience would be interested in so many of our problems." Mrs. Pearl Pachoaco, from the Richard B. Harrison Dramatic Club, admired "the dramatic force" of the play, but "would not care to invite the white sponsors of their club to attend the play."[65] The only theatre commitment Graham secured was for a two-day engagement at the International House of Chicago, but when the director came back from out of town (or got wind of the plot of the play), he pulled out, citing fear of "inter-racial hatred" as his excuse.[66]

These exchanges as reported by Graham suggest that the urban and for the most part professional, middle-class race leaders resisted mightily being lumped into what they considered a "typical" portrait of the African American citizen, especially one that depicted them as losers and second-class citizens. One must surmise that these people did not identify with Vic's family and others in their predicament or at least did not want such an identification made – and especially not by whites. The

NAACP as well as the funeral and church associations resented what they summed up as a defeatist portrait of the black community. Further, they were unwilling to give up gradualist politics for the revolutionary ending Ward offered. Graham was clearly sensitive to those who wanted to stress the successes of black people rather than the failures and was herself more comfortable with the rhetoric of celebration and uplift than with the strident criticism of racism and capitalism found in Ward's play. However, when the representative from the NAACP said that the play emphasized the "worst phases of Negro life," he was preoccupied with how the play would be interpreted by the white community. Expressing the same unease evinced by certain parts of the black community toward Richard Wright's *Native Son,* he implicitly worried how certain representations about black life may be used against them. The controversy over what a "typical" black family looked like or whether a certain play was politically progressive reveals that people are persuaded, or dissuaded, by ideas they hold about what is representative. To Shirley Graham, Ewing blundered the night she declared her belief that this was a typical Negro family. A realism based on the typical in this case only brought to the surface the differences between "the people," making it clear, at least within the black community, if not outside it, that the meaning of the typical was to be contested.

Graham made a further argument against producing the play in her letter to Minturn when she expressed her doubt whether this drama, because it was a problem play, could fill a theatre with a black *or* a white audience: "The average colored audience, even more than the average white audience wants to be entertained. Problem plays do not as a whole interest people not in the habit of going to the theatre."[67] Even F. T. Lane, an official from the Chicago Urban League who had written a letter supporting the production for its truthful portrayal of the racial situation, shared the reservation that the play probably would not have a wide appeal because it would seem too much like a "true story from a social caseworker's notebook." Could the playwright perhaps lighten the tension, he wonders.[68] This dichotomy between what the people "wanted" – entertainment – and what the socially committed playwright wished to give them – problem plays – haunted discussions about productions throughout the FTP. But in the case of the Negro units, it was heightened partly because the popular forms of entertainment – vaudeville, minstrel shows, and musicals – were so strongly associated with black actors. Black and white theatrical audiences apparently expected to be entertained, as ever, by familiar black stereotypes. Every political playwright on the FTP shared the problem of attracting a popular audience who wanted to be soothed and entertained in the theatre, not agitated toward change. Playwrights writing for the Negro units had a particularly difficult time bucking the tradition of popular black entertainment.

After receiving Graham's letter, Minturn was more than ever reluctant to place the play in a downtown theatre. In a letter to Flanagan, he argued that "serious thought" should be given to the problem of inciting race hatred: "If the script could be rewritten to eliminate that [race hatred], then I can see no reason for its not being done." Minturn doesn't make clear where the race hatred lies or even what sort it is. He complains that Ewing and Kopel have unfairly accused him of putting the play on hold, when the real reason for the delay is that all of the Loop theatres had been booked.[69] With Graham reporting serious dissension in the black community and with his own misgivings based on his theatrical experience, Minturn had more than enough reason to block production of the play without the excuse that all the theatres downtown had been booked.

Theodore Ward never forgot or forgave the principals in this case. He dismissed the fears expressed by Minturn and Graham as trumped-up excuses to sabotage his play. In an interview in 1976, Ward said that the problem, as he saw it, was Graham's jealousy over the appointment of Kay Ewing as director of *Big White Fog,* who happened to be not only white but rich, and a former student of Flanagan's at Vassar.[70] According to Ward's account, Graham spread the rumor that the play was defeatist in order to sink it: "I thought the whole thing was confined to the ambition of a Negro woman who was not prepared really to become the instructor or the supervisor of anything else in the Negro unit, but whose ambition was to be head of the project which she couldn't keep."[71] Ward went on to claim that Minturn was in league with Graham and that Minturn later showed him the letters from the black community in an effort to absolve himself of the charge that he obstructed the production.

Ward's accusation that his production was ambushed not by lack of black community support but by Graham's jealousy and ambitions is not entirely unreasonable. She clearly was ambitious and she was known to be the one black director with a track record in the Chicago unit, annointed by Flanagan herself. That Graham was passed over in this case for a white woman, one with her own ties to the head of the FTP, might well have galled her. The competition between black and white directors was fierce. In another interview about the Harlem unit, Leonard De Paur talks about the limited opportunity for black directors at the FTP. The Negro units were the only venue for them, so if jobs even there were closed, their despair was palpable:

De Paur: . . . the political lines had been very clearly drawn and there were black directors and white directors. And the black directors were fighting for primacy.

        Anyway, the point of it was there was one place on earth for a black director to do anything. I mean, there was no hope of our going down to 891 or the Living Newspaper or the Playhouse or name them, all the other projects around town where any number of white directors, albeit there were thousands of them scrambling for the opportunity, could have gone. There was just this one place that a black – in those days Negro – director had to operate. And if he lost his opportunities there, he had none anywhere. And that's why they were so jealous of those few.

Brown: It's your sense then there was a body of talent as far as playwrights, directors and –

De Paur: Oh, hell, yes; Good Lord, yes. My God yes, and it wasn't nearly capitalized. It wasn't nearly used.[72]

Ward's interpretation, however, ignored the fact that Graham's reading took the voices and concerns of parts of the black community seriously. Her sympathy for celebratory works of art was in line with a certain part of the black middle class, while such celebration to Ward seemed exactly the kind of cloudy obfuscation that hindered a clear view of reality. The differences between Ward's and Graham's political agendas played themselves out in the controversy over the production of *Big White Fog*.

    Ward did not blame Graham only, however. He also believed that the white politicians were confused as to what the black community really wanted. He remembers that after Minturn blocked the play, a prominent black woman named Mrs. Hale went downtown and said "her people" were eager to see *Big White Fog*. The white administration "didn't know which way they were going and they were not going to alienate [the] blacks on the South Side and prominent Negro businessmen."[73] In a surprising turnaround, perhaps because the Chicago city administration brought pressure on the WPA, *Big White Fog* did finally go into the Great Northern, a theatre on the Loop, home of the FTP's more experimental productions. It played in Chicago between April 7 and May 30, altogether for thirty-seven performances, and its success, in front of a mixed audience, no doubt surprised Graham and Minturn equally. Minturn described the enthusiastic audience of opening night and notes the favorable press reviews. The second night, Chicago was hit by a blizzard, which effectively closed downtown. And though Minturn noted that the box office did drop off for the play during the course of its run, he attributed this not to the play but to the "present slump" in the theatre business throughout Chicago.[74] All speculation about audience and culture was proved wrong. Whites seemed to be very interested in the problems of blacks; no race riots resulted, nor were the fires of interracial hatred fanned; and reviews in black as well as white journals were favorable. *Big White Fog* managed to find an audience willing to sit through a problem play. While it probably did not generate class or racial warfare, neither did it overcome class or racial schisms.

Each of the principals had acted like a cultural commissar, attempting to dictate the events surrounding this play. Each commissar had spoken of the black community as a monolithic entity: Minturn believed the community did not want to be instructed and preached to; Graham believed the black community did not want to be represented as defeated; the city administration did not know what to believe the black community wanted; Mrs. Hale believed that city hall did not know what the black community truly wanted and so she told them. Even now, looking back, it is hard to choose between conflicting stories: was it jealousy, ambition, or concern for people's feelings that motivated the dissent of Shirley Graham; was the FTP trying to protect itself from an increasingly hostile Congress about to launch a full-scale investigation into the perceived radical influence in the project? How much power should we assign to individual actions and how much to institutional policies or deep-set ideologies? All played a significant role in the bumpy road to the stage.

The assumption of a unitary black entity persisted in the reviews of the production. All of the objections and reasons for putting on the play reappear in these reviews but are reassigned to different effects. Consensus held it a talky but honest, sincere play, a description meaningless in its generality, except as a sign that the play struck reviewers as an authentic representation of black life.[75] While little mention was made about the form of the play or its direction, the quality of the acting received much attention. The actors' naturalness seemed to enforce the sense of realism: "It is a sheer joy to watch these federal theatre Negro players in action," one reviewer wrote: "Their voices are as sweet as honey. They are as much at ease on the stage as in their own homes. They have a mellow sense of humor through which runs the deep undercurrent of native pathos of their race."[76] "Native pathos" obscures the processes by which "pathos" comes to seem "natural." It implies a version of essentialism that constructs a passive and even doomed black race. To be "at home" equally on stage and at home effectively negates the skill of the actors as actors.

The review in the *Chicago Tribune* casts the play in a historical light that manages to distance the problem from contemporary society: "This work deals with the domestic life of Negroes in Chicago and in particular with one family whose head follows the Marcus Garvey movement ('back to Africa') into heartbreak and economic disaster. . . . In its handling of the Garvey episode the play has some value as an imaginative footnote to recent Negro history."[77] To cite Vic's adherence to the Garvey movement as the reason for the tragedy obscures the reasons why Vic chose to follow Garvey in the first place. An "imaginative footnote" further marginalizes any potency the critique of systematic racial prejudice in the play might have had.

Hallie Flanagan's brief recollection of Ward's play in her history of the FTP ignores any of the conflicts I have described. In her desire to defend the FTP from the charges made that the organization was riddled with Communists and Communist sympathizers, she soft pedals the working-class ending to emphasize instead the racial story:

> This script carried no political definition. . . . *Big White Fog* was important because it dealt with a racial problem by a member of the Negro race, and because, as Charles Collins pointed out in the *Tribune,* it afforded an authentic footnote to recent Negro history in recording the Marcus Garvey Back-to-Africa movement which originated in Chicago.[78]

Her official version glosses over the political controversies that arose *in* the play, not to mention those that arose over the production. To discuss the play only in terms of Marcus Garvey was to relegate the problems of blacks to one narrow version of the past. To sum up the play as dealing with "a" racial problem by "a" member of the Negro race undercuts Ward's pointed political critique of *American* racism.

As to the overtly political ending of the play, allowances were made for its enthusiastic support of a "brotherhood." Gail Borden of the *Daily Times* defends *Big White Fog* because a free America should not ban or suppress anything:

> Only recently . . . there have been letters passed around suggesting that the mayor do something about stopping the production of "Big White Fog" on the grounds that it is "Communistic" (which it probably is) and that it incites race prejudice (which it probably does not). And we disagree with these objec-

tions more than with the moral of the play, for the pure and simple reason that we believe in free speech whether on the stage or off. . . .

To oppose the use of the theater as a loudspeaker for a writer's social beliefs is to relegate the theater to the dullness of romantic, repetitive twaddle. Also when the playhouses are "controlled" America is showing that it is no better than those Utopias from which it tries to protect us and for which so many ardent young playwrights yearn.[79]

In this view the play functions as a Voice of America program booming around the world, touting the greatest feature of the United States: free speech. The play's content – class warfare, civil rights – its sharp critique of the United States, becomes absorbed in the general point that by allowing the play to be produced, America was to be congratulated for free expression and could ignore the criticism put forth. Ideas of what is natural or representative are used to contain and neutralize Ward's critique of racism and capitalism, so that what *Big White Fog* comes to stand for and celebrate is America's ability to tolerate criticism. Universalizing the historical specificity of Ward's play undercuts its usefulness as either a progressive or retrogressive political force. The reviews succeed in returning the play to the safer arena of "art."

The final performances of *Big White Fog* raised more questions about how people wanted to use the play and why some responded to the play in the ways they did. Ward tells how, in spite of the good reviews and the sizable mixed audience the play attracted, Minturn decided to move it to a black high school auditorium on the South Side. There the play closed in a matter of days. Why did Minturn pull the play from the Loop? And even more troubling, why did it fail to sustain an audience in the black community? A variety of explanations, none of which proves definitive, make a single master narrative inappropriate here.

Ward felt that the policies of the FTP at this moment in history were a convenient excuse for Minturn's personal antipathy to his political play. By 1938, funds for the FTP had been reduced by Congress several times; Flanagan had been forced to cut many of the project's regional units. In a Catch-22 situation, the FTP was then criticized by Congress for being too narrowly based in major cities. Wherever still possible, for political public relations and for ideological reasons, the FTP tried to maintain ethnic theatres in the big cities, thereby serving local communities. Minturn had earlier written to Flanagan that his idea was to book *Big White Fog* on the South Side as a community gesture; it would save blacks carfare and "would be a neighborhood theatre the same as many of your outlying theatres in New York, servicing that particular locality."[80] Noting that the Negro People's Theatre, a new dramatic organization on the South Side, sponsored the high school production, he wrote to Howard Miller:

> We have for some time wanted to know whether one of our Negro plays would draw on the South Side better than in Loop theatres, therefore were glad of the opportunity for this booking. There are no theatres available in the Negro district, but duSable is one of the two largest Negro High Schools in South Chicago, centrally located, with a fine auditorium.[81]

It may have been true that Minturn was using FTP policies as an excuse to close the show. Ward remembers Minturn's "official" reason for moving the play along these lines: "So Minturn retired the play to the South Side to a Negro high school, saying that *[Big White Fog]* was [a Negro play and that the] Negroes need to know [it]." But according to Ward, Minturn was out to destroy "black social theatre."[82] Ward believed that the administration in Chicago never really wanted to do contemporary plays like his:

> While whites could appreciate the depth of *Big White Fog* and it really went over here, it was sabotaged by members of the Administration, there was no question about that. And I hate to bring it up because it sounds like some kind of an excuse. But the Treasury Department itself told me it was making money only second to *The Big Blow*, which had been the most popular thing by Federal Theatre in Illinois which ran for a year. So it was retired not because of its inability to make money. They resented the fact that Hallie Flanagan forced them to do it and Kondolf was gone. . . . Hallie Flanagan had forced the Federal Theatre to do the show. She said, "That's precisely what we want is people writing plays, the indigenous thing. There's nothing wrong with that play."[83]

Moving *Big White Fog* out of the Great Northern where it was doing fine may have been a gesture to show continuing support for ethnic theatres, or it may have been a deliberate move to bury it in the black neighborhood. It could have been both.

The paradoxical situation of a black social theatre being destroyed when it is placed within a black neighborhood, remains most troubling. Ward continued: "So [Minturn] moved . . . [the play from the Loop to] the South Side, and that was the same as killing it, you see, because what do the Negroes know about going to the high school to see a play?"[84] One fact remains absolutely clear: the South Side production closed in four days because it had no audience. But why should it be the case that moving it to the South Side was the same as killing it? Here we can only speculate. The amount of advertising or promotional work done for this production is not known. No audience surveys were collected this late in the FTP's history. We have seen that the black community was divided about the play before it opened, but that black audiences *did* travel to see *Big White Fog* when it was on the Loop, when it seemed to be approved by establishment critics. It seems likely that the presence of whites in the audience, their visible support along with whatever complex validation they afforded the event, were important factors in attracting blacks. Perhaps the drop in attendance indicated that this audience was not attracted to the idea of a separate theatre; they *wanted* to go downtown and sit with an interracial audience. No matter what else it does, moving a production from an established theatre in the middle of the theatre district to a high school auditorium certainly sends a strong signal that the FTP did not think the play was worthy of a professional production.

The embarrassing contradiction of writing plays for the people who then reject them continued to plague Ward and this play. By 1940, just two years later, when the Negro Playwright Company revived *Big White Fog* in New York, what had been effectively buried or excused in reviews – the Popular Front labor ending – was blasted by reviewers as communist and un-American. Ward denied that he advocated communism as an answer for Negroes. "I see unity, interracial unity. Why do you have to be Communist for that? We have the theory of a democratic government, don't we, called Citizens of the United States?" But with such press, "the Negro middle class stayed away, and we couldn't get them. We played to about thirty thousand whites from the trade unions and, oh, I think we had a count. It might be a little more than that, but we counted fifteen hundred Negroes who attended that production after the opening night."[85] The black middle class was no different from the white middle class at this time regarding communism; they wanted no part of it. Leonard De Paur remembers that "the older people didn't like it [*Big White Fog*] worth a damn. . . . And it wasn't only the whites, it was the whites and blacks. This is that second-generation respectability I'm talking about."[86] Communist or not, Ward's radical drama emphasized the necessity of making interracial alliances between white and black workers within the play, and in order to have his play produced, Ward depended on white and black support. Eugene Gordon wrote in *New Theatre* in 1935:

> Radical drama comes closest to being a dialectical representation of life because it shows the relation of black workers to the

means of production, to class-conscious white workers, to the
ruling class, to the upper class of their own race, and to all
the other elements of society. . . . Alliances once unthinkable,
alliances between white workers and black workers, have
evolved from the changed relationships as shown in these plays.
The dramas fall short of "socialist realism" to the extent that
they fail to integrate these various relationships.[87]

The radical drama of *Big White Fog* existed in the friction between
different interests, different classes, different relationships to the theatre,
within and between races. But the creation of community on stage is
so much easier than the vexed, difficult, unresolved, and conflicted
relationships off stage.

Ward's explanation for the failure of his play to attract a black audience in 1940 echoes the sentiments of many others on the FTP: "We
thought that the Negro audience was ready for the theatre in 1940, but
the group needed a larger sense of understanding."[88] Langston Hughes
agreed with Ward that people weren't ready: "It is the greatest encompassing play on negro life that has ever been written. If it isn't liked by
people, it is because they are not ready for it, not because it isn't a great
play."[89] Politically progressive black artists like Hughes, Ward, and
Wright felt at times alienated from black audiences. In both 1938 and
1940, some blacks voiced their reservations about how others would
interpret black representation in the play. Problem plays and social
realism seemed the more acceptable medium to the progressives like
Ward and Flanagan, but such a form could offend (or bore) black
audiences who wanted to be uplifted or entertained. Ward's dilemma
mirrored the dilemma faced by the FTP: in reaching out to people who
hadn't been heard from before and who were given a chance to express
themselves, Ward and others like him might encounter the voice of a
nay-saying people. How problematic and fragmented the collective
noun "the people" proved to be. Expressions of diversity were never
fully honored by the progressive leadership of the FTP, the heads of
black organizations, or even by artists on the projects. Instead, everyone
involved in the FTP Negro units sought to present a consensus, to
suppress conflict in order to set themselves up as the true representative
of the "unheard" people.

Du Bois and Locke believed that they could fairly represent what was
most authentic about the entire race. The distance between the black
intellectual elite and the less educated became glaringly apparent, however, when the two groups were placed in proximity. The black migration from the South to the North meant that these black intellectuals

had to confront urban masses in Boston, New York, and Washington; they could no longer base their theories on a distant southern folk. And the black masses could "look toward a range of other representatives which included black union organizations, economic radicals, or Marcus Garvey and the Universal Negro Improvement Association."[90] Similarly, black artists like Wright and Ward had to confront actors and an audience who disagreed with their representations of them. The very call for the "real" raised conflicting ideas about what constituted reality and how one should go about getting people "ready" for it.

4

The Unpredictable Audience

No race can ever become great that has not produced a great literature.
— James Weldon Johnson

Without great audiences we cannot have great literature. —Sterling Brown[1]

Who were "the people" and how were their wishes to be known? The Federal Theatre Project did seem to be curious. In the archives at George Mason University, there are a series of photographs taken of the audience at a few of the Harlem Negro unit productions. None of the people in the photographs are identified; they are only marked as "crowds" or "celebrities." In a photograph, two young women in wool coats pose in the Lafayette Theatre, staring at the camera with excitement and pride (Figure 7). They are simply labeled "crowd." The smile and glint in the eye of the woman on the right makes me think she's about to have (or did she just have?) a good time. Perhaps what they are about to see (or just saw), *Androcles and the Lion,* is irrelevant to their pleasure. Perhaps it has everything to do with their smile. It is impossible to know. The "celebrities" also attending *Androcles* are more dressed up (Figure 8). Their tuxedos and furs distinguish them from those in the crowd. The lady on the right wears a hat with a veil; the lady on the left carries a beaded purse. The differences between the crowd and celebrities translates into wool and fur, leather and beads, but in both photographs, it is plain that these people are dressing up for a special night out. Going to the Lafayette Theatre was an event. The FTP's Negro unit's black audience dressed accordingly. Whether the night's entertainment promoted racial equality, class solidarity, American patriotism, or farce, the FTP, for both blacks and whites, was a medium for upward mobility, a middle-class affair.

136

Figure 7. LCFTP. "Crowds."

Of course, the presence of Mrs. Roosevelt and the mayor of New York at shows like the *Swing Mikado* (Figure 9) reminds us how interested the top echelons of the New Deal administration were in promoting the arts, which extended to patronage of the hit Negro shows. From Mrs. Roosevelt to the nameless couple taken over by the infectious spirit of the swing Gilbert and Sullivan, downtown whites sat and danced at Negro unit productions (Figure 10). Along with black audiences, they

Figure 8. LCFTP. "Celebrities."

would have to be reckoned with for every single Negro unit drama. So although it looks like the black crowd outside the voodoo *Macbeth* (Figure 11) in Harlem owned the streets and the theatre located in their community, in fact we know that the white reviewer for *Vogue* and the black reviewer from *Amsterdam News* had entirely different notions of what *Macbeth* meant to white and black audiences. What we don't know is whether their representations of audience response are accurate or, finally, only a reflection of their own opinion. In spite of audience surveys, reviews, and box office tabulations, it is still hard to know what those crowds and celebrities thought about Add Bates dressed up in a lion's costume once inside and seated at *Androcles and the Lion* (Figure 12).

I

Would the FTP only live up to its name as a people's theatre if directed by the people's choices? How was it going to forge links to the

Figure 9. LCFTP. "Mrs. Roosevelt and Mayor La Guardia at *Swing Mikado,* New York City."

community and how was it going to decide between communities if "the" community seemed divided? How was it to decide between peoples' desires? And how was it to know what the people wanted? Inconsistencies of intention abound: sometimes it seemed important not only to know but to honor a choice, but in certain instances some people could just as readily dismiss the audience's tastes.

One of the most difficult tasks the FTP had to confront, throughout

Figure 10. LCFTP. "Dancing at *Swing Mikado*."

its run, was "the old mystery of the theatre – what they want."[2] A theatre that depended upon public money must pay attention, at least rhetorically, to what the people wanted. Flanagan, who took such pride in the nickname of the FTP – "the people's theatre" – had a theory about that old mystery: never give them what they think they want because what they *think* they want is not what they *really* like, a somewhat dubious construction: "Take the *Showoff* in Harlem – we believed by taking a sure fire hit and doing it with the negro unit, we would make money – and we put on a swell production – it was a total flop as far as box office." Instead, she believed that experimental things "have paid. The things we did out of the fever of excitement and adventure were successful. When we kept our eye on the box office and played *Path of Flowers*, it was a miserable flop."[3] A popular theatre paradoxically avoids making box office decisions; a truly popular people's theatre refuses to produce sure-fire crowd pleasers thereby ensuring a popular success. The ambivalent relationship between the people and those serv-

Figure 11. LCFTP. "Crowds at voodoo *Macbeth*."

ing the people surfaced most often when somebody tried to solve that old mystery of the theatre: what they want.

Leonard De Paur testified that black audiences loved the theatre, especially in Harlem:

> Black audiences are great. Black theatre audiences are great. Blacks love theatre. They've always loved theatre. Blacks have always been, from the days of the first black company at the Ethiopian Grove down here at Mercer Street back in the early 19th century, blacks have loved theatre. And the opportunity to return to the theatre, for many of them who had known the theatre in the days when it flourished in Harlem, was a godsend and I honestly believe developed some new audiences. We really got some young people who had not been exposed to theatre earlier interested.[4]

Much attention was paid to the idea of an audience, its importance, participation, and support. But in spite of the audience surveys taken in

Figure 12. LCFTP. New York City. "Dancing, *Androcles and the Lion.*"

the early part of the FTP's history, much of what can be known about the audience is filtered through what other people said about it. The audience got to speak for itself through surveys, although those were mediated by interpretors, as we shall see; large portions of the audience never responded; and then there is no way of determining whether audiences answered in ways they thought were expected of them. The idea of the people as audience at the FTP and within the Negro units was crucial in maintaining the image of a community theatre. Much of the discourse around the idea of the audience aimed to speak for "it" as a singular entity. Attempts were made to define the audience, and so control it, train it in order to create a people's theatre. But the relationships *among* audience and producers, writers, directors were often reduced to the most elemental of considerations: did they fill the seats?

Despite the regional organization of the FTP, the theatre was largely judged by professionals who were looking at the quality of its New York City productions; most of the FTP professional theatre workers believed that only New York productions were worthy of judgment. Provincial audiences earned nothing but contempt from New Yorkers. Philip Barber, former stage manager for the Group Theater, had first been director for the entire state of New York before being shifted exclusively to New York City. His comments about audiences outside of New York sound a familiar theme in the writings of many a New Yorker:

> And you know, you spend a week in Buffalo, and what you come up with is that the Junior League might support a marionette show or puppet show, and that's a big achievement that you worked out there. Then you go and spend some time in Albany, and somebody thinks there that the thing to do is do a real bang-up production of *Charlie's Aunt.* You know, what have you got to work with? It isn't that the actors and the people weren't good. What was lousy was the audiences. You had no audiences at that time. You had a naive, dull, stupid audience to draw upon in those places outside of New York.[5]

Audiences outside the city of New York were hopeless. Even in other urban centers, Chicago and Los Angeles, the theatregoing audience might not conform to the sophisticated tastes of a New Yorker. On the other hand, what Flanagan liked about Los Angeles units, other than their efficiency and the absence of labor strikes, which plagued New York from the beginning, was their "audience spirit." The Los Angeles *Herald* in July 1936 characterized the FTP audience as "refreshing": "No show me crowd which feels it has paid its money and defies the theatre to divert it. That important part of the theatre's magic – audience spirit – is sensed in the crowded house – the feeling that this is the people's theatre doing something right down the people's alley."[6] Many critics both within and without the FTP described the audience as engaged and eager, an audience "which is not, I suspect, overfamiliar with the stage of flesh and blood and it has had moments of rather startling naivete. But it is an engaging audience. Its face is not frozen, it is not sitting on its hands, when it hisses it is not self-conscious and when it cheers it means it. It is young, lively, and I suspect, hard up."[7] Still, this naive audience might not be as adventurous as audiences in New York. As Howard Miller pointed out, "Plays flopped here [Los Angeles] that had played for years in New York."[8] In this, Los Angeles was typical of most of the projects. Although experimental and politically controversial plays made headlines, most of the FTP played to conventional audiences who demanded conventional plays. A lawyer for the project said:

> When I actually listed all the plays like so-and-so's aunt, etc., etc., and how many times that was produced, I wasn't particularly happy about – I should say at this far point that seventy-five percent of our stuff was the usual nonsense that was attracting audiences in the traveling theatres' stock companies prior to Federal Theatre. Twenty-five percent of it was on a higher level. This is a rough, arbitrary figure.[9]

Given the lists of plays in the appendix to Flanagan's history, *Arena*, 75 percent seems fairly accurate. Flanagan wished to give unconventional dramas, but a good proportion of the people seemed to be interested only in the conventional.

In one of the FTP's more populist gestures, audience surveys were handed out during the first two years of operation and on certain projects in order to find out just what it was the audience wanted. Did they go to the theatre often, did they enjoy the play they just saw, what sort of plays would they prefer to see, should there be a permanent federal theatre?[10] In addition, the FTP collected names, addresses, and occupations generating a list of supporters (they hoped) who would come to the aid of the FTP if and when they tried to begin a permanent national theatre. This effort, the FTP said, was the first "ever made by a theatrical producer to include in his theatrical scheme the audience, as well as the players and technicians."[11] The purpose of these surveys was generally to "bring the playwright and research workers into closer understanding and contact with our various units and with our audiences," to plan productions according to the people's wishes by learning precisely who the audience was. "Emergency surveys" were distributed to the directors and producers a week after the show opened, and in response, sometimes technical changes were made; for instance, in one case the director lowered the volume of music in *It Can't Happen Here*.[12] These surveys were discontinued after 1937 for lack of money. Although they weren't collected on every project or for every production, the samples taken seemed to suggest to the FTP that they had indeed been able to reach an entirely new audience, one that hadn't been able to afford to go to any other sort of theatre before the FTP came along.

When someone wanted to praise the "typical" audience of the FTP, they were impressionistically described as "lower middle-class, very hardworking people who for the night out wanted the cheapest night out and were serious about their theatre-going. They didn't just go for the lark. They went to be educated."[13] But the surveys suggested that the audience was "largely middle class, professionals, artists, business people, office workers, students, housewives, etc. Only 8.6% come under the occupational classification 'Trades and Manuals.' Of the middle-class groups, 'Professionals' account for 23.3% of the total, teachers alone being 9.17% of the total."[14] The question remains whether these were people who were going to the theatre for the first time or were going again because it was free. It seems safe to say that some of the audience surveys reflected the hopes of Flanagan and other progressives of the FTP: that the Federal Theatre brought the legitimate theatre within reach of the average wage earner, and that it spread theatre to areas and groups not reached by popular or regular theatre.

But when an audience asked for something the director did not wish to give them, it seemed that the audience wasn't an equal partner. Although "as far back as the early part of 1937 we knew that the negro audiences in New York City patronizing the Lafayette Theatre were clamoring for a negro revue," knowing this didn't persuade the directors to give Harlem a Negro revue.[15] When audiences surveyed in Los Angeles overwhelmingly asked for comedy and musicals, the supervisor of the regional research bureau in charge of audience surveys comments with a mixture of chagrin and contempt:

> It may be appropriate at this point to emphasize that when forty-eight people at the Mason Theatre express preferences for comedy, most of them mean "good clean comedy" on the order of "Abie's Irish Rose", and, that of the people who voted for drama, the majority thought of it in terms of "Madam X" and "East Lynne". Comments submitted by members of the audiences and quoted in this as well as in earlier surveys, are usually selected on a basis of constructive value. An apparent emphasis may, therefore, be given to the literate and articulate part of the audience. An attempt is usually made to corroborate the analysis with quotations from the audience. These quotations, however, do not necessarily indicate an accurate cross section of the audience. By recent analysis, the I.Q. of the great American public is not rated as high; in fact only 15% are

termed intelligent. It is, then, no mystery that "Abie's Irish Rose" grossed millions of dollars and that similar theatrical fare is always assured of success; the majority, in their quest for amusement, act their alleged mental age.[16]

Just as Flanagan thought it was her prerogative as director to override the wishes of local directors and local actors, so this surveyor skews the survey so as to reflect the "intelligent" part of the audience, the 15 percent who aren't captivated by "Abie's Irish Rose." Although the FTP congratulated itself, praised and publicized the audience surveys it conducted, if people were ignorant about what they really liked, if the box office couldn't be counted on as a reliable predictor of what they wanted, then audience surveys could also justifiably be ignored. While the regional supervisors found it relatively easy to scoff at local audiences, those who had to work directly with them, like the black directors of the Lafayette, found it much more difficult to dismiss the audience's desires for musicals, comedies, and revues.

The audience surveys reflected a commitment on the part of the FTP to find out something about their audience; without them they were "in the position of the Broadway producer who reads a play, likes it personally, produces it, and hopes that enough people will like it, so that he will make a profit from it."[17] At least one director enthusiastically praised the surveys: "Publicity and promotion for the production were greatly aided by the actual testimony of 'satisfied customers.' It was good to feel the authentic response of the audience, the real contact with that very necessary but hitherto despised silent partner of the theatre."[18] But apart from creating that wonderful feeling of being in touch with an "authentic response," it is doubtful whether the surveys had a deep or long-term effect on the theatre. Besides a few technical changes made and information gathered, directors could just as easily ignore an audience's wishes as respect them. In the end, the surveys only accounted for a small fraction of the population who did get to see a FTP play; outside of New York, Chicago, Los Angeles, Denver, and Seattle, few surveys were conducted, and those few only in that first year. The surveys never resolved the question of the identity of the people's theatre: would the FTP be a people's theatre only if directed entirely by the people's choices?

II

It is unmistakable that in spite of the assurances from Flanagan on down that the Negro units were not meant for "downtown whites," the units always had to contend with what James Weldon Johnson called the double audience:

> The Aframerican author faces a special problem which the plain American author knows nothing about – the problem of the double audience. It is more than a double audience; it is a divided audience, an audience made up of two elements with differing and often opposite and antagonistic points of view. His audience is always both white America and black America. . . . The Negro author can try the experiment of putting black America in the orchestra chairs, so to speak, and keeping white America in the gallery, but he is likely at any moment to find his audience shifting places on him, and sometimes without notice.[19]

The audience of blacks and whites sometimes had opposite points of view, but then opposite points of view could also be found within each race.

Black critics had been concerned about generating a black audience for theatre and making that audience behave a certain way for at least twenty years before the FTP came along. Black theatrical audiences were subject to the same middle-class disciplinary modes of behavior that Lawrence Levine outlined in his book *Highbrow/Lowbrow: The Emergence of Cultural Hierarchy in America.* Though vocal participation characterized an African American cultural practice in church and in theatre, the call and response woven into African American church practice no longer seemed appropriate for a middle-class theatre.[20] The popular black theatrical acts at the Apollo in Harlem continued to elicit audience participation, but quite clearly, the FTP in Harlem and elsewhere, though proud of its lively audiences, did not expect the same level of vocal participation.

Many critics from the twenties to the thirties objected to what seemed to them uncouth and unsophisticated habits. Black audiences came in for such criticism from black critics as well as from white critics. Du Bois had written in 1916 with contempt about the audiences who frequented the popular theatres in Harlem:

> Let us be frank. The colored audience as I have seen it recently in the colored theatres of large cities is not above reproach. We are an appreciative people certainly but our appreciation need not take the form of loud ejaculations and guffaws of laughter, particularly when that laughter breaks out in the wrong place. . . .

> Is this state of affairs due to ignorance or thoughtlessness? To
> a combination of both, I fancy. We cannot afford either. It is
> true one goes to the theater to be amused, in any event to be
> diverted, but the establishment and maintenance of the colored
> theater and the colored actor have at this point of our develop-
> ment a peculiar, though obvious significance. Our actors must
> be encouraged and not put on a level with mountebanks whose
> slightest gesture is the signal for laughter.[21]

The theatre becomes a place of acculturation, proper manners are
taught, and uncontrollable "ejaculations" squelched. But perhaps it
wasn't ignorance or thoughtlessness that provoked laughter "in the
wrong place." It might have been that people laughed because they
found the theatre absurd.

One of the most famous moments of "inappropriate" laughter in the
black theatre occurred when Jules Bledsoe came to Harlem to play
Emperor Jones. Randolph Edmunds, a black playwright and educator,
wrote:

> I was in the audience in the Lincoln Theatre last summer when
> Jules Bledsoe came there in *Emperor Jones*. This play had toured
> the country, and had even been produced in foreign countries.
> It is hailed as one of the best of the modern one act plays, and
> was for the first time playing in colored houses. Yet, this audi-
> ence howled, whistled, and hissed the actors until the acting of
> the play was impossible. The whole scene was disgusting as
> well as pitiable.[22]

Edmunds wants to be able to count on a certain response to a play, a
dignified response. Is the audience here simply unable to discern the
difference between tragedy and comedy, or are they laughing because
they find the performance pretentious and ridiculous? Langston Hughes
tells of the same reaction to *Emperor Jones* in his autobiography with a
good deal more sympathy for the audience:

> Somewhat later, I recall a sincere but unfortunate attempt on
> Jules Bledsoe's part to bring "Art" to Harlem. He appeared in
> Eugene O'Neill's *The Emperor Jones* at the old Lincoln Theater
> on 135th Street, a theater that had, for all its noble name, been
> devoted largely to ribald, but highly entertaining, vaudeville of
> the "Butterbeans and Susie" type. The audience didn't know
> what to make of *The Emperor Jones* on a stage where "Shake
> That Thing" was formerly the rage. And when the Emperor

started running naked through the forest, hearing the Little Frightened Fears, naturally they howled with laughter.

"Them ain't no ghosts, fool!" the spectators cried from the orchestra. "Why don't you come on out o' that jungle – back to Harlem where you belong?"

In the manner of Stokowski hearing a cough at the Academy of Music, Jules Bledsoe stopped dead in his tracks, advanced to the footlights, and proceeded to lecture his audience on manners in the theater. But the audience wanted none of *The Emperor Jones*. And their manners had been all right at all the other shows at the Lincoln, where they took part in the performances at will. So when Brutus continued his flight, the audience again howled with laughter. And that was the end of *The Emperor Jones* on 135th Street.[23]

To the audience at the Lincoln, used to talking back to the entertainers on stage, their response to *Emperor Jones* was perfectly legitimate behavior. It was the performance of a tragic *Emperor Jones* that seemed out of place, incongruous. When someone cried out to the Emperor, come "back to Harlem where you belong," at least some of the people in the audience asserted their proprietary rights over the Lincoln Theatre. Here they determined the rules of decorum and the appropriate genres. Just as the Emperor lords over his island but is ultimately brought down by the natives, so in this episode the voice of the Harlem "native" makes fun of the "art" play of Eugene O'Neill. The audience's laughter could have been a rejection of the premises of O'Neill's or any white man's sense of black tragedy; it certainly didn't seem real to the people who laughed, nor did it inspire pity or terror. O'Neill and Bledsoe's sense of "Art," as Hughes called it, capitalized and in quotation marks, was very different from the entertainment the Lincoln crowd was used to and liked. Du Bois, Edmunds, and Bledsoe wanted the audience to bow down to their idea of decorum: laughter, talking back, asserting the rights of an audience to be heard, perhaps part of an African American oral tradition, were to be outlawed in their idea of a theatre. The theatre could promote pride in its people but it would also teach them how to be a genteel audience, to become sophisticated enough to recognize serious "Art." It would teach them not to laugh. The gap between the educated elite and the people couldn't be wider in the different reactions to an evening at the theatre.

The same black critics who complained about unsophisticated lower-class audiences also were disappointed by middle-class audiences for their lack of support for "Art." In a January 1925 *Messenger* editorial, the rhetorical question, "Do Negroes Want High Class Anything?" is answered "No." They say they do, but they don't patronize the opera, the drama, literature. Why not? The editorial answers:

> They lack the actual financial and property basis to supply cultured wants. . . .
>
> Moreover, the culture of the large number of so-called edu-cated Negroes is very superficial. It is too new to have sunk deep. All of which is reflected in a pretense of loving the opera, drama and fine art, when in reality it bores them and is as pearls cast before swine. . . .
>
> Finally the shackles of slavery still bind the colored people. Their chains are broken but not off. They would rather, on the whole, duck into a dive, eat at a smoky, greasy fish joint, get their hair dressing done in a little junky den, than to go to some up-to-date, spacious, beautifully decorated cafes, restaurants, beauty parlors and theatres.[24]

The same charge had been leveled against all Americans: high culture was simply not a staple part of the daily American diet. If the Lincoln crowd threw the Emperor Jones off stage and the middle classes were more interested in getting their hair dressed than going to the theatre, who could be counted on for the experiments of "community" theatre, and ten years later who could be counted on to fill the seats of the Negro unit productions across the country? People would have to be persuaded that "Art" was not boring.

Whether lamenting the uncivilized behavior of the audience at the Lincoln Theatre, abhorring the white audience who only identified with a primitive black stereotype, or castigating the black bourgeoisie for their dismissal of anything but "dignified" representations of black peo-ple, black critics had worried about the black audience for years in black journals. If African Americans were supposed to be so naturally theatrical, why didn't black audiences support all kinds of theatre? The task was for black intellectuals to socialize newly urbanized blacks to appreciate something more than popular entertainment and convince the black middle class that social drama was worth its patronage.

III

Lovett Fort-Whitman had claimed in 1923 that it wasn't that the Negro audience was unrefined but that the *choice* of plays, Broadway hits, or plays not written by black playwrights were simply not relevant to the black community.[25] Carlton Moss, "the community man" in

Harlem, made it his job to visit all the fraternal organizations and churches in order to publicize the FTP's Negro unit and make the people "feel it was theirs, and then they would come."[26] De Paur claimed that black people loved the theatre, but the main task of the directors in Harlem was to figure out what would get them to come to the theatre, what would make them "feel it was theirs." Black audiences seemed to love theatrical entertainment and yet be estranged from theatrical institutions.

The question for the Harlem producers remained, What would play and to whom? The Harlem unit produced three problem plays, *Walk Together, Chillun, Sweet Land,* and *Turpentine,* all of which concerned racism in the South and received good press, but played to disappointingly small black audiences. The audience surveys hint at some of the dissatisfaction with problem plays. In audience surveys of *Sweet Land* and *Turpentine,* most of the critical remarks centered around objections from three groups. The first group wanted plays that spoke directly to it about northern life. A play about conditions in the South just wasn't sufficiently interesting to northern Negroes living in cities; they wanted a play about "New York Negro life and problems." More than once, the refrain "We want something more 'modern' " is recorded in the surveys, something that reflects "their lives" or their idea of their lives, not in the "backwards" South, but in Harlem, their home. A second group found all problem plays boring, too "preachy social. Audiences are not anxious to be preached to. . . . They want diversion, entertainment, not just morbid social problems." And a third group was embarrassed by the "low-brow" subject matter. "Why all this mess of backwoods. We want to improve like whites. The plight of Negroes is bad enough without making them appear so dumb and ridiculous." While white respondents were almost unanimous in their enjoyment of the plays (so much so that the compiler of the survey thought that *Turpentine* would transfer well to a downtown audience), blacks were very divided but also quite articulate about their objections.[27]

Some parts of the black audience did indeed look forward to what Lovett Fort-Whitman considered "relevant" material (and presumably these people would have also been delighted with *Big White Fog*). But another group found northern or southern problem plays boring, irrelevant to its desire to be entertained. A combination of class difference – the middle class does not want to be reminded of the degradation of the poor – and regional differences further fractured racial interests. The surveyor sensibly recommends that plays should be produced in repertory rather than one after another, which would allow for various tastes to be fulfilled at one time.[28] As Philip Barber notes, the purpose of the

Negro units was to produce plays by Negroes for Negroes, but that does not in itself assure popular success with the Negro audience:

> Seemingly, this was not specific enough, for "Walk Together, Chillun" and "Turpentine" fell into this category and their lack of appeal already has been recorded. The natural conclusion is that the Negro of the North is too much involved with his own problems to give much thought to the difficulties of his race in other parts. There is a basic flaw in such reasoning, however, for we know that only by maintaining an awareness of one another and keeping in mind the time when collaboration with other races will terminate their insufferable exploitation, can there exist a hope for deliverance.[29]

A theatre that could make different peoples aware of one another, even make it possible for the races to collaborate, certainly represented Flanagan's, Hopkins's, Locke's, and Johnson's views. But the audience that refused to see "low-brow" or preachy plays or considered the South too far removed wanted something different from its theatre. It wanted to see itself moving on up. An FTP administrator said of the Pennsylvania Negro units:

> One faction believes that the Negro should not always be pictured as a colorful and joyous individual, but should be shown as he really is; in other words, trying to elevate himself and better his conditions, trying to secure education and culture. The other faction also feels that such an attempt should be made but do not feel so strongly about it and consequently there is a tug-of-war every once in a while.[30]

"As he really is" continues to be the sticking point. Even in a passage that is forced to account for differences, confusion remains between "the Negro" as an individual (mostly always figured as "he"), and "the Negro" as representing the entire race.

The voodoo *Macbeth* and Shaw's *Androcles and the Lion,* both adapted for the Negro unit in Harlem, provoked a range of comments, critical and appreciative, revealing the different stakes different parts of the audience had in certain kinds of drama. One black reviewer hoped that the production would define a black audience. Roi Ottley wrote that *Macbeth* was a "spectacular production" and proved the worthiness of both the FTP and black actors. He took a strong separatist line, insisting that this play could only be truly understood by Harlem residents:

> The presence of Broadway and Park avenue in the theatre added to the glamour of the occasion, but they could hardly be consid-

ered a particularly sympathetic audience for what was being revealed. Nor were they entirely cognizant of the implications of such a production. We therefore warn downtown visitors that the play is purely for Harlem consumption, and is geared and produced accordingly.[31]

What was being revealed and what were the implications of a play produced purely for Harlem? If it were true that *Macbeth* was "geared and produced" solely for Harlem, then the beginnings of a community theatre, for Negroes, was being created. But this was wishful thinking.

Whatever the FTP bureaucrats said about creating a theatre of and for Negroes and not for downtown whites, a producer like John Houseman and a director like Orson Welles had no intention of forgetting about downtown audiences; indeed, they geared and produced with an eye to downtown audiences. Certainly Houseman and Welles had no interest in producing propaganda or social realism for socially minded black people in Harlem. They used the Harlem Negro unit to reinvent Shakespeare with their voodoo *Macbeth* and to promote their own careers. White reviewers certainly appreciated exactly how Harlem productions were geared precisely for white audiences. The reviewer from *Vogue,* Robert Littell, makes the voodoo *Macbeth* serve his own (and his culture's) very distinct needs. His review, entitled "Every One Likes Chocolate," begins with the ghost of Shakespeare watching one of his plays performed in a legitimate theatre in New York. Bored, he yawns and leaves the theatre to catch a train uptown to Harlem. There he finds himself watching the Harlem production of *Macbeth,* which he enjoys immensely. Littell describes the audience in the theatre as decidedly mixed: there are whites who have never been uptown before, people who never go to the theatre at all, and the white crowd familiar with Harlem. What are these people doing there, he asked?

> The whites went, not to see *Macbeth,* not to hear Shakespeare, who had bored most of them in school, but to get something different – that something at once innocent and richly seasoned, childlike and jungle-spiced, which is the gift of the Negro to a more tired, complicated, and self-conscious race. . . .
>
> We palefaces go to the Negro because the Negro has something that we have not, never will have, and dreadfully want. We go to Harlem not only to be amused, but out of homesickness for a land we have lost. In watching them, we recapture briefly what once we were, or like to think we were, long centuries ago before our ancestors suffered the blights of thought, worry, and the printed word. Civilization – call it that

> while it lasts – is for most of us poor white trash a barrier
> between ourselves and life. An ever-thickening pane of ground
> glass through which the wild, fiery flame of life shines feebly,
> like a fifteen-watt electric bulb through a washroom door.[32]

The familiar refrain is sounded here. Littell characterizes blacks as primitive, sensual, and uncivilized, a people who perform for whites to give
them a taste of life more deeply felt. Precisely what Ottley does not
want to occur takes place in this review. Littell describes the way a spirit
of a people can be siphoned off and taken like a drug by another people.
Ottley wanted to cordon off this spectacle and prevent a downtown
audience from sucking the vitality of this particular production, but he
can not stop the kinds of appropriation that go on by members of
the audience.

Other white reviewers were put off that a black company would even
attempt to interpret Shakespeare. Who owns a "classic" is, of course, a
question that arises, it seems, when "marginal" groups interpret the
classics. Some reviewers complained that the actors didn't speak their
lines in the proper Shakespearean manner. Houseman countered that
Welles wanted them to speak in a "simpler, more direct" style.[33] Other
reviewers were amazed that the play wasn't even more "jazzed" or
played in blackface than it was. The FTP backed the production arguing
that it hadn't attempted to be "classical":

> The scholarly critics, steeped in the tradition of the Bard, re-
> viewed our Negro Theatre's production as a conventional re-
> vival. From this point of view most of them found it somewhat
> disappointing. And they were quite right, too. This is not
> Shakespeare, in the tradition of Irving and Booth and Mac-
> ready. Perhaps it isn't even Shakespeare at all, except for his
> lines. But it is a rousing, riotous performance and a genuine joy
> to see. What if its brooding air of tragedy has been lost? This is
> not poetry, or literature, or even language. This is pure the-
> atre – Negro Theatre – the kind that is instinctive and inspired.
> Like Ptolemaic astronomy, it is geocentric. Everything revolves
> about it – including the mounted police who are necessary to
> hold back the crowds trying to buy tickets.[34]

The argument that blacks were natural actors had been contested
throughout the twenties by Alain Locke and others. The concept of a
"pure theatre" is not, after all, so different from Littell's view of the
uncivilized Negro, beyond language, skills, or training. Such a purely
racial theatre may be joyful, but it cannot lay claim to the canonical

tradition, to an "accurate" interpretation of Shakespeare. While there might be ways a racial theatre may be so strong and joyful that it makes its own circle of meanings, which others must read as something more than merely instinctive, neither the bureaucrats or reviewers found language to go beyond the "pure theatre" characterization of the Negro units.

In 1939, the last year of the FTP, the Negro unit in Harlem still struggled to find a large and loyal audience. Edward Lawson wrote a good review of Shaw's *Androcles and the Lion* in *Opportunity,* calling the play "one of the finest, most forcefully dramatic plays ever to grace the boards of the aging Lafayette. . . . It is amusing, it is timely, it is beautifully staged and well-directed, and its acting is as flawless as a superb all-Negro cast can make it." But the old mystery of the theatre had not been solved. He thought that the "biting satire, all the social protest that runs between the lines of this brilliant analysis of the plight of racial minorities" was "too subtle," far too "highbrow" for the average Harlem theatregoer. *Androcles* sold out to an almost "completely white" audience.[35]

The intellectual condescension of Lawson's position is much like Jules Bledsoe's when he stopped his performance to lecture the Harlem audience on the proper attitude toward the *Emperor Jones.* Perhaps *Androcles* simply seemed as irrelevant and silly as the *Emperor Jones* to some of the Harlem theatregoers. Edward Dudley, who actually worked in the unit, thought *Androcles* was ludicrous:

> We tried almost everything and some of the things we tried fell by the wayside because they apparently were real turkeys. This *Androcles and the Lion* that you talk about and some of the other things with grown men crawling around all over the floor in a lion's costume. We evoked more humor among people who saw it than we evoked real sense of theatre.[36]

One man's high-brow is another man's low.

Dutton Ferguson, special assistant of the Information Service of the WPA in New York, wrote to Lawson praising his review: "It carries a stinging message but should promote the cause of the Negro theatre and make articulate our sense of cultural value."[37] But the "our" Ferguson refers to – the middle-class Negroes who would choose to go to subtle, high-brow plays – might not be the "our" of greater Harlem. Lawson ended his review with the suggestion that the FTP bring to Harlem "a significant modern drama of Negro life that speaks its message directly to the masses and that entertains the Negro first, the white folks afterwards."[38] The problem remained of finding something that would be both significant and entertaining. Flanagan wrote a letter to the editor of *Opportunity*, quoting the last line of the review and asking for suggestions of plays from the editorial board of *Opportunity* or from its readers – plays that would be both significant and entertaining. She claims that the FTP administrators had always consulted "our Negro group as to choice of plays" and lists the plays produced at the Lafayette: *Conjure Man Dies, Turpentine,* and *Sweet Land* – all "modern drama."[39] Yet none of them were smash hits with the Harlem community.

Plays set in Haiti in particular seemed a good subject to Harlem producers. The story of Cristophe, the black general fighting for liberty in Haiti, seemed like it might please the Harlem audience. "Harlem wanted action, humor, colorful locale, superb acting, and – above all – a really outstanding play. 'Haiti,' judging by the unanimous approval of the metropolitan critics and generous patronage of the white folks at the Lafayette Theatre, IS THAT PLAY," a reviewer claims. But stating it, even in capital letters, didn't make Harlem respond in the way they should. Though more than 74,000 people had seen the play, "LESS THAN 20,000 OF THIS TOTAL HAVE BEEN NEGROES." Since white patronage had been much stronger than black, the FTP might decide to move the play downtown:

> In this projected move there is at stake vastly more than the success or failure of a play. If 'Haiti' must leave its native Harlem to receive its well-merited acclaim, the future of the Negro Theatre will be very bleak, indeed. The obvious conclusion will be that Harlem does not want a cultural mecca in its own community. . . . The issue, moral and cultural, is squarely up to the Negro people of Harlem.[40]

The stakes are high indeed when theatregoing becomes a moral as well as a cultural obligation. Harlem crowds continued to shirk their moral duty. Everyone wanted to figure out the mystery of the theatre, but no one yet seemed to have a clue.

IV

Playreaders were hired to evaluate the suitability of new plays, but they differed widely about what seemed acceptable to a Negro audience, and if they were white (and most were) they usually referred the question of what was appropriate back to someone who "knew" the "Negro" better. In the case of *Turpentine,* a drama about southern blacks who go on strike, ending when the vicious sheriff fires into the church where the strikers have gathered, playreaders varied sharply on the merits of the play. One praised its authentic voice: "The author writes with confidence and authenticity for much of the script. Make no mistake Mr. Morell knows his characters and the language they speak." Another reader leaves it up to "local producers" and their knowledge of local audiences to judge its effectiveness:

> To either reject or recommend the play seems almost impertinent for an outside critic or at least a critic who has not been in close contact with negro reactions towards this type of play. I should say that this is eminently a case where the reaction of the local producers, (especially if colored) should be allowed to exercise their own judgement on the basis of their knowledge of their audiences and their receptivity to the message of the play.

And a third reader, after noting the "real power in this play, humor and human feeling, natural dialogue and in general, writing that comes from the heart," decides it is too "dangerous" to be given a production, especially in Chicago:

> Is a play of warfare between blacks and whites, in which the whites are presented as murderers and traitors, suitable material for the theatre? "Turpentine" is propaganda pure and simple, with all the cards stacked against the whites. In the opinion of this reader, "Turpentine" should not be recommended to any Negro project anywhere – especially to Chicago. It is inflammable and dangerous. . . .
>
> These authors should be encouraged to go on writing for the theatre. They have a beautiful sense of comedy and of characterization. With a different theme, and some study of simple dramatic technique, they should write a play worthy of general production. [41]

We have seen before that what is deemed "worthy" must *not* be inflammatory. Playreaders and producers seemed to expect interracial warfare to break out in an instant. The fear of a volatile audience, ready to go up in flames over a drama haunts most of the deliberations of the FTP, though such fires never seemed to have occurred.

Sometimes a Negro unit, known to be cautious and inclined to produce entertaining plays, chose more inflammatory ones. Then playreaders responded in various ways to what seemed a bold and potentially dangerous choice. New Jersey existed in the shadows of New York, and the New Jersey units were felt, on the whole, to be more conservative than New York in their choice of plays. One state administrator wrote:

I have been egging them on to do some new things and blaze a few trails with courage. The overly cautious choices they claim were motivated by such things as local fear that our projects would emulate the naughty New York "Communists" or the double entendre vaudeville troupe. Others felt they had to try out the actors in a sure fire medium first. Once they got to know the troupe's potential powers, they would then take a chance on a new script.[42]

It is somewhat surprising then that the Newark Negro unit produced *The Trial of Dr. Beck* by Hughes Allison.

All of the playreaders had criticized the form of the play, the nondramatic courtroom drama, bad dialogue, repetitions. Some of these things could be corrected in production, some seemed part of the courtroom drama form. But the plot really stunned the white playreaders. Dr. Beck, who believes that light-skinned "blacks" are superior to dark-skinned Negroes, is on trial for murdering his dark-skinned wife so that he can marry his light-skinned mistress. Mrs. Beck's twin sister loves Dr. Beck, but because she has dark skin he doesn't notice her. We find out at the end of the play she killed her twin sister, Mrs. Beck, in a jealous rage. One white reader refused to judge the play:

> It has been pointed out that the conflict between the black and yellow constitutes highly explosive dramatic material. I cannot judge how deeply the Negroes might feel on this subject or in what degree resentments might be aroused. Most of the supervisors of the Harlem project feel strongly indeed on this subject. I recommend that this aspect of the play be studied carefully before a public performance is given.

Another reader felt that "There is, in the opinion of the reader, nothing to create race prejudice. It is, if anything, a strong appeal for the Negro without offense to the Whites." But Carlton Moss disagreed with him, and so he continued:

> After discussing the play with Mr. Moss, it was amazing to learn that there exists a deep racial feeling among the Negroes themselves – the light against the dark. He believes it would be a dangerous experiment to do this play in Harlem – in fact, anywhere – so it is suggested that for the good of the project a representative of Mrs. Flanagan see a rehearsal in Newark before the play is allowed to have a public presentation. Although the Play Policy Board does not feel as keenly about it, it recommends this procedure.

After a June 2, 1937 dress rehearsal, reports were filed about whether to proceed with a production. Again there were vastly different assessments of the play's merits. Some believed the plot was too creaky and imitative, others said it was structurally "well put together," with a "dramatic climax" and suspense, "these things [which] are essential to good melodrama." One reader, however, found the play offensive:

> The author has so imposed his personal prejudice in this work that it is hard for a reader to think of the play rather than the author. It is quite evident that the playwright suffers from a very deep-seated persecution complex. He blindly seeks an outlet for his passion and has selected the play form. He might better shout from the street corners and the neighborhood saloons for that is as close as his play comes to the theatre.

Converse Tyler, who had called it "good melodrama," still believed it unworthy of the FTP because the play "presents as its hero a negro who admittedly detests the darker skinned members of his own race." He acknowledged that it has "box-office value and for this reason I can understand a Broadway manager taking a fling at it. But on the whole it is vulgar and meretricious and would offend nearly every high minded member of the negro race." Yet another reader believed that with the author's "first-hand knowledge of the Negro background," he could make it "into an original and worthwhile play if the theme implied in the conflict between light-skinned and dark-skinned Negroes were developed and pointed up boldly."[43] White and black reviewers disagreed about the most fundamental things: what is vulgar, what is worthwhile and original, what is authentic, what is entertaining.

On the one hand, the Newark unit felt its audience would like *Dr. Beck;* on the other, it also chose to produce a play of Octavus Roy Cohen, *Come Seven,* at which point another tug-of-war ensued. It may be that the producers in Newark knew that different people would come to different sorts of plays, or it may be that they were responding to actors' desires for a variety of plays. It is impossible to know for sure what lay behind their decision. Cohen had written a great many popular "darky" plays in what passed for black dialect and black comedy in the early part of the twentieth century. By the thirties, progressives thought his plays full of terrible stereotypes. When the Newark Negro unit announced *Come Seven,* the Harlem Cultural Committee began to protest. Although the play was withdrawn from production by the FTP, Emmet Lavery, the head of the National Service Bureau, wanted it noted that the initial scheduling of *Come Seven* was not intended as any "adverse comment on the Negro race" and further that "members of

the company itself are insisting that the play go on."[44] In his letter to
Roy Wilkins of the NAACP, Lavery wrote that Wilkins should be
reassured by the fact that the particular producer of *Come Seven* was no
novice to the theatre, for the producer "happened to be Charles Hopkins, one of the most prominent Broadway managers of the last twenty
years."[45] Wilkins responded immediately:

> We are ready to admit that the Negro perhaps is inclined to be
> supersensitive on many points, but he has been misrepresented
> for such a long time on the stage and screen that there is justifi-
> cation for his sensitiveness. Our only concern, while noting the
> excellent work that has been done, is that the Federal Theater
> should not fall heir to the errors which have been made repeat-
> edly by Broadway and Hollywood producers. As a matter of
> fact, the poorest recommendation a judge of Negro plays could
> have would be to say that he is a Broadway producer, because
> that means that he tends to judge Negro productions for their
> commercial rather than artistic value. The public, overwhelm-
> ingly white, will pay to see delineation of certain traditional
> roles and themes by or about the Negro but will not support
> the portrayal of other themes even though the latter may be
> accurate, artistic, and expressive of true Negro life. . . .
>
> There is diversity of opinion among colored people on dra-
> matic themes treating the race and on literature, but except in
> the most sophisticated minority, there is unanimous opposition
> to the traditional stereotype treatment of the Negro in the
> drama and on the screen.[46]

Wilkins seemed to understand the various pressures on the FTP, but he
also wanted the FTP to understand his. Sensitive about the shuffling
black stereotype that makes up all of Cohen's plays, the vast majority of
African Americans found such portrayals offensive. Still, Lavery's point
had not been addressed: what about the Negroes in the Newark unit
who had thought *Come Seven* acceptable material? Did they have a
finger on the pulse of the black audience, a portion of the black audience,
or were they catering to a portion of their white audience? It is hard
to know.

Sometimes the most traditional of stereotypes were forgiven if people
thought the singing was good enough. Ralf Coleman, the only black
director to manage a Negro unit from its inception, wanted to appeal to
the "average audience" in Boston. He chose to work with the same
playwright Houseman used to open the Harlem unit – Frank Wilson.
Brother Mose like *Walk Together, Chillun* didn't challenge the status quo;

the "colored people" are good and bad but mostly comic and they sing and dance. The plays may not have pleased the more progressive minded literati, but they didn't ruffle anyone's feathers either. *Brother Mose* takes place in Texas and concerns the triumph of Moses over a racketeering black rival when oil is discovered on his land. In New Jersey, where the play was also performed, a reviewer wrote:

> The obvious shortcomings of a story that proved that the meek do inherit the earth were freely forgiven by the audience for the sake of the acting and the entertainment. . . . All the roles were more than adequately played. It was, however, the singing of such numbers of "Shortenin' Bread," "St. Louis Blues" and the better known of the old Negro spirituals that received the loud applause of the audience.[47]

The *Salem Evening News* called it "a story of typical life in a southern state with all the emotions and idiosyncrasies of the colored race contributing to a thoroughly entertaining and, at times, amusing vehicle."[48] In his director's report, Coleman evaluates the appeal of Wilson's play to various groups:

> This play by Frank Wilson, foremost Negro actor of the American stage, was performed over a period of several years by the Federal Theatre's Negro Drama Unit of New York. Mr. Wilson knowing his people and his public has in "Brother Mose" a play that appeals to the average audience combining broad comedy and deep pathos. This play was practically written to order for Federal Theatre audiences and as in New York has been played very successfully throughout the country.
>
> As a Negro director staging a play by a Negro author, this production was a "natural." Although the theme "The meek shall inherit the earth" and the pious old fashioned leading character "Moses" is objectionable to the so-called Negro intelligensia of Boston, the play to the average white audience is entertaining and enjoyable. Most Negroes object to it because it shows too plainly their idiosyncrasies and inhibitions. In playing Negro comedies there must be dialogue and situations characteristic of the Negro race, if the locale is laid in the south. This is true of "Brother Mose."
>
> As a director who believes that Negro folk plays are the greatest contribution of the Negro Theatre to the American stage, I heartily enjoyed staging and directing "Brother Mose."[49]

Coleman recognized that his audience was divided between black and white, within the black race, and between the "intelligensia" and those who simply wanted to be entertained. As a practical man of the theatre, one who had been involved in community theatre and Broadway, he tried to appeal to his idea of the "average audience." He saw his mission as entertainment, not instruction or uplift. He had 150 people to put to work, and as he says, "I tried to keep all the people busy – orchestra, chorus, dancers from vaudeville." When he found the play *Jericho* too countrified for Boston, he added music and New York nightclubs, adapting to his actors and to his audience. Coleman set out to please as many people as he could.[50]

Coleman had more training in the theatre than other black directors involved with the FTP, except, perhaps, Clarence Muse from the Lafayette Theatre and Hollywood. And he, like Muse, a fellow professional, thought of the theatre in the thirties as popular entertainment: "There was a deep appreciation away from Broadway and in the community for theatre and the arts. Say we go back to maybe '38, '39, '40, I mean, in those days people went to the theatre for entertainment. It was their only means of getting out of the house." A high school teacher who made Coleman memorize Shakespearean scenes "lit the candle" of his life-long attachment to the theatre. Coleman joined the first black community theatre of the arts in Boston, the Allied Arts Center; supported by wealthy people from Beacon Hill, the Allied Arts became the black center of the arts by 1926. Meta Warrick Fuller, the black sculptor, was in charge of the sculpture department; Coleman became director of the Allied Art Players, directing studio plays and at least three productions every year. The center became affiliated with the Ford Hall Forum, and Coleman met the Ford Hall program director who was interested in Negro theatre. Through this connection, Coleman directed plays under the auspices of the Ford Hall Players' Society. Although he wasn't paid, Coleman felt lucky to be able to direct and felt that by working he could learn more about the theatre and encourage the community to participate. With this strong background in community theatre, he was well placed to take the Paul Green play *Potter's Field* to Broadway in 1934, where it was renamed *Roll, Sweet Chariot*. Rose McClendon, Frank Wilson, the playwright-actor, and Coleman's brother, Warren Coleman, were in the cast. When the play closed after a month, Coleman went back to Boston and was chosen to direct the Negro unit of Massachusetts, with headquarters in Boston.[51]

Coleman remembers his tenure on the FTP as free of censorship, but clearly pressures from his audience, black and white, and from the FTP responding to the community limited the freedom of choice for directors. Coleman himself tells the story of his decision to put on *Stevedore* and the FTP's decision to book it outside of Boston, in Salem, Massachusetts.[52] Boston's black community raised their voices in declaring what was proper entertainment. In an article in the black newspaper, the *Boston Chronicle,* Coleman is quoted as saying that "white audiences do not want to see a Negro actor in plays written by white playwrights for white actors."[53] So he justified choosing Negro "folk" plays, plays that were "typed Negro." One of the playwrights on the Boston unit, Jack Bates, wrote about six plays: "At that time we called them 'folk plays.' We didn't call them 'black plays.' "[54] All were fantasies like *Green Pastures,* black reinterpretations of Bible stories. But the *Chronicle* wanted to see the Negro unit in plays that weren't specifically written for blacks because it considered those plays riddled with stereotypes: "Since last we wrote on this subject we have made searching investigation and are convinced that Coleman is entirely responsible for the stagnation of his group and showed neither ambition nor progressiveness in striving to give his players something worth while to do." Calling for him either to "go forward or step aside," the paper asserts:

> The Federal Theatre is the finest chance that the Negro actor has had to experiment and endeavor to educate white audiences in accepting characterizations without seeking to penetrate through the grease paint. Uncle Sam has provided the money for us to carry out just such an experiment and we must not allow either prejudiced white officials or half baked Negro directors to rob us of the opportunity. . . . In no event do we want to see on our stage Negro characters indulging in "gin-swizzling, crap-shooting and razor cutting" – no matter who is doing them.[55]

It was especially difficult to imagine in places outside of Harlem or Newark audiences that weren't mixed racially. In Chicago and in Boston, the demands of a divided audience were felt to be particularly acute. Certainly the black newspaper in Boston thought the FTP should be educating white audiences coming to see the Negro units, and Coleman thought his job was to entertain them. It was hard to find a play that could do both things and satisfy two audiences.

In Boston, as elsewhere, decisions about what plays to produce were made in response to pressure from what seemed to be portions of an audience. In 1936, a play called *Gold in the Hills* was suggested as suitable for the Boston Negro unit.[56] Hiram Motherwell, acting director of the FTP, thought the play terrible, although the state director liked the idea and backed the production. Motherwell wrote to Flanagan:

I suggest you ask Bill Stahl if there is any good reason why the Negro Unit should do trash like this. Ostensibly they have picked it as a relief from the folk plays they have been doing under Ralf Coleman. From several scraps of information I gathered I should infer that the choice of this play is some kind of makeshift. I know that the Boston Negro paper has been attacking the group on the grounds that Negroes should not do "Negro Plays" but any plays that any white actors do. Possibly the choice of this play is an attempt on Gallagher's part to placate that branch of Negro opinion, but if they want to do straight drama I don't see why they should pick a thing like this.

He asked Flanagan to veto it and someone must have killed it, for it seems never to have been produced.[57]

Years later, in an atmosphere in which black performers were judged by the quality of "protest" in their work, Coleman defended his choice of plays on the FTP, citing *Stevedore,* Green's *In Abraham's Bosom,* and plays by O'Neill as protest plays:

In the Federal Theatre we were doing protest plays. It isn't something new that these kids have just discovered, the black thing, you know. It isn't new. We were doing them long before they were born and suddenly we have built the foundation so that they can take over in a more violent way. We tried to do it subtly. We tried to inject entertainment into our message.

But thank God that in the theatre of my day the emphasis was on art. It wasn't on propaganda. Propaganda, yes, but we felt that we ought to have the little sugar coating over it like Ossie's "Purlie," a beautiful thing, satire tops. . . . You can't hit a person over the head like Baldwin did in his mad play on Broadway, you know, "Blues for Mr. Charlie," beautifully acted. Oh, it's a great thing but who do you depend on for your support in the theatre. Not Negroes. The Negroes have let many Negro plays go and let them down. When I was with "Lucasta," I could count the number of Negroes in the audience on my two hands unless they were friends of mine or friends of somebody in the cast you know, that way. But now I think it's different than it was then. Negroes are growing to support their own theatre because I've been reading that [at] the black movies some of the audiences are 90 or 99 percent black, which is a wonderful thing. We are training our audience to support black plays, but in my day, so far as the professional theatre was concerned, most of the support came from white audiences, you see. And that's another place where the theatre has advanced in attracting black audiences. And there's where the black relationship has helped theatre so far as black writers, playwrights, and black directors and black actors are concerned.

Coleman's relationship to his art and audience is a rich mixture of contradictory beliefs. But then his audience was a rich mixture as well. His central principle was to give the audience what it wanted, which, of course, is not the same thing as giving it what he (or others) thought it might have needed. And he chose which audience to placate; those who wanted to be entertained. Negro folk plays, he believed, would attract the biggest audience, composed mostly, but not entirely, of white patrons.

A Negro in charge of the Negro units, with very little, if any, cross over between units, Coleman refused to see his troupe as suffering from political or cultural segregation: "I wouldn't call it segregation, but it was sort of doing your own thing as a black or doing your own thing as an Italian, doing your own thing as a Jew and then all coming together and doing it all together." He directed a Negro unit but didn't believe it was segregated or separatist, just "doing its own thing." Directing a Negro unit for a mixed audience, he needed to figure out what kind of theatre he would direct on stage: folk plays of the sort that offended both white liberals and the black middle classes, social protest plays, or "universal" plays. Coleman claimed he was doing all three: "There's no such thing as an all-black play because that wouldn't be in keeping with life itself. . . . But so far as art is concerned, there is no demarcation line or demarcation so far as color is concerned. Art is art, whether you're black, green, blue or yellow. You're an artist."[58] As an artist, he made all of his decisions based on a desire to please his audience, which made him perhaps more sensitive to contemporary demands than some of the critics, bureaucrats, politicians, and playreaders working at the FTP, but his desire to be a director of the people, to direct what would appeal to the greatest number of people, did not make him a creator of a new visionary theatre. The Negro audience who would support a national race theatre that so many black critics had wanted never materialized for the FTP. What audiences there were fractured into various groups with various demands for various kinds of theatre.

The African American theatre had always to contend with the double audience described by James Weldon Johnson. Not only were there white and black differences; there were differences within the races as well. The FTP knew what the majority seemed to want – vaudeville, revues, musicals, "entertainment" – only this was *not* what some of the

FTP bureaucracy wanted to give them. Despite audience surveys and a professed belief in the necessity of listening to the people and of being guided by them, those with the power to make decisions often based them on what they thought was "good" and did not respect different tastes and sensibilities. Cultural elitism certainly afflicted the Negro units as well, but the audience for Negro plays was even more fractured, more sharply split than the general population who wanted to see a circus. A play that seemed highbrow and subtle to one reviewer seemed to someone else like just a bunch of grown men stupidly crawling on the floor in lion costumes. Gin swizzling seemed natural to one director, while to an editor it seemed derogatory and shameful. The mystery of the Negro theatre – the answer to the question "What do they want?" – was that "they" were plural and didn't exist except in the minds of everyone working in the theatre. The audience, all too often, was an idea, a figure of various people's expectations.

In 1924, Theophilus Lewis had wondered why the theatre wasn't more at the heart of the black community's spiritual culture:

> We have a great soul hunger for the bread of life, and we are so determined to get it that we don't give a hang about white people's prejudices or opinions. We go ahead and build our churches and endow our preachers so we can conveniently get the spiritual food we crave. If we really had the love and aptitude for the theatre we're supposed to have, it seems to me, we would at least make an attempt to do for our actors what we have done for our preachers.[59]

If blacks love the theatre as much as people claimed, then why is there not more dissatisfaction with what exists? Lewis wrote:

> What we call the Negro Theatre is an anemic sort of thing that does not reflect Negro life, Negro fancies or Negro ideas. It reflects the 100 percent American Theatre at its middling and cheapest. . . . You expect to find malcontents leading revolts, amateurs making exhilarating and novel experiments; kibitzers vociferously offering advice, criticizing; a considerable minority of the laity aware that something is wrong and disgruntled by it, even if not just sure what is wrong. No such healthy discontent exists among Aframericans. No torch bearers are trying to relieve the aridity of the so-called Negro Stage by starting little theatres.[60]

Reminiscing about the FTP, Leonard De Paur claimed that the Negro unit productions *had* been able to develop new audiences. Perhaps the red blood cell count of audiences did go up during the four years the Negro units existed. Audiences responded to some of the experiments and rejected others.

If the mission of the FTP and certain black critics was to generate a national people's theatre and, in the case of the Negro units, a national race theatre, they had to contend with divided audiences – white and black – and races internally divided. They couldn't avoid divided audiences or segregate them, but didn't necessarily try to embrace all of the audiences' desires either. This was perhaps the biggest missed opportunity. More of a willingness to provoke the reactions some playreaders were so fearful of (short of race war), might have been a good thing. More explicit confrontations might have made the theatre less arid, more exciting, and vibrant. In order to be a people's theatre in more than name and intention, the FTP bureaucracy should have listened to the people in communities more attentively. Within the black community, directors were forced to deliver entertainment and uplift. While this may have prevented a single philosophy of what constituted a race theatre from crystalizing, it allowed the expression of a kind of vitality that Lewis hoped to see: in the letters registering complaints and in audience surveys, we can see how kibitzers, the disgruntled, amateurs, and critics of all sorts kept the FTP's Negro units hopping from one drama to another. The more kibitzing, fighting, and disgruntlement, the livelier the theatre.

5

Acting Properly

If you want to know who we are:
We are gentleman from Japan,
On many a vase and jar –
On many a screen and fan
– *The Mikado*[1]

Perhaps there are natural actors, but to believe that an entire race is made up of such fantastic beings seems equally fantastic. To use the theatre to make a break with the old way of seeing and the old way of being African American, to use the theatre to create a new culture, critics knew there had to be a different point of view, a different direction, different writing. Many critics, directors, and writers tried consciously to break with the tradition of African American theatre. But when it came to thinking about acting, the very traditional language of racialism, the description of black actors as "natural," seemed effectively to preclude all attempts to break free. The mainstream white culture had invested in a particular view of black acting that minimized artifice or "playing," and most black critics, even when they saw what was at stake in being called "naturally dramatic," also used the same words, if not exactly with the same intent when describing black actors. Perhaps there was less interest in changing what seemed most successful and what seemed so deeply embedded in American culture: the belief that black acting was "natural" and "spontaneous." The idea was that black actors did not seem to choose to play a part one way rather than another. They had no cause to interpret because they were too much the subject without being accorded any subjectivity. They could only "play" what they knew, what people conceived of as their "own" lives.

From realistic dramas like *Big White Fog* to musicals like *Run, Little Chillun* set in the United States and adaptations like the *Swing Mikado,*

168

Figure 13. LCFTP. Los Angeles, July 21, 1938. "Church Revival, *Run, Little Chillun.*"

the claim would be made that every production of the Negro units was successful because actors delivered a natural rendition of their lives. Nowhere was this rhetoric more strong than in the descriptions of black musicals; for African American music had always enjoyed a unique status as the art best reflecting the special quality of the African American people. Music seemed to embody a racial spirit and the songs and dances at the heart of popular black performances seemed to enact a kind of ecstasy. Actors and audience alike are taken over by the spirit. In *Run, Little Chillun* (Figure 13), the southern Baptists get their chance to take part in a church revival. With the singers' backs turned away from the audience, they seem deliberately to focus on their own audience, those churchgoers in front of them. Taken over by the spirit of God and music, the actors do not need to pay attention to the audience. A denial of the immediate theatre audience is part of what constitutes the natural. In Figure 14, another kind of song and dance is enacted in *Run, Little Chillun,* these supposedly from Africa. As much as Hall Johnson, the writer, and Clarence Muse, the director of the production in Los

Figure 14. LCFTP. Los Angeles, July 22, 1938. "African Chants, *Run, Little Chillun*."

Angeles, insisted on their accuracy, the staging and costumes look like every other voodoo African Caribbean production the FTP put on for their Negro units. This was a theatrical tradition, not an authentic African dance. The same bone necklaces and earrings and feathered hats and bare legs can be seen in photographs from *Macbeth* and *Black Empire* as well as in *Run, Little Chillun* (Figures 15 and 16). Here, the dancers are front and center, acting for the audience, consciously performing this exotic dance.

The musical adaptation of *Swing Mikado* doesn't attempt to replicate a natural rendition of black life, except that it surely makes reference to "natural" black entertainment through the swing songs, the mugging, and comedy that marks the opera. In Figures 17 and 18, the actors dance and camp it up. Is this an updated minstrel show or a Gilbert and Sullivan opera? What part is mimicry of a Gilbert and Sullivan tradition, what part a reference to black forms of popular entertainment? What part is posed and rehearsed and what part is natural? These are questions that may be asked of every Negro unit production. Rather than thinking about what is natural, it may be more liberating to think about how artificial acting is. The actors on the Negro units may have been a good

Figure 15. LCFTP. New York City. "Voodoo Men, *Macbeth*."

deal more conscious than the audience was willing to acknowledge of different styles of acting and the skillful demands of their craft. After all, it would take a certain amount of skill to satisfy the audience's demand that they "be" natural.

I

Throughout the twenties and thirties, black and white critics ring variations on this theme: blacks are more natural (sometimes this translates to more primitive), more lyrical, less self-conscious than whites. Eugene O'Neill considered Charles Gilpin the best actor he ever worked with, the one who came closest to O'Neill's own intentions as playwright. In 1925, O'Neill wrote in the *Messenger*:

> The Negro artist on the stage is ideal from an author's stand-point. He interprets but he does not detract – and when his own personality intrudes it is usually (unless he has learned too much rubbish in the conventional "white" school of acting) an enrich-ment of the part. I think Negroes are natural born actors –

Figure 16. LCFTP. Seattle, WA. "Voodoo Man, *Black Empire*."

Figure 17. LCFTP. Chicago/New York City. "The Mikado and Chorus, *Swing Mikado*."

(speaking in generalities) – while whites have to learn to lose their self-consciousness before they begin to learn. As to voice and innate lyric quality of movement and expression, there is no comparison. You have it "all over us."[2]

W. E. B. Du Bois said much the same thing in 1916: "The Negro is essentially dramatic. His greatest gift to the world has been and will be a gift of art, of appreciation and realization of beauty."[3] Even Alain Locke, who recognized that the "natural born actor" type had been used to justify the belief that black actors need no training, restricting them to the "mimic and the clown," nevertheless argued that the "natural gifts of temperament" of Negro actors gave them the potential to "revolutionize the drama quite as definitely and perhaps more vitally than a coterie of dramatists":

> A comprehending mind knows that the very life of drama is in dramatic instinct and emotion, that drama begins and ends in mimicry, and that its creative force is in the last analysis the interpretative passion. Welcome then as is the emergence of the Negro playwright and the drama of Negro life, the promise of the most vital contribution of our race to the theatre lies, in my opinion, in the deep and unemancipated resources of the Negro actor, and the folk arts of which he is as yet only a blind and hampered exponent. Dramatic spontaneity, the free use of the body and the voice as direct instruments of feeling. . . . It is this

Figure 18. LCFTP. Chicago/New York City. "Pooh-Bah (William Franklin), Ko-Ko (Herman Green), Pish Tush (Lewis White) in *Swing Mikado*."

sense of something dramatic to the core that flows movingly in the blood rather than merely along the veins that we speak of as the racial endowment of the Negro actor.[4]

Arguing that his people are dramatic "to the core," Locke never gets closer than this to racial essentialism. In this same essay, he plays with the metaphor of culture, referring to the "sub-soil" of African American drama, the underground of vaudeville and minstrelsy where the greatest talents lie, like Williams and Walker. On the whole, he believed the talent is wasted in stereotyped shuffling darky minstrel shows. Locke wanted more "serious" dramas for these performers, richer stories to match the "natural" talents of these actors. But by invoking and praising the natural, Locke risked trapping actors in conventionally "natural" roles. The discourse, so pervasive in black and white culture of the "naturally musical and naturally great Negro actors," gave actors the right to act as long as they seemed like they weren't acting. A *Macbeth* set in Scotland played by African Americans would have been inconceivable, unrealistic, inauthentic, while the voodoo seems not at all to be a stretch. Certain parts are natural, others are not. Shakespeare continued to be the test for critics and audiences. Could blacks be "trained" to speak the lines?

Theophilus Lewis consistently refused to take the natural route. Great acting would never, in his opinion, be enough to create a great theatre. While black and white critics praise the natural genius of an Aldridge or a Gilpin, thereby "proving" a "racial genius for the theatre," to Lewis "it merely proves that Robeson is a mighty fine actor."[5] Lewis understood that the star system would swallow up the best in the black community, further weakening any attempt to create an alternative Negro theatre. Stars like Robeson and Gilpin would be tempted by white producers who could pay higher salaries than black producers and guarantee them bigger audiences:

> This condition makes a prominent part in a show assembled for white audiences the goal of the colored actor's ambition. Naturally, only the more talented performers can make the grade; and instead of making an effort to reform the Negro theater for the better, the more competent and versatile colored actors spend their best years developing themselves for a career under a white producer. . . . Hence that most useful factotum who has appeared early in the history of almost every other group or national theater, the actor-dramatist, striving to express the group character and problems esthetically, has never been evolved by the Negro Theatre. In his stead the Negro Theatre has produced the actor-showsmith who sought his material, not in Negro life, but on the Caucasian stage.[6]

Even the most serious of scripts available to black actors in the twenties and thirties were objected to by some as filled with stereotypes.

Stars like Robeson and Gilpin had to defend the plays that made them stars – O'Neill's *Emperor Jones* and *All God's Chillun Got Wings*. Although the plays were "serious," not typical black theatrical fare, Robeson found himself arguing that the *Emperor Jones* was not primarily about blacks in America but an "exultant tragedy of the disintegration of human soul."[7] By insisting that the play's subject was the "human" soul not the particular black one, Robeson avoided seeing that the portrayal of the Emperor was as stereotyped in the tragic mold as Bert Williams was in his comic one. From those who think the journey backward in time to a racial (and primitive) heritage was another kind of pernicious stereotype, Robeson justified the ending on the grounds that it was simply dramatic: "We are too self-conscious, too afraid of showing all phases of our life, – especially those phases which are of greatest dramatic value. The great mass of our group discourage any member who has the courage to fight these petty prejudices" (369).

Lewis acknowledged that great acting can sometimes mitigate the unrealistic plot or dialogue in a given play. In a "morality play" adapted from a monograph entitled *Black Boy,* Paul Robeson's performance shades the idealized character, humanizing and complicating the character, investing "the flimsy role with dignity and charm."[8] A great actor can, however, only do so much to dignify flimsy roles. Charles Gilpin became notorious because he identified so strongly with the part of Emperor Jones that he began to change some of O'Neill's lines in order to bring even more dignity to the Emperor. O'Neill is quoted as saying to Gilpin: "If I ever catch you rewriting my lines again, you black bastard, I'm going to beat you up." O'Neill's biographers write that Gilpin became more and more erratic, substituting words and drinking, "less and less willing to 'play the game,' " and was eventually fired.[9] An actor must stick to the letter and try his best within those limits to change the spirit.

How much could any actor affect the course of events in the FTP? The records are only indirectly revealing about the kinds of black actors there were and what they wanted. And of course, local conditions, a particularly sympathetic director or a racist bureaucrat could make all the difference in the world. Most FTP actors were not stars. Even in Harlem, the Negro unit included vaudevillians and amateurs. Carlton Moss remembers:

> Then you had people who had been supers in Broadway plays like *The Green Pastures,* where they – you see, the language was that when they wanted to do a black play, get a lot of blacks and put 'em on the stage or just have one who could make a lot

of noise. So you had a lot of people who were actors and you'd say, "What were you in?"

"Oh, I was in *Green Pastures.*"

"What did you do?"

"Oh, I was in it."

"Yeah, but what did you do?"

"Well, I was in *The Green Pastures.*"

You had a lot of that. Then you had, when the word got out that they were hirin' actors, then you had people who knew they were actors. That's all, they just knew.[10]

Often actors in the FTP, white and black, according to Flanagan, needed to be retrained in diction, voice, and movement.[11] In Philadelphia, a Negro vaudeville unit put on a play called *Jericho*. It was reported at an FTP conference that the director had been "able to retrain these actors because the characters in the play were close enough to their own lives and people and transitions could easily be made."[12] Although directors never expected much from white or black vaudevillians, the expectations for black actors were exceptionally low. In Philadelphia, they found a play in which the actors would not have to "act" but only act naturally since the play mirrored their lives so closely (or so the FTP bureaucrats believed).

The Negro unit in Seattle surprisingly put on some of the most experimental of productions of any Negro unit, partly due to its directors, Florence and Burton James, who taught at the University of Washington. They produced a wide range of shows, from *Little Black Sambo* to *Lysistrata;* a new play by a black playwright, Theodore Browne, called *Natural Man* about John Henry; *Noah;* a version of *It Can't Happen Here;* and the labor play *Stevedore*. Being encouraged to write new plays, improvising Brer Rabbit stories for children's theatre, and composing music for productions allowed playwrights, actors, and musicians to exercise direction and some autonomy in the theatre. Equally important was the large and talented pool of amateurs and professional black actors in Seattle who struck the white director of the western region of the FTP as remarkable precisely because they *didn't* fit the standard portrait of the "natural" black actor:

> The Negro group is to work under Burton Jones and is, I think, their most interesting activity. They have, however, a curious difficulty – while the Negro population of Seattle is very large, they are mostly educated Negroes, and they are actually having to teach dialect to many of the players in their opening produc-

tion of *Porgy*. This makes me wonder a little if our whole white approach to the Negro theatre question isn't wrong.[13]

Indeed! Education and skills undermine the notion of authentically natural performances and might shake the foundations of a Negro theatre based on certain notions of what a white audience expects a black audience to sound like. In Seattle, it seems that at least some of the time, the actors taught the white directors what they would and would not do. During a rehearsal of the Brer Rabbit children's play, the white director, Esther Porter Lane, tells how one actor

> sat out front and started as a mammy telling stories out on the side to get us going on the whole Joel Chandler Harris stuff. And thoughtlessly, in those days, I had costumed her or asked her to be costumed in an Aunt Jemima red kerchief with little knots here and little knots there and she looked adorable. And then I found something was wrong, they were unhappy, she wasn't singing very well and, you know, the scene wasn't clicking. And they finally said, "Anything but that." And her mother had been a slave, her grandmother had been a slave, and even in those days, "I'll do anything but I won't put a red kerchief on my head."[14]

Perhaps those actors who refused to act in Paul Green's play in Chicago objected to "acting" the parts of convicts because they believed, just as this woman did in Seattle, that this acting wasn't just make believe. Putting on a red kerchief wasn't a symbol; it signified, it signaled slave without the quotation marks.

II

The Los Angeles Theatre Project had been noted for its efficiency as well as its aesthetic and political conservatism.[15] Actors here seemed particularly powerless in the hands of a white bureaucracy. Dale Wasserman, who lighted one of the shows for the Negro unit, recalled that there were a great many black actors, but added:

> In general they were kept rather segregated and did their own material. . . . I think ostensibly they were part of the general pool, but in actuality they didn't get very much work unless a production was being put together that was a Negro production. I do know that we could borrow them. . . . But they were, in general, kept as segregated as the Yiddish unit.[16]

Claude Miller, a director from Broadway, was in charge of the unit. He hired about fifty actors and technicians in the beginning and hoped to use some of the former Lafayette Players who were in town.[17] Its one hit, *Run, Little Chillun*, came late in 1938. Before that they produced the standard plays of the FTP's Negro units: *Androcles and the Lion*, a *Macbeth*, *Noah*, *Black Empire* (about Haiti), and *Natural Man*, written by Browne in Seattle. None of the plays were radical or about current events like *Big White Fog* or *Turpentine;* the plays in Los Angeles were all safe period pieces and had all been produced elsewhere.

Max Pollock directed *Macbeth* because

> Mrs. Flanagan wanted me to do it. So she said, "It went great in New York and you've got Negroes sitting on their fannies." So I saw it and Mr. Welles did a remarkable job with the script but to me it was all false. He took the script and made a theatric thing out of Shakespeare. They had acrobats who fell on the floor, they did tumbling, he had drums on it.

Pollock cut the voodoo:

> And my actors were acting and I had wonderful luck because they could be taught. I had a man who couldn't read the text. The fellow who would knock on the door says, "Knock, knock." . . . And I taught him how to read it so it was marvelous. . . . I rehearsed *Macbeth* six months. Imagine doing that in the theatre. Well, six months we sat around the table, an idea of mine that we sit around and discuss the play and add a speech to some of them and so forth, the voices and so on.[18]

On the one hand, he seems to have encouraged participation in the process of directing the play, but on the other, he remained firmly in control, teaching one actor literally and figuratively how to read. Out of the 120 Negro actors he had to work with, 40 of them, he said, knew nothing about acting, and he fired those 40 rather than teach them all how to act.

The reviews and audience surveys reiterate the conventional range of opinions regarding the unconventional practice of black actors acting Shakespeare. Those who liked the production praise the "ablest" actors who "bring to their roles a zest born of some hot inner fire that so often is lacking among the palefaces." "Gives new light to Macbeth" an audience survey records.[19] A good many people considered the experiment unnatural, while those who enjoyed the production enjoyed it because it seemed utterly natural. Those who felt the performers should "present a theme and story native to the background of the African people" criticize the "inability of most of the cast to project Shakespeare's dialogue explicitly enough to make it understandable and in many cases audible."[20] "Were I a Negro, I should not consider this distortion of Macbeth a compliment to my race." "Fancy white people presenting 'Emperor Jones' or 'Green Pastures.' "[21] The conservative compiler of the survey comments that the pros and cons are almost evenly divided, but she disqualifies the people who liked the play because, in her words,

> they patently had no conception of Shakespeare's original tragedy *Macbeth,* or else because they saw in the production merely a gorgeous riot of color and sounds, an exciting melodrama. On the other hand, the critics who objected, did so vehemently, and usually backed their criticisms with sound arguments and many suggestions of plays more suitable, in their opinion, for a Negro cast.[22]

Clearly Los Angeles did not seem a place open to a great deal of experimenting when such rigid conceptions of acceptable roles for black actors existed.

But while reviewers and the audience vented their opinions about what suited black actors in Los Angeles, the actors themselves began to agitate for more autonomy over who should direct them and what they should be directed in. A petition had been circulated demanding more jobs for skilled African American technicians and artists, but it had been tabled. A newspaper reported on a mass meeting that took place in 1938, in which actors brought up a promise made the year before by Howard Miller, the western regional director for Federal Theatres, "that the Negro unit would be given a theatre manned from front to back by race artists and technicians, similar to the one operating so successfully in Harlem." But nothing had come of this:

> "We have been advised that if we can get the community interest aroused, we may get the theatre," Jess Brooks said.
> "There are over 40 thousand colored citizens in Los Angeles county," Brooks stated. . . .
> "We feel," he continued, "that it is a matter of taxation without representation for politics of this project to be molded and handed down to us without a single Negro having a word in that policy. We have been denied a single director or supervisor in our drama unit with the curt announcement that 'the time is not ripe for Negro directors.' "
> Disclaiming any effort to establish a jim-crow theatre, Webb

> King clarified the committee's aims by stating that it was asking
> for opportunities to train their people in the various positions
> connected with the operation of a theatre unit.[23]

These issues of actor training, directorial control, and authenticity get
mixed up all the time in everyone's discussion of a Negro theatre. One
assumption is that a black director would better represent black drama,
that is to say, black drama would be represented as more authentically
natural if a black director was in control. But in Seattle and in Los
Angeles, there is evidence that black and white directors alike were
training actors, sometimes to *seem* naturally "black"; actors had to be
trained to act authentically. The notion of what was "authentic" was
discovered in rehearsals, thus undermining the idea of natural acting.
Actors gained professional control by being subjected to a director's direction.

No doubt in response to this protest, the FTP announced *Run, Little
Chillun,* a respectable hit on Broadway in 1933, as the next production
of the Los Angeles Negro unit. Clarence Muse, a black actor who had
performed with the Lafayette Players, directed the musical by the well-
known black chorus leader Hall Johnson. It turned out to be the last
show and the most popular of all the black and white shows in Los
Angeles, perfect for the Hollywood audience: flashy, musical, colorful,
decidedly *not* propaganda.[24] Was this what the Los Angeles actors had
in mind?

A Mr. Glenn, wishing to publicize the strengths of the FTP, wrote to
Washington pleading for material and chose this particular production
as an example of just what the project did right:

> GIVE ME, and other trained publicists like me willing to foster
> such genius, the DISPLAY MATERIALS THE PUBLIC WANTS AND WILL
> REACT TO and you do more, with one such stroke, to offset
> ignorant criticism, and gain favorable tax-payers reaction to
> continuance, than when you stage a flock of propaganda plays
> and then expect people to accept them, as they often don't. . . .
>
> Can use not only the popular "Run Little Chillun" photos so
> many times requested before, promised, but never yet pro-
> duced – but also your own selection from the plays which
> went best back East and produced the most in cash returns.
> Incidentally, not the least of such a display right now, should be
> figures to accompany – to show box-office results. That will
> talk turkey to many who will accept what the Negro dramatists
> and players have done (if not TOO bizarre – just as well to "can"
> some of the super-jungle effects out here as we are not especially

Harlem minded,) – when they may resent the Communistic tinge of far too many of the plays that were produced by whites. What the darkies do often carries, as did "Little Chillun", an *inner message* which helps people in these trying times. Had so many tell me they had been thus helped by the "Little Chillun" play – and some I know went several times, just to get the benefit of it. And box receipts tend to show that people prefer that type of natural folk-play to the propagandic fantasies far too often produced by the "philanthropoid" type. So – if you can let the Negro actors help pull you out of this mess, better do it – but PLEASE MAIL PHOTOS PROMPTLY, as the time is NOW.[25]

Here, the publicist believed he could use Negro actors to sell the entertaining quality of the FTP and to reassure a conservative and presumably white audience that any kind of radical social propaganda was not being promoted under FTP auspices, at least not in Los Angeles. Negro actors were purely entertainers who could be relied on to control Great Depression anxiety about radical change. While Glenn cautions against promoting the "TOO bizarre," "jungle effects," or plays with a "Communistic tinge," none of which appeals, he believes, to a California audience, *Run, Little Chillun* suits precisely because it stays away from all those things with its "*inner message* which helps people in these trying times." His idea of Negro actors and of this particular play served a wholly conservative agenda.

One of the inner messages of the play emphasizes the trouble caused when anyone tries to break out of their "suitable" role, their traditional obligations. The play takes place in a small town in the South, and the plot revolves around different spheres of influence, competing loyalties. Jim, the married Baptist minister's son, has to decide between his wife, his church, and a woman, Sulamai, who has bewitched him. The Baptist Church has to contend with a rival church, the Outdoor Pilgrims, who have set up camp across the river. One of the chief Pilgrim priests also becomes entranced by Sulamai and must choose between his fiance, his church, and Sulamai. In the end, the men decide to take their rightful place as leaders in their communities, and Sulamai is struck down dead outside the church, her trouble-making days over for good. Unlike *Big White Fog*, *Run, Little Chillun*'s plot reinforces the necessity of finding and sticking to one particular community; defying the rules, going it alone only brings down the wrath of God. As a play about the benfits of conformity and the dangers of transgression, the play suits the conservative nature of Los Angeles theatre and its mainstream audiences.

Even though the text of the play can be read and performed conservatively, there might have lurked in the rehearsals leading up to the performance a self-conscious theatricality that undercut its conservative plot. Clarence Muse directed his flock of actors with a strong hand and with a very different attitude from either the director of *Brer Rabbit* in Seattle who encouraged the actors to improvise or from the director of *Big White Fog* who portrayed the rehearsal experience as a group process in which the entire cast arrived at a consensus of what constituted a realistic portrayal of Negro life in a big city. Muse assumed these actors needed to be taught how to act properly. He had been a character actor with the Lafayette Theater in Harlem in the teens and had worked as a "race adviser" on certain Hollywood films. He was experienced and from accounts of people who knew him, a man who commanded center stage at all times.[26] "Of course, you don't know me, just hearin' about me on this thing. I'm getting in charge of this thing. I think that's one thing that George Washington and I had in common. What I had to say was law, l-a-w." According to Muse, the actors didn't know if the people who had protested the lack of black representation on the FTP would approve of *Run, Little Chillun:*

> They weren't sure if that was the kind of play they wanted to have. It had been kind of whitewashed, you know, into you got to do plays of great dignity and all the rest of that yap yap. Well, I had to work on that for a while and dye it up and treat it along and sent some of them home. I think I fired two or three of them wise guys before they got a chance to disrupt everything.[27]

It isn't entirely clear exactly what Muse thinks about *Run, Little Chillun.* He has no patience for the argument that he should only direct plays of "great dignity," dismissing it as a bunch of "yap yap." Like Ralf Coleman, the other professional black director in Boston, Muse wanted a hit, to please the biggest audience he could by entertaining them. It seems that he had to do his own "whitewashing," painting the play as dignified enough, and he got rid of anyone who didn't like the dye he used. Muse describes how he cast Sulamai and then how he handled the actors:

> I said, "That girl's gonna be it." The main man that kicked on it was Hall Johnson himself, but I said, "That's the one." . . .
>
> Well now, naturally, you see I caused some friction there, you know, a little yap yap. I said, "Well, times are tough, folks, and I got two assignments, two picture assignments. I put 'em

> aside to come here to do this. Make up your mind whether you
> want to go back in the hills where you were or go down the
> line where I'm carryin' you and walkin' on red carpets." That's
> the kind of talk you have to do with these people, you know.
> They've been pushed around and told so many lies by silver-
> tongued orators. When you get into a deal like this, you've
> gotta be real flat and down-to-earth. What do you call it, gim-
> mick talk? . . . But we were so far down as a people into the
> real technique of good theatre, I had no other choice.[28]

Muse knows how to talk more than one talk. He knows the appeal of
silver-tongued orators insisting upon plays of dignity, but he also knows
that the language of the down-to-earth and threats can motivate as
well. Perhaps Muse sounds manipulative, dictatorial, condescending, or
perhaps he seems merely professional, eager to transform people into
actors, versed in the "real technique" of theatre.

Muse relied on professional talk to get the play on: what he noted
about an actor was, on the one hand, the natural sway of a woman
walking across the room and, on the other hand, how untrained in the
"technique" of acting these "actors" were. He underscores the ways in
which the actors had to *learn* their parts. None came by them "naturally":

> In approaching this play from the point of production, I find
> that great care must be taken in casting, unusual stress must be
> instilled in the actors of the sincerity of the religious motif; it is
> absolutely impossible to complete the form and maintain the
> definite design, if one of the many hundred cues is missed or
> improperly timed.

Set in the rural South, the play would be performed to an urban audience by urban actors who needed to be convinced, persuaded, or taught
how to convey the idea of the sincerity of religion. In contrast to most
of the reviews, black and white, of this play, all of which applaud
the natural sincerity of these guileless "actors," Muse emphasizes the
professional qualities of the production, the many hundreds of lighting
cues, the importance of the music in creating the needed effects. He did
not take for granted that the actor would be a Baptist or Pilgrim; but
that in both cases research was necessary to make the play believable. "I
might add that the strange original music of the 'Pilgrim Scene' demands
the attention of well schooled musicians and singers who can act as well
as sing. And research on African culture is very important before the
spirit can be understood."[29] Research, technique, attention to details,

training, all bespeak a professionalization; a person might have a natural walk, but a natural walk didn't make a natural actor. These actors might be of African descent, but it didn't necessarily follow that they would automatically know how to sing "African" chants or be able to convey the sincerity of a church revival. Though written by an African American, the songs are of dubious "authentic" value as African chants.

Muse trains these actors to act naturally by teaching them skills. He does such a good job that black and white reviewers wrote about the actors as natural and authentic. There was no controversy about *Run, Little Chillun* as there had been about *Macbeth*. Almost all of the reviews praise the show for its authenticity. One reviewer for the black newspaper, the *California Eagle,* claims:

> I have always believed that when a truly great Negro show would ever be produced it would be DONE by NEGROES. Hall Johnson proves that decisively with "Run, Little Chillun."
>
> Those of us who witnessed the performances of "Run, Little Chillun" saw a different Negro. Not the Nordic man's idea of a Negro, but the Negro as he actually is. Hall Johnson has painted the most vivid portrait of a lovable carefree and "Amen Corner" Negro ever presented on the American stage.

The reviewer believes the characters represent the Negro "as he actually is," although Muse never thinks about the play or the characters in those terms. And some other Negroes might strenuously reject the "lovable" and "carefree" portrait as authentic descriptions of "the Negro." But there is no room to question the authentic *belief* of this reviewer when he writes that he lived this play himself: "I spent most of my early childhood in just such a church enacted on that stage. I knew all those characters intimately. Possibly as no other person, save one like myself who had lived in just that same atmosphere." Only a black director and a black writer can tell the truth because they are "direct" descendants and so "very aware of this wealth of material handed down for generations by an oppressed people."[30] The play becomes the property of an audience, most of whom like it, because it seems to belong to a tradition they recognize and does not threaten their sense of what constitutes that tradition. The review in the *Daily News* expresses admiration for the show, though what it admires is the mix of "realism" and the "barbaric fantasy": "This paradox becomes as refreshing a piece of drama as ever swept healthy vigor into the theater." The reviewer exclaims that black actors have the gift of acting naturally: "Their complete naturalness is replete with an unstudied dignity that might well be the envy of the most talented artists." In the white newspapers, *Run, Little Chillun* is valued because it seems to reinvigorate the audience: "It is a glorious, emotional, and melodious debauch. Its cast of several hundred Negroes sing, dance and generally emote in a production so amazingly beautiful and vital that one almost feels the Roosevelt administration has not been in vain." The review in the *Jewish Community Press* captures all of the general white preconceptions of a black show. A Negro show differs from anything else on stage: "This is the quality of Negro plays: reflecting the primitiveness of a people, they arrest our attention the stronger, though their appeal is toward our instincts rather than toward our intellect."[31] Born actors, these Negroes did not act in a play; they were living out their lives on stage.

In the play *Run, Little Chillun,* all passions and desires to see new things, to ask questions, to be led out of the ordinary are either contained by the community or ruthlessly expelled. Perhaps this made it such a popular play in the thirties, comforting both whites and blacks about the stability of their communities. How much stronger the containment becomes when all black acting becomes natural acting and further, when the language of lived experience becomes the only way to authenticate art: "No one from the South could help appreciating the authentic reproduction of a Negro community. The actions in church were not exaggerated – I have witnessed just such a scene in a Negro church."[32] People perceive that the only appropriate drama for black actors is not imitation but natural representation of their own lives. It seems in the published reviews of this play, black actors' lives have been made the property of those who watch, delighting in their authenticity.

But there are signs that actors and some directors knew that the authentic was just one more mask to be learned. Houston Baker describes "mastery of form" as a minstrel mask that conceals, disguises, floats like a trickster.[33] Actors could subvert a constricting and racist notion of authenticity by consciously and strategically mastering the form of "authentic" black life – which is thought to be rural and religious. They might *learn* how to play it naturally like those actors singing "African" songs and singing in the rhythms of southern black life. Certain directors knew there was nothing at all natural about the "natural" effect they got from actors. Directors and actors could have been involved in a sort of deformation, a self-conscious wink at "vernacular" speech, signifying on it, thereby fooling both white and black critics. Such a reading may call into question for us what is authentic and what is learned and who has what at stake in continuing to think about African Americans as natural actors.

III

What is appropriate for a revolution or for a race certainly will always be contested, and who decides what constitutes a revolution will change over time. Sometimes cultural appropriation is racist, sometimes theatrical, and sometimes liberating; and sometimes it can be racist, theatrical, and liberating all at once. Sometimes even the most conventional of plays can spark an unconventional response somewhere, sometime, though perhaps not in ways that can be known or historically documented.

The last big hit of the FTP in Chicago took place in the Negro unit, with a play it is impossible to believe either Richard Wright or Theodore Ward would have thought revolutionary: an adaptation of Gilbert and Sullivan's 1885 *The Mikado*. The *Swing Mikado* played in Chicago for five months to 250,000 people and made $35,000; in the weeks before Christmas, it grossed between $5,000 and $5,500 a week, a far higher gross than any other Chicago FTP production.[34] The show was so successful that producers in New York tried to buy out the show and move it to New York. Whether one appreciates the *Swing Mikado* because one believes it to be a properly theatrical and liberating show or dismisses it as derivative and inappropriate because it forced white standards onto black actors depends on how one conceives of cultural property – what is appropriate and what is appropriative. Were the actors in this opera subjected to old racial stereotypes or were they able to make of themselves new subjects?

The plot of *The Mikado* is comic opera at its silliest: a beautiful young girl, Yum-Yum, has fallen in love with the Mikado's son who is disguised as a second trombone player. But she is unfortunately betrothed to an older man, Ko-Ko. The Mikado has ordered that anyone who "flirted, leered, or winked / (Unless connubially linked) / Should forthwith be beheaded," and Ko-Ko has been condemned to death for such crimes to humanity. The people release him and make him Lord High Executioner because they reason that "Who's next to be decapited / Cannot cut off another's head / Until he's cut his own off." And he won't want to do that, so everyone breathes safely. On it goes with twists and turns to a happy ending. A typical Gilbert and Sullivan opera, with tuneful songs and generalized satire against pomposity and highhandedness, *The Mikado* is both very very English and very very common.

There's a long history of appropriating Gilbert and Sullivan and in particular this play. In the twenties in Berlin, a naked Yum-Yum sang in the bath and Katisha rode onto stage in a taxi; more recently at the Civic Light Opera in Chicago in the 1980s, Peter Sellars opened the first act with a Northwest Airline jet taking off for Japan where the entire opera was set in a corporate office with a big Sony sign on the other side of the glass window. Boston had seen a black minstrel troupe in 1886 perform *The Black Mikado or The Town of Kan-Ka-Kee*.[35] The FTP's swing opera signifies another updating of the opera; white Americans casting African Americans to play Victorian England's idea of Japan has its own crazy kind of postmodern play.

Gilbert said he got the idea for *The Mikado* when a Japanese sword hanging in his study fell from the wall. It's as good as any other genesis story. The sword was in Gilbert's study because of the particular historical moment when Japan had been forced to communicate with the West, and all things Japanese had become fashionable. Gilbert had no doubt seen the Japanese village that had been set up in Knightsbridge. Japanese people would demonstrate how to serve tea every day at a certain time. Gilbert hired one of the geishas employed in Knightsbridge to instruct his three little maids on how to walk "Japanese style." How similar to Billy McClain and Nate Saulsbury's production of *In Black America,* the southern plantation reproduced in Brooklyn in 1896 with five hundred people pretending to be slaves, living in cabins for the summer and who would, Nathan Huggins writes, "assemble under a tent for a standard musical review in the minstrel tradition."[36]

The English bought fans and Japanese material at Liberty House; the Americans bought black entertainment and assuaged their consciences in Brooklyn: life as a slave couldn't have been all that bad because they certainly looked like they were having fun. Both spectacles involve a deliberate confusion between reality and style; they trade off on it. The tea ceremony becomes translated into an aesthetic style, to be reproduced on Liberty material; the actors playing slaves make music, rendering history entertaining. Spectators wanted to believe they were seeing the real thing, although they must have also known they were watching a performance out of context, out of state, out of time. What could the actors have been thinking? Perhaps in the interplay between "the real thing" and "the performance" actors may have experienced some liberating notion of playing a particular style.

On the surface, of course, *The Mikado* seems ripe for equity protests of all sorts. English or African Americans playing Japanese? Should it be played at all? There have been ongoing protests against Gilbert's depiction of Japan since 1907, when a Japanese prince was about to visit England and the Lord Chamberlain banned a revival of *The Mikado* out of deference to Japanese tastes. Most Englishmen, including Gilbert, found this act of censorship ridiculous, since they contended that the opera was a satire of England not of Japan. The *Daily Mail* invited a Japanese correspondent to see a production of *The Mikado,* and he was quoted as finding the music quite pleasant and fine, though the plot was not realistic: no Japanese girl would kiss as demonstratively as Yum-Yum, he said.[37] A very few Englishmen protested that the opera ought to be permanently banned as it was "galling and humiliating in every way" to Japanese who revered their Mikado, much as Roman Catholics honored the Pope. The Lord Chamberlain kept the ban in place for six weeks, though productions went on anyway; neither side won their case.

What made it seem appropriate for the Negro unit in Chicago? In the fall of 1937, Harry Minturn, the white acting assistant director to the national director for the FTP, had to find a vehicle for the Chicago Negro unit. His background was almost entirely in vaudeville and popular shows as theatrical manager and producer, actor and director. He had only rather reluctantly sponsored Theodore Ward's *Big White Fog.* Clearly, he was no New Dealer with a cultural mission to erase stereotypes or create new roles for blacks. His theatrical instincts probably told him that social realism wouldn't entertain white or black folks. It seems natural that since he felt at home with the song and dance forms of the musical, he turned to a musical opera when he had to find a way of putting to work fifty or so black actors and actresses.[38]

Many of the actors in the Chicago Negro unit had been vaudevillians. Herman Green, who played the part of Ko-Ko, the low-class tailor in *Swing Mikado,* had been acting since he was eight, joining his father in a vaudeville troop, playing "eight a daze" – the lowest rung of vaudeville where an actor would do his shtick eight times a day. Maurice Cooper, who played the romantic lead Nanki-Poo, was born in Kansas City and had come to Chicago and gone to Crane Junior College; he won a National Broadcasting Company and *Chicago Daily News* contest as a singer and toured thirty-seven states as a concert singer.[39] A third principal, William Franklin, had played the main role in *Aida* recently with the Chicago Civic Opera Company.[40] These actors were all professionals who had done quite well. A big musical comedy would make the most use out of these particular actors' strengths as well as Minturn's strengths as director. Minturn decided to try to do something with *The Mikado,* changing the locale from Japan to a coral island in the Pacific, with swing versions of some of the songs. He started rehearsing the unit in February 1938 and planned to present it during the summer, first in a downtown Chicago theatre and then in outdoor parks. The new director for the Illinois project, John McGee, saw the show in rehearsal and was so impressed that he asked Minturn to wait until the fall to open the show as part of the new season. Minturn agreed.[41]

The production served different cultural needs. Minturn designed the *Swing Mikado* to display the musical talents of his cast, both as swing and straight operatic singers. Minturn always emphasized that he directed the show "straight"; he swung only three numbers and used these only on the choruses (and numerous encores). In this, he was following the tradition of the early Lafayette Theatre in Harlem, which produced Broadway shows not by any means written *for* blacks, but popular nonetheless among the black audience. These plays gave actors the opportunity to play parts that they couldn't do on Broadway. Although no script has been found or conclusively identified as belonging to the Chicago production, one script of *The Mikado* at George Mason University has some notations that might indicate it was used as a script. "Gentlemen of Japan" has been crossed out, replaced with "High Steppers from afar." On the other hand, what must have seemed an offending reference to "nigger serenader" has not been crossed out, though perhaps it was in rehearsal. To act in a Gilbert and Sullivan show meant either adhering to the traditional business that had grown up around each opera or risking the boos of fanatical Gilbert and Sullivan fans. Gilbert had been a notoriously stern director in his attempts to stop actors from inserting their own ideas of gags into the script. But by 1938, certain additions had become tradition, and a diehard fan would expect to hear the Mikado's blood-curdling screams in between his verses of "The Punishment Fit the Crime." The Negro unit stayed close to the tradition.

The Chicago *Defender* raved about the show:

> No private producer would have risked his 'roll' on a stupendous production of this nature, and yet I predict this production will demonstrate to the nation that audiences will go to the theatre, and see living people perform, and that it will not only have a long run in Chicago, but will equal 'Green Pastures' in general interest nationally.

With surprise, the white reviewers remark that these actors *can* do the Gilbert and Sullivan business:

> I think the D'Oyly Cartes would have the time of their lives at this sometimes minstrel version of their acutely specialized business. I think they would marvel at the way this Negro cast turns intricate phrases of patter lyrics. . . . When unadulterated Gilbert and Sullivan meets this gifted Negro cast, something universal happens by way of entertainment.[42]

The black cast transcends the particular markings of swing and produces a "universal" entertainment. Harry Hopkins reportedly said "that in Chicago the WPA WAS the *Mikado*. He said he had gone to a lot of shows all over the country – some of them pretty bad ones – but that this was the first time he really had a good time and added that this was so even though it was without social significance."[43] The show could be universal and therefore decidedly *not* political. Hopkins breathed a sigh of relief and enjoyed himself.

But most of the white reviewers wanted more primitive business, more dance, more specifically "black" markers: "The cast mugged here and there and now and then gave a burlesque touch to the lines and situations, but not much nor often. It was evidently trying to be legitimate in a setting which clamored for parody – and for 'swing.' "[44] For them, the *Swing Mikado* proved what needed no proof in their minds – that African Americans could sing and dance superlatively. One reviewer rejoiced when he saw a "half-hundred grinning, joyous and richly voiced Negroes suddenly explode into modern rhythm after toying with the limpid coolness of Sullivan's music," and many white critics couldn't get enough of it and felt cheated when the cast moved back into the "legitimate" style of singing.

Hallie Flanagan wrote that the production of the black *Swing Mikado* fulfilled all of the FTP's aims: "It is rehabilitating human beings and conserving their skills; it is bringing entertainment to thousands who without Federal Theatre would not be able to afford theatre going; and it is stimulating the theatre industry itself by new ideas of stagecraft, brilliantly executed." She supported Minturn's decision not to swing the entire show, but she was in the minority.[45] Her support didn't necessarily mean that she thought about Negro actors in untraditional ways; indeed, the successful Negro units confirmed her belief that Negroes were naturally talented and could be used to entertain all Americans with universally accepted entertainment. The *Swing Mikado*, the voodoo *Macbeth*, and *Run, Little Chillun* were popular because they catered not exclusively to Negroes but largely to white expectations of black entertainment. But sometimes those white expectations were challenged when they saw that black actors could take on different masks, as was the case with the *Swing Mikado*.

So little is recorded about *who* the actors were and what they thought they were doing. A contemporary reviewer believed that he knew what the actors wanted: "Not only the audience resented the use of the original script as a ball and a chain. The boys and girls in the cast showed their sentiment plainly in their reaction to the chance to let loose with tap dancing, swinging tunes, and specialty numbers."[46] But could this reviewer simply have projected his desires onto the actors? Can we be sure that the actors wanted to dance more? Actors never seem to have left their own words in the voluminous records of the FTP; often directors, playwrights, and bureaucrats, black and white, speak for them. In the case of the *Swing Mikado,* records reveal the machinations that went on almost immediately to take this particular production to Broadway. One document may offer a glimpse of actors' interests or what the production meant to them.

John McGee, the regional and state director of Illinois who had already asked that the play be postponed until the fall, seems to have begun negotiating with New York producers in the summer of 1938 and into the fall to take the show to New York. The FTP fired him by December for conspiring with private producers, in the middle of the *Swing Mikado*'s run in Chicago. From the beginning, Harry Hopkins had made it clear that the WPA could never compete with private business. Technically then and in the spirit of the FTP, when a commercial producer offered to take the show, the FTP should have "sold" it immediately. (In its deliberations over the FTP, Congress cited the *Swing Mikado* episode as part of the FTP's many transgressions; in their minds the Chicago production should have been given to a commercial producer.) Flanagan hoped that she could arrange a joint production with a private producer in which the FTP and the producer would share costs and profit, though she realized that the WPA might rule against this.[47] But Minturn and others didn't want to give up their show. Minturn wrote to Flanagan: "The *Mikado* is bringing in money which we well need and is accomplishing what we have been striving to do in Chicago for three years, namely, to get a favorable general reaction from the Chicago public, both artistically and financially, for the Federal Theatre."[48] The government didn't receive any assurances from the New York producers that its cast would be used. Minturn expressed some worry that if the show closed in New York, the performers would be thrust back into the FTP but without the prospect of opening another *Swing Mikado;* once a show closes, it is almost impossible to reopen, he explained. In the end, the FTP simply didn't want to give up a hit they had devised.

Minturn became furious when he learned that John McGee had managed to coerce (at least from Minturn's point of view) the nine principals in the cast to sign an option that would guarantee the use of their services for a production of the *Swing Mikado* in New York for six months. The actors signed, making it impossible for any other private producer *or* the FTP to use them in any other production in New York without securing a release from McGee's designated producer. McGee had also held auditions without telling the actors what they were for; rumors started that a second *Swing Mikado* company would be formed. Three days after McGee was fired, he called a meeting of the actors. When Minturn found out about the meeting, he had the stage manager cancel it and held his own the next day.[49]

In the transcript of the meeting, the actors voiced some of their concerns. Minturn spoke first:

> Boys and girls, there have been a lot of rumors pro and con about this play going to New York. I have not been in a position before to talk to you as a group. You will all believe me when I say we have come a long way together – all of us – from the start of this thing until its success at the present day. I do not believe that any one of you feel that I have not been thoroughly honest and thoroughly in accord with you. Have you? (Applause). . . .
>
> Therefore, if I had been free to talk to you I would have a long time ago.

The transcript reveals the mix of condescension and pride Minturn felt toward the troupe. He presents himself as the good master, paternal, looking after his charges. "You have become one of our outstanding efforts here and I am terribly proud of you." Then Minturn turns to the options the actors had signed. Although he refrains from ever directly saying so, he wants to talk them out of going to New York. The actors ask questions; only Herman Green is identified, the rest are simply named "member of cast." Perhaps speaking for the principals who signed the option, Herman Green asks Minturn point blank for advice. Should they take the option or not? Minturn replies that if it is a bona fide contract, then they are free to take it, although he "personally" doesn't believe in that kind of a contract. Green replies: "I am for you 100%. That's why I asked you." The group remained legitimately confused and said so. Is there a second troupe, are they going to New York, are only some of them going? What will happen if the principals take off? Will the FTP keep the Chicago production on stage, and how? One member of the cast says: "Something unconventional has been going on. We are all skeptical. We don't know where we're going." Some of the members of the cast were angry that the stars had been singled out and had the power seemingly to wreck their chances to continue the show in Chicago. "A great many people have no contracts and have not been consulted about any. Most of us feel that our allegiance is to the Federal Theatre and it does not seem exactly ethical for members of the Federal Theatre to be called out for meetings for contracts for productions of the Federal Theatre." And "there seems to be a feeling of doubt as to what the principals are going to do, and also that they were a little selfish in going ahead." At the end of the transcript various members of the cast express loyalty to Minturn: "I feel this way. It was your idea in putting on this play. You said down in Decatur once that you had a grand idea for the colored theatre. You had the worry and grief of putting on this show. We owe the success of the *Mikado* to your supervision." And "Mr. Minturn was the only one with vision. We should not get out of an airplane going up. Mr. Minturn has brought us this far and his vision will not stop now" (Applause).[50] The actors who had *not* signed contracts temper their loyalty with a shrewd sense of the main chance; their strategy shamed the principals back into line with the entire group. Ultimately, the FTP took their production to New York in March, played it until May, and then sold it to a commercial producer. It reopened right across the street from Mike Todd's *Hot Mikado* with Bill Robinson. Neither one lasted long; the "Swing" for twenty-four performances; the "Hot" for eighty-five. Todd updated the music and swung the entire version.[51]

In the anxious questioning of the cast, there are traces of professionalism and pride, ambition and caution, and schisms too, of course, between the principals and the others. A unit may be forming, dedicated to something more than a simple fulfillment of white expectations. In spite of what was said about the *Swing Mikado* by reviewers, the actors did attempt to negotiate roles for themselves. For some of these actors, playing a part in the *Swing Mikado* may even have been a theatrical and professional liberation.

When the African American male chorus began to sing the first lines of the opera in 1938 –

> If you want to know who we are,
>   We are gentleman from Japan:
> On many a vase and jar –
>   On many a screen and fan,
>   We figure in lively paint:
>   Our attitudes queer and quaint –
>   You're wrong if you think it ain't –

surely they knew very well the ways in which screens and fans and masks of all kinds constituted their "authenticity" in the dominant culture; at the same time, the self-conscious identity of themselves as "art" unravels the authenticity of their depiction. They are not what they seem to be. More than the Japanese geishas, these African American actors knew that they were expected to be queer and quaint by at least one part of their audience, while another part of their audience could be expected to see behind the screen to enjoy their skillful performances. Unlike *Run, Little Chillun* and *Big White Fog*, which were written and directed naturalistically, the *Swing Mikado* delighted in artifice; it was an opera about style. The actors' skill in duplicating the Gilbert and Sullivan style indicates how masterful they were in performing a play of screens and fans and masks.

In his book *Sambo: The Rise and Demise of an American Jester*, Joseph Boskin writes:

> Whites don't read black newspapers or journals and don't listen to or even hear black speeches or protests. They are laughing too hard. . . . Does it really matter that Bill 'Bojangles' Robinson possesses dignity and charm when he dances with Shirley Temple. . . . What *do* whites see? Are they aware it is all act, all put on, all comic survival within imagery long established?[52]

Can humanity be glimpsed behind the condescending, limited stereotypes still so apparent in the thirties? At one pole, Boskin believes that black actors *were* acting, that the song and dance was a role taken up deliberately. Nathan Huggins asks at what point the mask becomes the self and the whole notion of acting is lost.[53] Both Huggins and Boskin presuppose that there are private and public worlds, that they are separated or should be, that one is truer than the other, more authentic, less corrupted. Under what circumstances can the public role be redeemed? Listening to the actors who were anxious to keep their jobs, one may hear notes that counter the stereotype of actors as simple vessels, easily filled.

Clearly the *Swing Mikado*'s cast cannot be said to have exploded the song and dance discourse that surrounded them then. But in the tentative groping to an identity as a unit, perhaps (who knows?) one actor or two may have stepped from behind the screen of minstrelsy to some other part history hasn't recorded for us. And certainly it is also possible to read this episode deliberately (as I have tried to do here at the end) as a self-conscious attempt to call attention to the artifice of their role, forcing an audience or a reader to consider the boundaries of propriety, property, the appropriate, which, if not exactly revolutionary, may be a liberation of sorts – if not then, then now.

Afterword

We are creatures of history, for every historical epoch has its roots in a preceding epoch. The black militants of today are standing upon the shoulders of the "new Negro radicals" of my day – the '20s, '30s, and '40s. We stood upon the shoulders of the civil rights fighters of the Reconstruction era and they stood upon the shoulders of the black abolitionists. These are the interconnections of history.
— A. Philip Randolph

Attempting to fix cultures or stop them from changing is like trying to end or annihilate history.
— Richard Schechner[1]

Everyone recognized that the FTP provided a great opportunity for those who had been shut out from mainstream theatre movements, but the theatre was threatened both within and without by its necessary embrace of diversity. At the Negro unit in Harlem, some, like Leonard De Paur, were frustrated by the compromises and seeming lack of a single direction. He praised the Communists because at least they had a clear and consistent plan about what they should be doing:

> Because they were genuinely doing – at least attempting to do something. At first they were trying to organize some sort of resistance within the project so that the project itself had a sense of direction. And this we sorely needed. We had no idea where the hell we were going. And I just couldn't figure that one out to save my life. I said, "Well now, all right, so Gus wants to do this. And then we're going to do that. And we ought to do a musical. And then there's the children's thing." What the devil? We should sit down and say, "Let's plan, even if we're not gonna be here for two years, let's plan the next two years and see what we can accomplish in two years." And somebody's gonna look at it and say you're crazy but at least they're gonna

196

give us credit for having thought in some orderly and constructive fashion about what should happen to this project.[2]

Some people who worked at the Lafayette agree that the Negro unit was without a point of view or a philosophy of the theatre arts "in which we heartily believe[d] and to which we [could] consecrate ourselves."[3] Thomas Anderson, an actor on the unit, said:

> *Anderson:* Remember that, other than when Orson did Shakespeare and you did the *Swing Mikado,* the rest of the things were just ordinary things. And regardless of the fact you were doing *Turpentine* and regardless of the fact you were doing *Conjure Man Dies* . . . you were doing *Androcles and the Lion.* You were doing nothing that was going to be extraordinary and to really make people stand up and shout about.
>
> *Lorraine Brown:* There was no idea abroad that you might have the basis there for something comparable to the Abbey or the Yiddish Theatre?
>
> *Anderson:* Oh, yes. All of this sort of thing was there. It was talked about, but there was nobody really to make it work. There was so much jealousy about doing *Macbeth.* "Why can't we do this other blank play? Why can't we do this? Why can't we do the other?" And no one could take charge and pull it together. So when Houseman left, then there was nothing to hold it together.[4]

It would have been impossible (even for Houseman) to "pull it together" because there were too many irreconcilable points of view. The Negro units produced plays celebrating the working class and performed musical revues. Each represented a different sense of direction, a different constituency, a different consecration of belief. Though the debates were constant within and between communities, most everyone agreed that the experiment was too precious to be lost altogether. When it seemed that the Negro unit in Harlem might be absorbed into other units downtown, people protested immediately.

Congress had cut the WPA's budget so drastically in 1938 that rumors flew that the Lafayette would close. The FTP never planned to shut down one of their most famous units, but they did decide to centralize by moving the coordination of the Lafayette unit downtown. A letter from someone at the YWCA branch in Harlem expressed dismay:

I would like to call your attention also to the fact, that attendance at plays in the Times Square Theatrical District is prohibitive for the great majority of people living in this community, not only because of the prices charged, but because so many of the people are called upon to work very late and it would be impossible for them to cover the long distance necessary to come home, get dressed for attendance at a play, and then go back down town in time for the show. If the showings of the legitimate stage are to be preserved for our young people, these shows must be presented in our own community. Many of these young people know nothing but the moving picture presentations. Certainly all of this is presented from the view point of the public – to the participants also it is encouraging, inspiring and a personality developing experience to present their abilities among their friends.

Certainly, years ago I would never have thought of writing such a letter to any government official, but in these days when, "government for the people" is something more than a phrase, I thought you would be interested in community reaction.[5]

Du Bois's manifesto for a Negro theatre had called for a theatre of the people, by the people, for the people, and also *near* the people. Perhaps this last requirement was not as important in certain cities like Chicago or Los Angeles, but Harlem considered itself a separate community, and at least some of the people involved in the Negro unit there believed that their theatre should not be for "downtown whites." For the writer from the YWCA, the theatre clearly was a bulwark against mass entertainment; it was an educational tool of the middle classes. For others, like those represented by the Negro Arts Committee, the Negro unit in Harlem was an opportunity for jobs and artistic control. In a brief submitted by them to the FTP, they complained about the continuing racism that hampered black progress, and they continued to demand better representation and Negro supervisors. Not one member of the Planning Board of the FTP was black, and since each production was assigned a member of the Planning Board as producer there had been no black producers of black productions. Without such representation, their concerns were always going to be secondary.[6]

In December 1938, Charles Taylor of the Negro Arts Committee had asked Flanagan to allow the Lafayette to remain autonomous. Flanagan hedged: "It is not possible to set up every individual group in Federal Theatre as a separate autonomy. I think you have only to look at such productions as have used Negro and white casts to see that both companies gain in many productions by the presence of each other." In a reply, Taylor explains that centralization would destroy the project for blacks:

> Decentralization gave us practically what we are now asking for, a chance to exploit ourselves thereby showing what our capabilities with the presentation of opportunity are. Recalling our splendid record to you, our plays given during that period numbered ten and many white productions were augmented with our personnel. This within itself is a singular achievement. Our directors had a chance to further develop themselves (opportunities having been few in private industry) and the Negro was marching on happily, feeling that the apex of our art would some day be reached. Under centralization there is no place for the Negro director, producer, or supervisor unless it is obscure. We call your attention to the fact that we have never had a Negro director to put on a white production, we again recall we have never had a Negro stage manager among white companies and again we cite our never having had a Negro company manager among the white units.
>
> We wish to make known that it is not our intention to desire complete isolation; we merely wish a unit where our progressiveness which existed in the past will continue.[7]

Facing increasing budget cuts from Congress and pressure to suppress units perceived critical of the government or of American culture, Flanagan and other national directors had tried to lower the profile of the Negro unit in Harlem and elsewhere. In the end, the Negro units were kept open and autonomous, and they shared the fate of the entire FTP – slashed by Congress in 1939.

The Negro units had paradoxically enjoyed positive press and generated support and good publicity for the FTP, and yet they were also the subject of the final attack by Congress. As the first WPA Art Project to be closed by Congress for its "un-American" activity, the Negro units were front and center as targets of hostile congressmen. The idea of autonomous Negro units, leading to a national Negro theatre or a fully integrated American theatre, including whites and blacks equally, threatened the status quo. The question of what part the Negro or a Negro theatre was to take in American life – part or whole, autonomous, segregated by choice, or by fiat – was no closer to being resolved.

II

Randolph believed that historical movements were linked, that the militants of the sixties "stood on the backs of" militants from the twenties, thirties, and forties. Those writing about the theatre during the sixties, as well as some who wrote about the sixties twenty years later see a greater disjunction between everything that came before, say, 1964 and everything that comes after. Paul Carter Harrison writes that "black theatre was born in the crucible of the Civil Rights Movement of the '60s." Everything that came before was Negro theatre in which the "black experience became mired in an appropriation of the more exotic aspects of black life." In the sixties, a "renewed sense of Afro-centric identity . . . freed [artists] from the ambivalences of a dual-consciousness."[8] Larry Neal's manifesto on theatre and the black arts movement written in 1968 sets out the differences between pre- and postsixties. It is striking, however, how similar in certain important respects his manifesto is to Du Bois's: both wish to create a theatre about, by, for, and near the people:

> The Black Arts Movement is radically opposed to any concept of the artist that alienates him from his community. Black Art is the aesthetic and spiritual sister of the Black Power concept. As such, it envisions an art that speaks directly to the needs and aspirations of Black America. In order to perform this task, the Black Arts Movement proposes a radical reordering of the western cultural aesthetic. It proposes a separate symbolism, mythology, critique, and iconology. The Black Arts and the Black Power concept both relate broadly to the Afro-American's desire for self-determination and nationhood. Both concepts are nationalistic. One is concerned with the relationship between art and politics; the other with the art of politics.[9]

Like Du Bois, Neal emphasizes the importance of a community-based art, one that looks backward and forward to nationhood. The critical importance of linking artist to community is seen as the key to empowerment for artists and for politics. The belief that cultural nationalism and separatism were possible, that a black audience could be identified and a white audience ignored, perhaps marks the greatest differences between the experiences of those involved in the FTP and those working in Harlem in the sixties. The new plays, Neal writes,

> are directed at problems within Black America. They begin with the premise that there is a well defined Afro-American audience. An audience that must see itself and the world in terms of its own interests. . . . Implicit in the Black Arts Movement is the idea that Black people, however dispersed, constitute a *nation* within the belly of white America.[10]

Neal rejected what he called "protest plays" because they appealed to a white audience's concept of fairness and morality. Under this restriction, therefore, much of the social realism of the FTP – *Big White Fog, Turpentine, Sweet Land* – would have to be rejected because each clearly targeted white as well as black audiences.

The critique of the Harlem Renaissance and, implicitly, the FTP's Negro units is that neither was deeply embedded in the black community, that in having to placate a divided audience, they could not properly pay attention to the differences that constituted black culture or a black nation. It is certainly true that the FTP and the Negro units held sometimes contradictory positions in relation to the community, speaking for the people instead of listening to them. But in studying the ways in which different people within the organization attempted to formulate a policy about community and about culture, we see some attempts to refashion and establish new coalitions, sometimes around politics (interracial labor in *Big White Fog*), sometimes around genres (the living newspaper format in the unproduced *Liberty Deferred*). A study of the FTP Negro units should give pause to anyone who thinks communities speak with single voices.

Larry Neal's belief in the necessity of reaching the black community in the sixties was predicated on too simple a notion of a single black community that would respond in unison to his idea of cultural nationalism. While black nationalism has waned since the sixties, the sense that there *is* something different about African American culture and the African American experience has not. Perhaps now, however, there may be a way round the essentialism and "ghettoization" that Locke and Johnson feared would attend the acknowledgment and celebration of such differences. The successful Pulitzer playwright August Wilson may be an example of someone who attracts the divided audience Neal scorned with plays rooted in African American history. Each of his plays, *Ma Rainey's Black Bottom, Fences, Joe Turner's Come and Gone, The Piano Lesson, Two Trains Running,* covers a particular decade of African American life as he focuses on stories that embody black history and family narratives. In an interview with Bill Moyers, Wilson insists on the African difference:

Moyers: Do you think those people in Pittsburgh must find the African in them or in their past before they really know who they are?
Wilson: Yes, they are African people. We are Africans who have been in America since the 17th century. We are Americans. But first of all, we are Africans. We have a culture that's separate and distinct from the mainstream white American culture. We

have different philosophical ideas, different ways of responding to the world, different attitudes, values and linguis-
tics, different aesthetics – even the way we bury our dead
is different.

Moyers: But if blacks keep looking for the African in them, if they
keep returning spiritually or emotionally to their roots, can
they ever come to terms with living in these two worlds?
Aren't they always going to be held by the past in a way that
is potentially destructive?

Wilson: It's not potentially destructive at all. To say that I am an
African, and I can participate in this society as an African, is to
say that I don't have to adopt European values, European
aesthetics and European ways of doing things in order to live
in the world. We would not be here had we not learned to
adapt to American culture. Blacks know more about whites in
white culture and white life than whites know about blacks.
We *have* to know because our survival depends on it. White
people's survival does not depend on knowing blacks.[11]

Wilson has this wider sense of being able to hold at least two kinds of
aesthetics, values, and ways of doing things in his mind at the same
time. He may not want to adopt the values, but he has adapted to them.
There may be more choices available to him in the hybrid mix of
African and European influences he has had to grapple with. At the end
of the interview, Moyers asks if Wilson ever grows weary of "thinking
black, writing black, being asked questions about blacks?" And Wilson
responds: "How could one grow weary of that? Whites don't get tired
of thinking white or being who they are. I'm just who I am. You never
transcend who you are. Black is not limiting. There's no idea in the
world that is not contained by black life. I could write for ever about the
black experience in America."[12] Here is the rejoinder to some of the
fears expressed by participants in the Harlem Renaissance: "Black is not
limiting." Wilson's plays prove it. There is universalism in the particular
so that even Moyers can weep at *Fences* because it is not only a black
story about segregation but also about a son's relationship to his father.

But if some wonderful African American writers and directors like
George C. Wolfe – author of *The Colored Museum* and just appointed
director of the New York Shakespeare Festival at the Public Theatre –
Adrienne Kennedy, and Ntozake Shange have joined August Wilson in
deepening the life of the theatre, theatre itself has not become deeply
embedded in daily life the way Flanagan, Hopkins, and Du Bois had
hoped. It remains a middle-class institution, a treat, a rare and expensive

night out. The hopes of the FTP and the black arts movement of the sixties was that the theatre might change the way people think and act in culture. But this greatest expectation has not been fulfilled. And African Americans' habits do not differ much here from the habits of other Americans. Theophilus Lewis partly blamed the lure of fame and fortune of the legitimate theatre, partly the lack of training or access to training, as well as the continuing desire by the dominant culture to see only certain roles performed by blacks for the lack of a strong black community theatre in the twenties. But this cannot be the whole problem and he knew it. Then as now, theatre – Broadway, regional, experimental, or political – simply has not sunk into the everyday life of American culture. The task of attracting audiences to any sort of theatre continues. Lindsay Patterson, writing in 1974, claimed that "black audiences want realistic plays . . . why should they go through changes to go into a theatre. . . . Mass black audiences, like mass audiences anywhere, want, especially to be entertained."[13] Making theatre popular, joyful, accessible, and affordable just hasn't happened.

Finally, the theatre remains inhospitable on the most practical level to ethnic representation. A study in 1986 from Actors' Equity made this clear: over 90 percent of all productions in the United States were filled by all-Caucasian casts.[14] Although nontraditional casting and color-blind casting have been tried by various companies, not a great deal of headway has been made, partly because our society is anything but color-blind, willing or able to see beyond a very narrow sense of what constitutes realism. A black Gertrude and a white Hamlet would be so startling a concept that the casting choice would guide the conception of the entire play. That color-blind casting seems problematic to producers reflects the ongoing color coding and color bias that seems perfectly natural in our society.[15] Whether, given such conditions, color-blind casting even makes strategic sense is another question. Operating in such a firmly entrenched color-coded environment, theatres producing ethnic work employ all those actors still locked out from the majority of productions in the United States and showcase the work of authors committed to telling their separate ethnic story. In any case, to think in terms of either erasing all distinctions or foregrounding them continues to set the narrow terms of what constitutes a proper or appropriate dramatic representation of "authenticity," "realism," or the "natural."

III

Frank Lentricchia, whose quotation of Kenneth Burke began this book, turns to the metaphor of "conversation" as a way to show

how the activity of people talking together can be both an act of conversation, maintaining certain topics and decorum, and an act of revolution, including a certain voice in the room of speakers and thereby producing a break in civility. A new voice, a different angle, a slight recasting of the tenor of the conversation and history itself might be changed, though this is never assured and never easy:

> Cultural action is a shaping power, but it is not original; it is underwritten by something else. You cannot jump into this conversation and do what you please. It is hard to get into; harder still to speak on your own once you do get in; tougher yet to move the conversation in any particular direction that you might desire. For this conversation has been propelled and constrained mainly by collective voices, sociohistorical subjects, not by private ones, not by "autonomous" intellectuals. The involvement of cultural conversation in the social has always borne purpose, but the rhetoric is generally masked and the telos (the exercising – channeling, influencing, distributing, imposing – of a form of social power) is generally invisible.[16]

Ways of seeing, traditions of discourse, a particular social history, the constraints of habit and collective voices make it hard for individuals to change the flow of a cultural conversation. But in the end, Lentricchia believes that conversation may be one of the only ways to intervene in cultural history. History

> "makes" us, and yet, at the same time, at any moment in the process, our active willing "makes" the conversation, gives it the propulsive energy that forces it on. So even though we may feel "mastered," by putting in our oars we do two things: we help to shape our own experience of history *while providing the shape of things to come for those who will enter later,* after we are gone.[17]

The conversation in the United States about racial identity always seems to swirl back to the proper relationship between hegemonic culture and "minority" interests. What is the relationship between a national "American" literary tradition and the various hyphenations: "Asian-American" or "African-American" or "Italian-American"? What does it mean to drop the hyphen altogether: African American? What is the relationship between a national culture and a racial subculture? The construction of racial identity seems to fall into two trajectories: either to separate from other groups by emphasizing cultural difference or to join the dominant group by rejecting difference. The marketing of culture still divides products between the particular (provincial) and general (universal). And critics still manage to impart a moral and aesthetic hierarchy to these oppositions – separate or dependent, provincial or universal – one more politically and aesthetically successful, one more moral than the other.

But conversations and the interconnections of history are like culture, never purely original. Richard Schechner claims, and I agree, that

> borrowing is natural to our species. . . . No culture is "pure" – that is, no culture is "itself." Overlays, borrowings, and mutual influencings have always made every culture a conglomerate, a hybrid, a palimpsest. So much so that we probably should not speak of "culture" but of "cultures." Racism is basically a myth of desired cultural purity played out against "others" who are perceived as being not only different but inferior.[18]

Yes, there is appropriation, and yes, dominant nations may exercise dominion over cultures, but this does not necessarily mean that political and economic subjugation extinguishes all traces of a subjugated people's culture. In the complicated case of African Americans, so much at the heart of popular American culture, we have seen the ways in which they have been constructed through white eyes and through black eyes, and then reflected back into each others. The reflections have produced artistic expression powerful enough to transform all New World cultures.

To be able to specify the *intersections* among class, gender, family, nationality, and race makes generalizations difficult but might be one way to move the conversation forward, to rechannel the fundamental ways people enjoy and experience particular cultures. To be able to envision cultures not divided into mine–yours, major–minor, universal–provincial, dominant–marginal, or high–low, but to construct theories and illuminate practices that circumvent such polarities might also compel us into thinking and practicing sympathetic exchanges, to break up the idea that there are "natural" ways of behaving and "natural" audiences. The theatre may be one cultural site that could transform such simple categories, perplex and unsettle our natural ways of reading, listening, figuring. It may be that there are other forms better suited to popular expression at this moment in history to do transcultural work. In the tradition of Johnson and Locke, a contemporary cultural critic writes: "By adding discourses, and emphasizing process and cultural specificity rather than 'universality' and reified 'tradition,' the interaction might become too complicated to reduce to simple binaries. The dislocation of a centered hegemony might lead to the progressive borderization of culture, to a sharing, rather than crossing, of borders."[19] It is the idea of the "borderization of culture," of a sharing exchange, that is perhaps the most utopian of all notions, but one that I cannot give up.

When I turn to my local scene here in Los Angeles and, in particular, the theatre, it becomes apparent both how difficult it is to find an audience for the theatre today and yet how committed people are to making theatre about, by, for, and near various peoples. At the recently disbanded, financially bankrupt Los Angeles Theatre Center, Bill Bushnell oversaw the production of new African American, Chicano, and Asian American plays. The LATC was a victim of many things: a location in a depressed downtown Los Angeles, a failure to raise money, and the absence of wide subscriber interest. Although Chicanos went to Chicano shows and blacks to black shows, very few crossed over and saw fit to subscribe to an entire rainbow season. The LATC became a theatre about, by, for (but not very near) different groups of peoples, insular communities, islands unto themselves. What people gained was a voice, representation, and what they lost was an audience of others and, ultimately, the whole theatre. Peter Sellars follows closely in Flanagan's footstops when, as the director for the Los Angeles Art Festival in 1990, he deliberately booked Asian dance companies in Chicano neighborhoods and Australian aboriginal dancers in Griffith Park. Like Flanagan, Sellars wanted to emphasize a federal model, the differences between people, but he also wanted people to experience the community of others. Such a theatre may risk mistranslation and misappropriation, but it may also inspire a conversation and a culture to new twists, new turns, new understandings, and greater sympathies.

Notes

Preface

1 Since "Negro" was the term preferred by most black artists and intellectuals during the period of U.S. history I cover, when writing about that period I conform to this usage. However, there are also many times throughout the book when I use "black" and "African American," more modern terms, as racial markers: the latter, most often, in cases when questions of mixed cultural identity are invoked, the former, when the unifying notion of race is invoked.

2 An example of such a methodology can be found in Karal Ann Marling, *Wall to Wall America: A Cultural History of Post-Office Murals in the Great Depression* (Minneapolis: University of Minnesota Press, 1982).

3 See Alain Locke, "The New Negro," in Alain Locke, ed., *The New Negro* (1925; New York: Atheneum, 1970), 3–16.

Introduction

1 Quoted from Frank Lentricchia, *Criticism and Social Change* (Chicago: University of Chicago Press, 1985), 160.

2 Dick Netzer, *The Subsidized Muse: Public Support for the Arts in the United States* (Cambridge University Press, 1978), 53.

3 See Raymond Williams, *Keywords: A Vocabulary of Culture and Society* (New York: Oxford University Press, 1976), 76–82.

4 Theatre remained the second largest project after music, employing between 12,500 and 14,000 at its peak (see William F. McDonald, *Federal Relief Administration and the Arts* (Columbus: Ohio State University Press, 1969), 496–543). See the following works for material on the FTP and, in particular, the Negro units: Hallie Flanagan, *Arena: The Story of the Federal Theatre* (1940; New York: Limelight, 1985); Jane De Hart Mathews, *The Federal Theatre, 1935–1939: Plays, Relief, and Politics* (Princeton, NJ:

207

Princeton University Press, 1967); Lorraine Brown and John O'Connor, *Free, Adult, Uncensored: The Living History of the Federal Theatre Project* (Washington, DC: New Republic Books, 1978); E. Quita Craig, *Black Drama of the Federal Theatre Era: Beyond the Formal Horizons* (Amherst: University of Massachusetts Press, 1980); Glenda E. Gill, *White Grease Paint on Black Performers: A Study of the Federal Theatre, 1935–1939* (New York: Lang, 1988); George Kazacoff, *Dangerous Theatre: The Federal Theatre Project as a Forum for New Plays* (New York: Lang, 1989); Ronald Ross, "The Role of Blacks in the Federal Theatre, 1935–1939," *Journal of Negro History* 59.1 (January 1974): 38–50.

5   The case of the vaudevillians was especially problematic because there were so many of them unemployed both because of the Depression and because the form was becoming less and less popular. How to use them or retrain them caused many a headache on the FTP; see Brown and O'Connor, *Free, Adult, Uncensored,* 136–49.

6   See "Finding Aid" at George Mason University (hereafter GMU) for figures.

7   Flanagan to McClure, September 12–18, 1935, WPA Central Files, 211.2 (Drama), National Archives (hereafter NA).

8   General Correspondence National Office, Record Group 69, NA (hereafter RG69, NA).

9   J. Howard Miller to Lawrence S. Norris, January 9, 1939, General Correspondence National Office, RG69, NA.

10 W. E. B. Du Bois, "KRIGWA Players Little Negro Theatre," *Crisis* 32 (July 1926): 124; William Farnsworth to Alfred E. Smith, June 26, 1936, Correspondence of William P. Farnsworth, RG69, NA.

11 GMU, Maurice Clark, Interview by Lorraine Brown, March 3, 1979, tape side A.

12 Michael Rogin, "Blackface, White Noise: The Jewish Jazz Singer Finds His Voice," *Critical Inquiry* 18 (Spring 1992): "Just as the white man in classic American literature uses Indians to establish an American identity against the old world, so the jazz singer uses blacks. If regeneration through violence against Indians won the West, then rebirth through mass entertainment (expropriating black music) won the city" (441).

13 Rejecting a notion of art that is "essentially referential" and a people who are "essentially" black, nevertheless, Gates believes that there are black tropes, black figurative language, black narrative forms, and a black idiom from which the principles of criticism of black literature should be found. " 'Blackness' is not a material object, an absolute, or an event, but a trope; it does not have an 'essence' as such but is defined by a network of relations that form a particular aesthetic unity"; see Henry Louis Gates, Jr., *Figures in Black: Words, Signs, and the "Racial" Self* (New York: Oxford University Press, 1987), 40, 45–46.

14 Michael Awkward, "Negotiations of Power: White Critics, Black Texts, and the Self-Referential Impulse," *American Literary History* 2.4 (Winter 1990): 593, 595.

15 Paul Gilroy, "One Nation Under a Groove," in David Theo Goldberg, ed., *Anatomy of Racism* (Minneapolis: University of Minnesota Press, 1990), 266–7.

16 See Cornel West, "Minority Discourse and the Pitfalls of Canon Formation," *Yale School of Criticism* 1.1 (Fall 1987): 197–98; and Cornel West, "The New Cultural Politics of Difference," in Russell Ferguson, Martha Gever, Trinh T. Minh-ha, Cornel West, eds., *Out There: Marginalization and Contemporary Cultures* (New York: Museum of Contemporary Art, 1990), 29.

17 Eugene O'Neill, "Eugene O'Neill on the Negro Actor," *Messenger* 7.1 (January 1925): 17.

18 Charles Johnson, "Editorials," *Opportunity* 4.44 (August 1926): 239.

19 See Pierre Bourdieu, *Distinction: A Social Critique of the Judgement of Taste,* trans. Richard Nice (Cambridge, MA: Harvard University Press, 1984; 1979: Paris, Les Editions de Minuit): "Intellectuals could be said to believe in the representation – literature, theatre, painting – more than in the things represented, whereas the people chiefly expect representations and the conventions which govern them to allow them to believe 'naively' in the things represented" (5).

20 Stuart Hall and David Held, "Citizens and Citizenship" in Stuart Hall and Martin Jacques, eds., *New Times: The Changing Face of Politics in the 1990s* (London: Routledge, Chapman & Hall, 1989), 181.

21 William Stott, *Documentary Expression and Thirties America* (New York: Oxford University Press, 1973), 104.

22 GMU, Howard Miller, Interview by Bert Holland, January 1976, 19.

23 See Lionel Trilling, *Sincerity and Authenticity,* (Cambridge, MA: Harvard University Press, 1971), for a discussion of the rise of sincerity and its eventual replacement by the concept of authenticity:

> A very considerable originative power had once been claimed for sincerity, but nothing to match the marvellous generative force that our modern judgement assigns to authenticity, which implies the downward movement through all the cultural superstructures to some place where all movement ends, and begins. . . . It is a word of ominous import. As we use it in reference to human existence, its provenance is the museum, where persons expert in such matters test whether objects of art are what they appear to be or are claimed to be, and therefore worth the price that is asked for them – or, if this has already been paid, worth the admiration they are being given. That the word has become part of the moral slang of our day points to the peculiar nature of our fallen condition, our anxiety over the credibility of existence and of individual existences. . . . *Authenteo:* to have full power over; also, to commit a murder. *Authentes:* not only a master and a doer, but also a perpetrator, a murderer, even a self-murderer, a suicide. These ancient and forgotten denotations bear upon the nature and intention of the artistic culture of the period we call Modern. (12, 93, 131)

24 See Richard Wright, *American Hunger* (1944; New York: Harper & Row, 1977), 113–16, and my Chapter 2 for a fuller discussion.
25 Lentricchia, *Criticism and Social Change,* 77–8.
26 Ibid., 79; Kenneth Burke, *Attitudes Toward History,* 2d ed. (Berkeley: University of California Press, 1959), 328.
27 Raymond Williams, *Marxism and Literature* (Oxford University Press, 1977):

> Thus in advanced capitalism, because of changes in the social character of labour, in the social character of communications, and in the social character of decision-making, the dominant culture reaches much further than ever before in capitalist society into hitherto "reserved" or "resigned" areas of experience and practice and meaning. The area of effective penetration of the dominant order into the whole social and cultural process is thus now significantly greater. This in turn makes the problem of emergence especially acute, and narrows the gap between alternative and oppositional elements. (125–6)

28 Ibid., 114, 112; my italics.
29 Houston A. Baker, Jr., *Modernism and the Harlem Renaissance* (Chicago: University of Chicago Press, 1987), 12–13.
30 Houston A. Baker, Jr., *Afro-American Poetics: Revisions of Harlem and the Black Aesthetic* (Madison: University of Wisconsin Press, 1988), 4-6.

1. A New Deal (or Not) for Culture

1 Warren I. Susman, *Culture as History: The Transformation of American Society in the Twentieth Century* (New York: Pantheon, 1973), 178.
2 Arthur M. Schlesinger, Jr., *The Age of Roosevelt: The Politics of Upheaval* (Boston: Houghton Mifflin, 1960), 411.
3 Otis L. Graham, Jr., "New Deal Historiography: Retrospect and Prospect," in Otis L. Graham, Jr. ed., *The New Deal: Critical Issues* (Boston: Little, Brown, 1971), 171.
4 Barton J. Bernstein, "The Conservative Achievements of Liberal Reform," in Graham, ed., *The New Deal,* 161.
5 *Ibid., 161.*
6 *Graham, "New Deal Historiography," 171.*
7 *Hallie Flanagan, Arena: The Story of the Federal Theatre* (1940; New York: Limelight, 1985), 24–5.
8 Susman, *Culture as History,* 152, 183.
9 Schlesinger, *The Age of Roosevelt,* 425.
10 Harold L. Ickes, "Not for 'Special Consideration' but a 'New Social Order for All,' " in Howard Zinn, ed., *New Deal Thought* (New York: Bobbs-Merrill, 1966), 342.
11 Ibid., 343.

12 Jane De Hart Mathews, *The Federal Theatre, 1935–1939: Plays, Relief, and Politics* (Princeton, NJ: Princeton University Press, 1967), 8; Raymond Moley, cited in Ronald D. Rotunda, *The Politics of Language: Liberalism as Word and Symbol* (Iowa City: Iowa University Press, 1986), 74.

13 Robert H. Bremner, "The New Deal and Social Welfare," in Harvard Sitkoff, ed., *Fifty Years Later: The New Deal Evaluated* (New York: Knopf, 1985), 86.

14 Although the Civil Works Administration over the winter of 1933 was the boldest experiment in work relief (Hopkins put 2 million people to work without having them undergo means tests and investigations; they were paid prevailing wage rates as opposed to security wages, and produced consumer goods), Roosevelt terminated the program within months, and Hopkins didn't protest. The Federal Emergency Relief Act and the Works Progress Administration that followed the CWA both employed means tests, but even so, relief projects organized around people's skills was a relatively new concept, and social workers like Hopkins showed a sensitivity to the psychological needs of workers. See William W. Bremer, "Along the 'American Way': The New Deal's Work Relief Programs for the Unemployed," *Journal of American History* 62.3 (December 1975): 637, 642.

15 Ibid., 638.

16 Ibid., 648.

17 Bremner, "The New Deal and Social Welfare," 75.

18 Harry L. Hopkins, *Spending to Save: The Complete Story of Relief* (New York: Norton, 1936), 173, 174.

19 Ibid., 177, 175.

20 Lewis Mumford, "A Letter to the President," in Zinn, ed., *New Deal Thought,* 171.

21 Library Congress Federal Theatre Project/George Mason University Special Collections (hereafter LCFTP), Florence S. Kerr, "The American Answer," Saturday June 3, 1939.

22 See Joanne Bentley, *Hallie Flanagan: A Life in the American Theatre* (New York: Knopf, 1988), 16, 186–9.

23 GMU, Philip Barber, Interview by Round Table, November 1975, 64.

24 Bentley, *Flanagan,* 37.

25 Ibid., 176.

26 Ibid., 230.

27 William F. McDonald, *Federal Relief Administration and the Arts* (Columbus: Ohio State University Press, 1969), 500.

28 Lawrence W. Levine, *Highbrow/Lowbrow: The Emergence of Cultural Hierarchy in America* (Cambridge, MA: Harvard University Press, 1988), 24; see also Robert C. Allen, *Horrible Prettiness: Burlesque and American Culture* (Chapel Hill: University of North Carolina Press, 1991), n. 296, 51.

29 See Robert Károly Sarlós, *Jig Cook and the Provincetown Players: Theatre in Ferment* (Amherst: University of Massachusetts Press, 1982), 2–4; Emil John Poggi, *Theater in America: The Impact of Economic Forces, 1870–1967*

(Ithaca, NY: Cornell University Press, 1966), 99; Kenneth MacGowan, *Footlights Across America: Towards a National Theater* (New York: Harcourt, Brace, 1929).

30 McDonald, *Federal Relief,* 484.

31 Lary May, *Screening Out The Past: The Birth of Mass Culture and the Motion Picture Industry* (Oxford University Press, 1980).

32 Mathews, *The Federal Theatre,* 30, 12. A charter for an American National Theatre was mandated by Congress in 1935. It was supposed to be an organization that would be privately funded, tax-exempt, and for the entire nation. No money was pledged by Congress, and the aspirations of such a theatre were subsumed by the FTP.

33 Flanagan, "Conference of Stage Directors of Eastern Region," April 29, 1937, General Correspondence, RG69, NA.

34 Susman, *Culture as History,* 157, 154.

35 Alfred Haworth Jones, "The Search for a Usable American Past in the New Deal Era," *American Quarterly* 23 (December 1971): 718.

36 GMU, Howard Miller, Interview by Bert Holland, January 1976, 9.

37 LCFTP, Flanagan, "Not in Despair," *Federal Theatre* 2.4 (May 1937): 5.

38 LCFTP, Flanagan, "Theatre and Geography," *Magazine of Art,* August 1938: 2–3.

39 Flanagan, *Arena,* 372.

40 LCFTP, Flanagan, "Theatre and Geography," 3.

41 When Irwin Rhodes met Lee Pressman, general counsel of the WPA, in New York, to ask him questions about how to proceed as lawyer for the FTP, Rhodes was told to forget all about legal precedent. He tells the story this way:

> I had had a list of questions that I really was very dubious about the answers. . . . I had never met Lee Pressman, but I said, "Who is my boss? Who can I ask questions?" So finally I decided Lee Pressman must be the man, and one day I got in touch with Lee and he said he was coming to New York. I said, "I have some questions to ask you." So we had lunch and I had these 15 or 20 questions. And I remember asking all the questions, and he made me feel very good about everything. I realized when I had gotten done that he hadn't answered anything, but he'd given me a new viewpoint. And I accepted that and played it to the hilt to the end of Federal Theatre. That was: "Decide what you want to happen." In other words, I didn't decide based on legal precedents. There weren't any, which was, of course, the exact opposite of what we had been taught in law school. But decide what you want and let it be that way. (GMU, Irwin Rhodes, Interview by Lorraine Brown, February 1977, 21)

42 Jane De Hart Mathews, "Arts and the People: The New Deal Quest for a Cultural Democracy," *Journal of American History* 62 (September 1975): 320.

43 LCFTP, Flanagan, "Spirit of New York Workers Praised by National Director," *Federal Theatre* 1.1 (November 1935): 3.

44 LCFTP, Flanagan, "Federal Theatre Project," *Theatre Arts Monthly* (November 1935): 865–6.

45 LCFTP, Flanagan, "Speech to New York City Project Production Supervisors," *Federal Theatre* 2.1 (June 1936): 5–6.

46 LCFTP, Flanagan, "Federal Theatre: Tomorrow," *Federal Theatre* 2.1 (June 1935): 5.

47 LCFTP, Editorial, "The People's Theatre Grows Stronger," *Federal Theatre* 1.6 (May 1936): 6.

48 LCFTP, Flanagan, "Federal Theatre: Tomorrow," 5, 26.

49 LCFTP, Flanagan, "What Are We Doing With Our Chance?" *Federal Theatre* 2.3 (November–December, 1936): 5.

50 Ibid., 6.

51 Mathews, *The Federal Theatre,* 178–9.

52 LCFTP, Editorial, "The People's Theatre Grows Stronger," 5.

53 LCFTP, Flanagan, "Theatre and Geography," 1.

54 Mathews, "Arts and the People," 329.

55 Actors' Equity was adamant that all nonprofessionals be excluded from the project, that its people be taken care of, insisting that auditions had to be held and classification boards set up to verify that the actors applying for relief were truly actors. William McDonald, in his book on the Federal Arts Projects, notes that Boston was a center of dramatics under the Federal Emergency Relief Administration. In that city, popular community theatre had been sustained largely by amateurs. But when the drama groups were transferred to the WPA, officials discovered that many of the people involved were not professionals and hence unqualified to meet WPA standards. Consequently, the Boston FTP dwindled in size and energy. The decision to cut support of a nonprofessional cast may have been necessary if the WPA was charged with taking care of professionals first and also may have been necessary if the kind of theatre Flanagan wanted to support was different from the popular plays the Boston FERA was doing, but such moves undermined the second aim of the WPA Arts Projects: to take the theatre to the people and allow them to shape it themselves. See McDonald, *Federal Relief,* 508, 493; Mathews, *The Federal Theatre,* 55.

56 Susman, *Culture as History,* 179–80.

57 LCFTP, Flanagan, "Theatre and Geography," 1.

58 Flanagan, *Arena,* 28.

59 See Mathews, *The Federal Theatre,* 62–70, for a full account of the problems of Elmer Rice's production of *Ethiopia.* Hopkins did in the end ask that it be stopped altogether and it was.

60 One of Flanagan's friends and co-workers remembers how she was ready to quit:

> If Rice was going, she had to go, too. And it was really deep. When you get to, you know, remarks like Lorraine's "Maybe she wasn't a liberal," like Hellman, she was not only a liberal but she had this kind of integrity that you're not going to touch. And if Rice says he has to

go, she doesn't have that kind of professional support. She's being axed, all the promises are being broken. And that was a long evening. . . . And those government workers said right in her teeth, they said, "It's your choice right now tonight. This is probably the last minute you can leave with integrity." They really said it to her that night. If she walked off that night, she'd be like Elmer Rice, untouched. If she stayed on, they were saying, those old government workers, "Look, it's happened once. It's gonna happen again. If you care so much about your integrity that you can't take it," like – who was it, Truman, "if you can't stand the heat, get out of the kitchen." In very wise words, both of those men worked with her and they were honest that way. "If you want to go now, as we know you want to go, we're saying that you're right if this is more important to you." And somehow, you know, they talked her into – "I've got all these people on the payroll and I'm tied up in this integrity thing. The line goes a little and I'm gonna be damaged and have arrows at me and so on and so forth." (GMU, Esther Porter Lane, Interview by Mae Mallory Krulak, September 1976, 22)

61   Bentley, *Flanagan,* 298.
62   Ibid., 240.
63   Richard H. Pells, *Radical Visions and American Dreams: Culture and Social Thought in the Depression Years* (New York: Harper & Row, 1973): 317.
64   Jones, "The Search for a Usable American Past," 715.
65   GMU, Howard Miller, Interview by Bert Holland, January 1976, 19–20.
66   Mathews, *The Federal Theatre,* 296–314.
67   LCFTP, Published Reviews, "WPA Federal Theatre Adverse Publicity," *New York Journal-American.*
68   Loren Kruger, *The National Stage* (Chicago: University of Chicago Press, 1992), 183.
69   GMU, Irwin Rhodes, Interview by Lorraine Brown, May 1977, 14–15.
70   GMU, Howard Miller, Interview by Bert Holland, January 1976, 18.
71   GMU, Philip Barber, Interview by Round Table, November 1976, 82.
72   GMU, Leonard De Paur, Interview by Lorraine Brown, December 1976, 41.
73   LCFTP, Published Review, Brooks Atkinson, "Ought We to Found a National Theatre?" *New York Times Magazine* (March 24, 1940).
74   Bentley, *Flanagan,* 18.
75   Flanagan to Glenn Adams, Supervisor, Professional and Service Division, WPA Chicago, October 30, 1935, Correspondence of Regional Office, RG69, NA.
76   McDonald, *Federal Relief,* 557.

2. Critical Directions

1   Alain Locke, "Steps Toward the Negro Theatre," *Crisis* 25.2 (December 1922): 68.

2 Hazel V. Carby, "Policing the Black Woman's Body in an Urban Context," *Critical Inquiry* 18 (Summer 1992): 754.
3 Henry Louis Gates, Jr., *Figures in Black: Words, Signs, and the "Racial" Self* (New York: Oxford University Press, 1987), 3–58.
4 James Weldon Johnson, "The Opportunity Dinner," *Opportunity* 3.30 (June 1925): 177; Charles Johnson quoted in Patrick J. Gilpin, "Charles S. Johnson: Entrepreneur of the Harlem Renaissance," in Arna Bontemps, ed., *Harlem Renaissance Remembered* (New York: Dodd, Mead, 1972), 238; Alain Locke, ed., *The New Negro* (1925; New York: Atheneum, 1970), 15.
5 See Arnold Rampersad, *The Art and Imagination of W. E. B. Du Bois* (1976; New York: Schocken, 1990), 184; Abby Arthur Johnson and Ronald Maberry Johnson, *Propaganda and Aesthetics: The Literary Politics of Afro-American Magazines in the Twentieth Century* (Amherst: University of Massachusetts Press, 1979); Theodore Kornweibel, Jr., *No Crystal Stair: Black Life and the Messenger, 1917–1928* (Westport, CT: Greenwood, 1975). New York, with a black population of over 150,000, was the home of seventeen black publications, including four newspapers, as well as nationally circulating monthlies like the *Crisis,* the *Messenger,* and the *Crusader.*
6 Rampersad, *The Art and Imagination of W. E. B. Du Bois,* 201.
7 Kornweibel, *No Crystal Stair,* xi–xiii, 43–4.
8 Hazel Carby points out that "black people were becoming increasingly urbanized before they left for northern cities" and that they came with some experience of urban forms of entertainment such as blues singers, musicians, and vaudeville performers. See Carby, "Policing the Black Woman's Body in an Urban Context," 739.
9 See Maxine Schwartz Seller, ed., "Introduction," in *Ethnic Theatre in the United States* (Westport, CT: Greenwood, 1983), 6.
10 Nathan Huggins, *Harlem Renaissance* (New York: Oxford University Press, 1971), 248.
11 James Weldon Johnson, "The Dilemma of the Negro Author," *American Mercury* (December 1928): 477–81, writes about the divided audience – black and white – that African American writers must address. See Chapter 4 for further discussion.
12 Joseph Boskin, *Sambo: The Rise and Demise of an American Jester* (Oxford University Press, 1986), 44–5.
13 In Caryl Phillips's novel of 1989, *Higher Ground,* the African interpreter who had worked for white slave merchants is sold into slavery. As he is about to be taken to the ship, he remembers an African chant:

> Under my breath I begin to mutter. Other lips move independently, and without organization we swell into a choir. I realize that this is the same choral chant that I would listen to when I was the man next to Price, the same hitherto baffling rebellious music that now makes a common sense for we are all saying the same thing; we are all promising to one day return, irrespective of what might happen to us in whatever land or lands we eventually travel to; we are promising

ourselves that we will return to our people and reclaim the lives that
are being snatched away from us. (Caryl Phillips, *Higher Ground* [New
York: Penguin, 1989], 59–60)

14 A handbill in the *New York National Advocate* states: "The gentleman of
color announce another play at their Pantheon, corner of Bleecker and
Mercer Streets on Monday Evening. . . . They have graciously made a
partition at the back of the house for the accomodation [sic] of the whites."
The *Advocate* also surmises that the attendance of whites led to the closing
of the theatre. It may have reopened in 1823. See Jonathan Dewberry, "The
African Grove Theatre and Company," *Black American Literature Forum* 16.4
(Winter 1982): 128–31.

15 See especially Boskin, *Sambo,* 76–7, for a discussion of minstrelsy and its
critics; and Eric Lott, " 'The Seeming Counterfeit,': Racial Politics and
Early Blackface Minstrelsy," *American Quarterly* 43.2 (June 1991): 223–54.

16 See Lott, "Early Blackface Minstrelsy," 225, 223. Lott sets out some of the
"conflicted set of responses" minstrelsy excited:

> Blackface is perhaps the best place to study the contradictions of popu-
> lar racial feeling in the nineteenth century. . . . The minstrel show
> indeed was based on a profound white investment in black culture
> which occasionally surfaced in certain less malign ways. This produced
> a popular form in which racial insult was twinned with racial envy,
> moments of domination with moments of liberation, counterfeit with
> currency – a pattern at times amounting to no more than the two faces
> of our particular mode of racism, at others gesturing toward a specific
> kind of political or sexual danger; and all of it comprising a peculiarly
> American structure of racial feeling. This structure began to take the
> form of a complex dialectic: an unsteady but continual oscillation
> between fascination with "blackness" and fearful ridicule of it, under-
> scored but not necessarily determined by an oscillation between sym-
> pathetic belief in blackface's authenticity and ironic distance from its
> counterfeit representations. (227)

Lott agrees with Huggins that the image of the black minstrel becomes
central in the white American psyche. While the Protestant Yankee had to
be hard working and repressed if he were to succeed in an increasingly
competitive world, his alter ego, the African American minstrel character,
becomes a vicarious and necessary release for the white audience, serving
white people at the expense of black humanity. Lott goes on, however, to
describe not only psychological identifications but *political* identifications
white working–class audiences made with the minstrel character.

17 Anyone who worked with blacks in the theatre or portrayed them on stage
had to face the terms of a pervasive historical racism. The range of available
parts had been rigidly defined; roles were narrowly, racially circumscribed.
The minstrel stereotype, popular in the nineteenth century – childlike,
innocent, slow, lazy, unrestrained, self-indulgent, irresponsible, vulgar –

was still operative in the early twentieth century, in films, on stage, in popular culture. See Huggins, *Harlem Renaissance;* Hans Nathan, *Dan Emmett and the Rise of Early Negro Minstrelsy* (Norman: University of Oklahoma Press, 1962); Robert C. Toll, *Blacking Up: The Minstrel Show in Nineteenth-Century America* (New York: Oxford University Press, 1974); Lott, "Early Blackface Minstrelsy," 223–54; Michael Rogin, "Blackface, White Noise: The Jewish Jazz Singer Finds His Voice," *Critical Inquiry* 18.3 (Spring 1992): 417–53. For histories of African American theatre, see Ethel Pitts Walker, "Krigwa, A Theatre by, for, and about Black People," *Theatre Journal* 40.3 (October 1988): 347–56; Dewberry, "The African Grove Theatre and Company," 128–31; Henry T. Sampson, *The Ghost Walks: A Chronological History of Blacks in Show Business, 1865–1910* (Metuchen, NJ: Scarecrow, 1988); Leslie Catherine Sanders, *The Development of Black Theater in America: From Shadows to Selves* (Baton Rouge: Lousiana State University Press, 1988); Jack Schiffman, *Harlem Heyday: A Pictorial History of Modern Black Show Business and the Apollo Theatre* (New York: Prometheus, 1984); Doris Abramson, *Negro Playwrights in the American Theater, 1925–1959* (New York: Columbia University Press, 1969); James V. Hatch, *Black Image on the American Stage: A Bibliography of Plays and Musicals, 1770–1970* (New York: DBS Publications, 1970); Errol Hill, ed., *The Theater of Black Americans I: Roots and Rituals/The Image Makers* and *The Theater of Black Americans II: The Presenters/The Participators* (Englewood Cliffs, NJ: Prentice-Hall, 1980); Loften Mitchell, *Black Drama: The Story of the American Negro in the Theatre* (New York: Hawthorn, 1967).

18   Sampson, *The Ghost Walks,* 140–1.
19   Mitchell, *Black Drama,* 69–70.
20   Sister M. Francesca Thompson, O.S.F., "The Lafayette Players, 1917–1932," in Hill, ed., *The Theater of Black Americans II,* 1–32.
21   Sampson, *The Ghost Walks,* 280.
22   Thomas L. Riis, *Just Before Jazz: Black Musical Theater in New York, 1890–1915* (Washington: Smithsonian Institution Press, 1989), xxi, 18–19, 161–2, 31–2.
23   Boskin, *Sambo,* 87–8.
24   One group of writers and intellectuals, centered at the University of North Carolina, Chapel Hill, devoted their careers to (or owed them to the success of) Negro-related writing: Paul Green, Julia Peterkin, DuBose Heyward, T. S. Stribling, Elizabeth Lay Green, Edward Sheldon. Frederich Koch, the director of the Carolina Players, and former student of George Pierce Baker, particularly encouraged plays that made an artistic use of Negro themes. Liberal social scientists Frank Graham and Howard Odum published important studies of the Negro from 1927 to 1929; *Carolina Magazine* devoted one issue entirely to work by Negro contributors. See Amritjit Singh, "Black–White Symbiosis: Another Look at the Literary History of the 1920s," in Victor A. Kramer, ed., *The Harlem Renaissance Re-examined* (New York: AMS Press, 1987), 31–42.

25 Loften Mitchell names some of the groups in his book *Black Drama:* the Harlem Experimental Theatre, Negro Art Theatre, Harlem Community Players, Dunbar Garden Players, and Negro People's Theatre, among others. Also see John G. Monroe, "The Harlem Little Theatre Movement," *Journal of American Culture* 6 (Winter 1983): 63–70, for a discussion of the Colored Players' Guild, the Acme Players, and the National Ethiopian Art Theatre; and Jervis Anderson, *This Was Harlem: A Cultural Portrait, 1900–1950* (New York: Farrar, Straus, & Giroux, 1981), 275–6.

26 Willis Richardson, "The Negro and the Stage," *Opportunity* 2.22 (October 1924): 310.

27 Raymond O'Neil, "The Negro in Dramatic Art," *Crisis* 27.4 (February 1924): 155–7.

28 Anne Cooke, "Third Moscow Theatre Festival," *Opportunity* 14.2 (February 1936): 59.

29 Sterling Brown, "A Literary Parallel," *Opportunity* 10.5 (May 1932): 153.

30 Sanders, *The Development of Black Theater in America,* 10–11.

31 See Roland Wolseley, *The Black Press, U.S.A.,* 2d ed. (Ames: Iowa State University Press, 1990), 58–9.

32 Du Bois, "Obituary," *Moon Illustrated Weekly* 1.14 (March 1906).

33 Nor was he afraid to change his mind and criticize what he once praised. He was a man with a Victorian aesthetic sensibility, yet his journal, the *Crisis,* published many of the modern black writers. He was a cultural elitist who advocated folk art and a socialist suspicious of Russia in the teens who became a Communist in 1961; opposed to a segregated army, he nevertheless advocated black enlistment during World War I. He rose to prominence in the first decade of the twentieth century fighting Booker T. Washington's segregation policies, but he broke with the NAACP in the thirties, denouncing integration as unworkable and calling for blacks to support black institutions.

34 Du Bois, "Our Book Shelf," *Crisis* 31.3 (January 1926): 141.

35 Du Bois, "Criteria of Negro Art," *Crisis* 32.6 (October 1926): 290–7.

36 Paul Robeson, for instance, in 1925 will echo the James Weldon Johnson line that there can be no great culture without a great literature:

> One of the great measures of a people is its culture, its artistic stature. Above all things, we boast that the only true artistic contributions of America are Negro in origin. We boast of the culture of ancient Africa. Surely in any discussion of art or culture, music, the drama and its interpretation must be included. So today Roland Hayes is infinitely more of a racial asset than many who "talk" at great length. Thousands of people hear him, see him, are moved by him, and are brought to a clearer understanding of human values. If I can do something of a like nature, I shall be happy, I shall be happy. (Paul Robeson, "An Actor's Wanderings and Hopes," *Messenger* 7.1 [January 1925]: 32)

37 David Glassberg, *American Historical Pageantry* (Chapel Hill: University of North Carolina Press, 1990), 283–5; 112–13. Glassberg points out the

various tensions and interest groups that endorsed pageants: there were those who wanted to sponsor recreational pageants for schoolchildren in playgrounds and those who wanted to organize a professional core of pageant directors who would police the form. Some people, like George Pierce Baker, Flanagan's teacher at Harvard, believed the pageant could combat commercial, popular forms of mass art. Some wanted to emphasize the importance of Anglo-Saxon history; others wanted to dramatize the newly emerging pluralistic society of immigrants.

38 Du Bois, "The Drama Among Black Folk," *Crisis* 11.4 (August 1916): 169. The Ethiopian tradition in poetry was "typical of the thinking of black middle-class intellectuals during the first two decades of the twentieth century." Du Bois was following in this tradition, a tradition that relied on "symbols of stability, permanency, and high culture"; see Wilson J. Moses "The Poetics of Ethiopianism: W. E. B. Du Bois and Literary Black Nationalism," in William L. Andrews, ed., *Critical Essays on W. E. B. Du Bois* (Boston: Hall, 1985), 102.

39 Du Bois, "The Star of Ethiopia," *Crisis* 11.2 (December 1915): 91.

40 Du Bois, "The Drama Among Black Folk," 171, 173.

41 Du Bois, "KRIGWA Players Little Negro Theatre," *Crisis* 32 (July 1926): 134.

42 Walker, "Krigwa, A Theatre by, for, and about Black People," 355; also see Monroe, "The Harlem Little Theatre Movement, 1920–1929," 67.

43 See Mark Naison, *Communists in Harlem During the Depression* (New York: Grove, 1983), especially the chapter "Communism and Harlem Intellectuals in the Popular Front – Anti-Fascism and the Politics of Black Culture," 193–226. Even more than Du Bois, Randolph and Owen exemplify this cultural paradox. Both grew up in houses where learning was respected. Both Randolph and Owen were born in the South, and they came to New York City along with thousands of other southern blacks in the teens to make their way. Like Du Bois, Randolph appeared to be aloof, correct; his speech sounded British. Everyone noticed the Oxford accent that he had acquired after hiring a voice teacher. Like Du Bois, he was interested in the theatre, joining in Harlem "Ye Friends of Shakespeare," an amateur theatre group, thinking he might become a stage actor. But Randolph didn't go on stage; he became a Socialist and confidently assumed a privileged position as a leader of his people. See Benjamin Quarles, "A. Philip Randolph: Labor Leader at Large," in John Hope Franklin and August Meier, eds., *Black Leaders in the Twentieth Century* (Urbana: University of Illinois Press, 1982), 142.

44 See Quarles, "A. Philip Randolph," and Kornweibel, *No Crystal Stair*.

45 Editorial, "Helen E. Hagan," *Messenger* (October 1921): 200.

46 Quoted in Kornweibel, *No Crystal Stair,* 124.

47 Jervis Anderson, *A. Philip Randolph: A Biographical Portrait* (New York: Harcourt, Brace, Jovanovich, 1972), 145, 147.

48 Theophilus Lewis, "Theatre," *Messenger* 8.6 (June 1926): 182.

49 Lewis, "Theatre," *Messenger* 8.12 (December 1926): 362.

50   Lewis, "Theatre," *Messenger* 6.5 (May 1924): 145.
51   Lewis, "Theatre," *Messenger* 8.6 (June 1926): 182.
52   Schiffman, *Harlem Heyday*, 17.
53   Lewis, "Theatre," *Messenger* 6.5 (May 1924): 145.
54   Lewis, "Theatre," *Messenger* 6.12 (December 1924): 380.
55   Lewis, "Theatre," *Messenger* 9.3 (March 1927): 85.
56   Lewis, "Theatre," *Messenger* 9.7 (July 1927): 229.
57   Lewis, "Theatre," *Messenger* 8.11 (November 1926): 334–5.
58   Lewis, "Theatre," *Messenger* 6.8 (August 1924): 250.
59   Lewis, "Theatre," *Messenger* 9.7 (July 1927): 229.
60   Lewis, "Theatre," *Messenger* 8.9 (September 1926): 278.
61   Lewis, "Theatre," *Messenger* 9.7 (July 1927): 229.
62   "After all, they were Americans and affected by the good and bad taste of
     their countrymen. Like other Americans, blacks knew a commerical suc-
     cess – even when they might not know whether or not it was good – and
     their entertainment was tailored to the standards of mass culture." See
     Huggins, *Harlem Renaissance*, 293.
63   Locke, *The New Negro*, 3–4. Charles Johnson, editor of *Opportunity*, had
     included Locke from the beginning in his plans to boost the fortunes of
     black artists, and Locke used the journal to judge which candidates should
     be included in his canon of the Harlem Renaissance. Like Du Bois, Johnson,
     Randolph, and Owen, Locke was highly educated, a bona fide member of
     the talented tenth. Unlike the others, he never attended a segregated school.
     After completing a Ph.D. in philosophy at Harvard, he was the first black
     man awarded a Rhodes scholarship to Oxford. Had he been white, he
     would have been employed by Harvard; instead, he went to the Harvard of
     black universities – Howard in Washington, D.C. – with a great deal of
     bitterness. Locke always railed against what he felt to be the narrow society
     of Washington and Howard; he longed for escape and did so as often as he
     could to New York and Europe. In a letter to Charlotte Osgood Mason,
     he writes:

>   I do so wish I was in New York this week-end – seldom have I had so
>   long an unbroken stay in Washington – and it's like being in a damp,
>   musty attic. Really you have no idea what mental stagnation it has
>   brought on – I've reached the point where I just can't account for my
>   time – the days go on, – nothing much gets done beyond mere
>   routine, – and the whole thing in retrospect looks like a foggy road
>   that you've been walking on a long time – you know the distance, but
>   just can't believe your eyes. . . . Of course the second affliction is being
>   cut off from the news – one gets nothing here but petty gossip and
>   intrigue – all of which is Zulu to you, even if I dared want to bother
>   you with it. (Locke to Mason, November 20, 1932, Washington D.C.,
>   Locke Papers, Howard University)

As formal in his manners as Du Bois, aristocratic and elitist, and gay, Locke
seemed to attract more criticism than any other critic during the Renaissance perhaps because

more than any other figure, he represented the attempt of the black intelligentsia to define and label the Renaissance as a literary movement. . . . This made him a target for writers who resented being defined, categorized, or labeled, who, although emotionally attached to the Renaissance, also were thoroughly individualistic in their literary philosophy.

Zora Neale Hurston accused him of trying to dominate the Renaissance because he had academic degrees (see Cary Wintz, *Black Culture and the Harlem Renaissance* [Houston, TX: Rice University Press, 1988], 119, 116). Arnold Rampersad, Langston Hughes's biographer, makes Locke out to be fairly villainous, a slippery character who played Hurston off against Hughes in order to retain the favors of the rich lady who at various times supported all of them – Charlotte Osgood Mason (see Arnold Rampersad, *The Life of Langston Hughes: 1902–1941* [New York: Oxford University Press, 1986], 200).

64 Alain Locke, "A Note on African Art," *Opportunity* 2.17 (May 1924): 136.
65 Locke, *The New Negro,* 5.
66 Locke, "To Certain of Our Philistines," *Opportunity* 3.29 (May 1925): 155.
67 See Locke, "Roland Hayes: An Appreciation," *Opportunity* 1.12 (December 1923): 356.
68 Locke, "A Note on African Art," *Opportunity* 2.17 (May 1924): 135.
69 Locke, *The New Negro,* 210.
70 Perhaps the most famous exchange over the categories African and American and Negro art took place in the *Nation* in 1926, when George Schuyler wrote an article entitled "The Negro-Art Hokum" to which Langston Hughes replied. These two reiterate the debates about the possibilities of identity for black, Negro, African, African American artists. Schuyler, a young, independent-minded socialist of sorts at that point in his life, claimed that there was no such thing as an African American art distinct from American forms. African roots, even the particular Afro-American historical differences, have been erased, Schuyler argued; and at any rate, art must escape the particular circumstances of its location and historical moment in order to become great, that is, universal. Schuyler maintained that nationality was more influential than race, that the American Negro was "just plain American" and that "the Aframerican is subject to the same economic and social forces that mold the actions and thoughts of the white Americans" (662). Education and environment are the determining factors. Langston Hughes, already a much praised race poet, responded the following week. He insisted that difference created by history had constructed racial characteristics. The Negro artist has his "racial individuality, his heritage of rhythm and warmth, and his incongruous humor" (693). Hughes made one more careful distinction about the Negro artist: the "great" Negro artist will come from the common people, and great race art will spring from popular art – the blues and jazz. But in a note that would be sounded by the younger New Negroes of the Harlem Renaissance, Hughes wanted to be free to be whatever kind of artist he wanted to be,

free of any critical injunctions: "An artist must be free to choose what he does, certainly, but he must also never be afraid to do what he might choose. . . . If colored people are pleased we are glad. If they are not, their displeasure doesn't matter either. We build our temples for tomorrow, strong as we know how, and we stand on top of the mountain, free within ourselves" (694). Nurtured by the community of common folk and yet able to ignore "colored people" if they don't like what he has created, Hughes seems to argue that he should be able to create art freed from any standard – white or black. George Schuyler, "The Negro-Art Hokum," *Nation* 122.3180 (June 16, 1926): 662–3; Langston Hughes, "The Negro Artist and the Racial Mountain," *Nation* 122.3181 (June 23, 1926): 692–4.

71 Charles Johnson, "Editorials," *Opportunity* 4.44 (August 1926): 238. Trained as a sociologist, not as an aesthete, Johnson clearly thought these arguments frivolous and beside the point. He wasn't interested in developing critical judgments: he simply wanted to encourage all black artists. A graduate of Virginia Union University, in 1916 he went to the University of Chicago to study sociology. His first real work occurred in the aftermath of the Chicago riots of 1919 when he was appointed associate executive secretary of an interracial commission assigned to investigate the cause of the riots. The study, *The Negro In Chicago: A Study of Race Relations and a Race Riot,* published in 1922, emphasized the problems attending the huge migration of rural blacks to the urban North and established Johnson as an expert in race relations (see Patrick J. Gilpin, "Charles S. Johnson: Entrepreneur of the Harlem Renaissance," 215–16). In 1921, Johnson moved to New York as director of research and investigations for the National Urban League, where he would direct the economic and sociological research of the entire league. Johnson's scientific training in the conditions of city life made him a perfect match for the Urban League and its progressive ideals, principally that the gathering of facts would lead to reform. Nancy Weiss describes the differences between the NAACP and the Urban League in the following way: the NAACP would "occupy itself principally with the political, civil and social rights of the colored people," while the Committee on Urban Conditions would deal "primarily with questions of philanthropy and social economy." Precisely because the Urban League was less militant in its method, it was better able to raise money from philanthropists. While the NAACP called for direct action, the Urban League leaned toward investigation and persuasion. See Nancy Joan Weiss, *The National Urban League: 1910–1940* (New York: Oxford University Press, 1974), 65).

72 Johnson, "Public Opinion and the Negro," *Opportunity* 1.7 (July 1923): 206.

73 Johnson, "Out of the Shadow," and "Jazz," *Opportunity* 3.29 (May 1925): 131–3.

74 Cornel West, "The New Cultural Politics of Difference," in Russell Ferguson, Martha Gever, Trinh T. Minh-ha, Cornel West, eds., *Out There: Marginalization and Contemporary Cultures* (New York: New Museum of Contemporary Art), 27.

75 Black journalism continued to be an important outlet for African American writers debating cultural questions:

> As the Depression worsened, the black editor as businessman and as political radical came increasingly to the fore. The more conservative editors and writers of organizational journals experienced a difficult time gathering a following. And thus it was that the black popular magazines made money, at least for a while, the leftist little magazines established literary policy, and the house journals lost support. Through periodicals, the older generation of writers tried to shape the development of a new literature. Dorothy West looked to the left, Claude McKay to the right, and Alain Locke remained discreetly in the middle, both in politics and the arts. Newer Negroes made up their own minds, after first consulting with Richard Wright. (Johnson and Johnson, *Propaganda and Aesthetics*, 124)

76 See especially Locke, "Toward a Critique of Negro Music," *Opportunity* 12.11–12.12 (November–December 1934): 328–31; 365–67, 385. While Charles Johnson praised jazz precisely because of its popularity, Locke deplores it because of its commercial vulgarity and the exploitative nature of its production. Locke refuses to see that anything oppositional or beautiful can come from art catering to or taken up by the popular market. In all of his writing in the twenties and thirties, he argues for the necessity of artists remaining independent from commercial ties. Opposed to the popular artist is the rare genius who creates art that will last for the benefit of the select few.

77 Locke, "Steps Toward the Negro Theatre," 66.

78 Locke, "God Save Reality!" *Opportunity* 15.1 (1937): 12.

3. Producing New Dramas

1 GMU, Leonard De Paur, Interview by Lorraine Brown, December 28, 1976, 3.

2 George Sklar, "Editorials," *New Theatre* 2.7 (July 1935), 3. The New York Suitcase Theatre, organized in 1931, presented working-class plays before labor organizations. When Langston Hughes said in 1938 that he wanted "a theatre . . . of my own" and named it the Harlem Suitcase Theatre, this was one more attempt to build a people's theatre in Harlem. See Arnold Rampersad, *The Life of Langston Hughes: 1902-1941* (New York: Oxford University Press, 1986), 356-7

3 Alain Locke, "The Negro and American Theatre," in Addison Gayle, Jr., ed., *The Black Aesthetic* (1927; rpt. New York: Doubleday, 1971), 268.

4 Alain Locke to Charlotte Osgood Mason, June 30, 1935, Locke Papers, Howard University. In *Opportunity*, he comments that "certainly two of

the most powerful issues of the contemporary scene have met in 'Steve-dore,' and a synthesis of race and class as a new type of problem drama may just as well be taken for granted." See Alain Locke, "The Eleventh Hour of Nordicism," *Opportunity* 13.1 (January 1935): 12.

5 Jay Plum, "Rose McClendon and the Black Units of the Federal Theatre Project: A Lost Contribution," *Theatre Survey* 33 (November 1992): 152.

6 Alver Napper, "Aims Values and Possibilities," General Correspondence National Office, RG69, NA.

7 The Lafayette was fully equipped to put a production together from start to finish. It had a costume department, carpentry shop, and lighting depart-ment, as well as grip men to move scenery, prop men, and a composer. Although it lacked modern machines, built as it was in 1911, it had plenty of manpower to handle scenery. Three men moved the asbestos curtain, which weighed four hundred pounds. The FTP employed ushers, box office men, porters, and firemen. A playreading committee turned sugges-tions over to the central planning board, after which the script would be sent to a director. The Lafayette was the city's largest project employing the greatest number of Negro workers in one place – up to 750 people in the beginning, 122 actors waiting to be cast. In May 1936, 502 people were employed at the Lafayette; in December 1937, the number had been cut in half to 253, 122 of which were actors; 38 were in the technical department, 25 house workers, 7 in records, 5 stage managers, 3 shop carpenters, 2 time keepers, with clerical and department heads making up the rest. All were black, except one secretary. See "WPA Negro Theatre," December 21, 1937, General Correspondence National Office, RG69, NA.

8 Hallie Flanagan, *Arena: The Story of the Federal Theatre* (1940; New York; Limelight, 1985), 63; John Houseman, *Run-Through* (New York: Simon & Schuster, 1972), 178–9. Houseman may have exaggerated his own impor-tance in his autobiography.

9 Leonard De Paur said:

> Well, you see there were people like Houseman who were capable of selling an idea whether they had any track record or not. And then there were blacks who had reasonable track records within a very limited sphere who just could not be trusted. Because it was assumed immediately that this black person just didn't have the qualifications. It's an old story and it's no secret. (GMU, Leonard De Paur, Interview by Lorraine Brown, December 1976, 18)

10 GMU, Carlton Moss, Interview by Lorraine Brown, August 6, 1976, 11.

11 See Plum, "Rose McClendon and the Black Units of the Federal Theatre Project," 144–53. Plum argues that McClendon played a pivotal role in the particular organization of the FTP's Negro units. In 1935, along with Dick Campbell, she founded the Negro People's Theatre, which was committed to the idea that theatre should be "intimately connected to the world around it" (149). She wrote that the NPT would "present plays that [were] vital to

Negro life, thereby developing the creative and artistic talents of the Negro, fostering the high ideals of the race, and illuminating the forces of social realism through the medium of the theatre" (149).

12 GMU, Carlton Moss, Interview by Lorraine Brown, August 6, 1976, 11.

13 Houseman, *Run-Through*, 186.

14 "WPA Negro Theatre," December 21, 1937, General Correspondence National Office, RG69, NA.

15 GMU, Philip Barber, Round Table Interview, November 11, 1975, 27.

16 Flanagan, "Negro Theatre," April 13, 1937, Correspondence of New York City Office, RG69, NA. Alternative plans had been proposed by a group of thirty-nine workers who petitioned for a more hierarchical distribution of power. They proposed that there should be just one managing producer with an administrative assistant responsible for coordinating all of the various departments of the unit. This particular group proposed Carlton Moss to be assisted by John Velasco. See "To the Directors of the Negro Theatre," April 7, 1937, Correspondence of New York City Office, RG69, NA.

17 GMU, Leonard De Paur, Interview by Lorraine Brown, December 2, 1976, 11–13.

18 "Negro Theatre," unsigned letter to Philip Barber, February 25, 1937, Correspondence of New York City Office, RG69, NA.

19 GMU, Thomas Anderson, Interview by Lorraine Brown, May 24, 1978, 10.

20 Alain Locke, "We Turn to Prose," *Opportunity* 10.2 (February 1932): 42; Locke, "The Eleventh Hour of Nordicism," 12.

21 Montgomery Gregory, "The No 'Count Boy," *Opportunity* 3.28 (April 1925): 121.

22 Eugene Gordon, "From 'Uncle Tom's Cabin' to 'Stevedore,' " *New Theatre* 2.7 (July 1935): 22.

23 W. E. B. Du Bois, "In Abraham's Bosom," *Crisis* 34.1 (March 1927): 12. The play began as a one act, which Green worked into a full-length play. Abraham, a mulatto, works for his white father who owns the turpentine stills. Though Abraham has been promised by his father that he can open a school for other Negroes, his father reneges on this promise. In the full-length play, Abraham goes off to open the school but loses it after striking a pupil. His son isn't interested in education, and when Abraham tries to start a trade school that will become a Negro university he speaks out of turn, is beaten, and when he kills a white man in a fight, is shot.

24 Theophilus Lewis, "The Theatre," *Messenger* 9.2 (February 1927): 53.

25 Lewis, "My Red Rag," *Messenger* 10.1 (January 1928): 18.

26 LCFTP, Playreader Report, *In Abraham's Bosom*, Rose E. Flanell; Katharine Robert.

27 Lewis, "The Theatre," *Messenger* 5.12 (December 1923): 924.

28 Sterling Brown, "Concerning Negro Drama," *Opportunity* 9.9 (September 1931): 288.

29 George Zorn, April 1, 1937, "Report of the Activities and Accomplishments of Negro Dramatists Laboratory," Correspondence of New York City, RG69, NA.
30 GMU, Carlton Moss, Interview by Lorraine Brown, August 6, 1976, 14.
31 GMU, Leonard De Paur, Interview by Lorraine Brown, December 28, 1976, 17.
32 Flanagan, *Arena,* 289.
33 GMU, Abram Hill, Interview by Lorraine Brown, February 27, 1977, 2–3.
34 Emmet Lavery to the Negro Arts Committee, March 31, 1939, National Service Bureau, RG69, NA.
35 LCFTP, Playscript, Abram Hill and John Silvera, *Liberty Deferred,* 3.
36 Philip Barber continues:

> You see, the two people I had immediately that were next to me in the later years when I was chairman of the Production Board were essentially looking up scripts. They never in all the time they were there, and I knew them personally quite well, never ever submitted one single script that they read. They always had a negative outlook. "No good. No good." So I never got anything to read. . . . Jack Gibbs was one of them. . . . a very academically, a very tight kind of theatre would be what he would conceive of. He had no use for anything else. . . . But there he would be in a job where he could block all kinds of things. But that we had nothing to do with. That was under Roz and Hallie. They ran that absolutely. In the beginning that was all under Elmer, but Roz got it out from under Elmer inside of two months. She wasn't going to play. I should think – this is one of the things that I would like to find out. I think that there's an awful lot that has not been said, and I'm not even sure that whites can get at it. But it's worth a try. (GMU, Philip Barber, Interview by Lorraine Brown, November 11, 1975: 150–1)

37 GMU, Carlton Moss, Interview by Lorraine Brown, August 6, 1976, 34.
38 LCFTP, Playscript, Hughes Allison, "Foreword to *Panyared,*" May 22, 1939, 27–8.
39 Marion Brooks to Emmet Lavery, March 28, 1939, Correspondence of Hallie Flanagan, RG69, NA.
40 Emmet Lavery to Hallie Flanagan, March 29, 1939, Correspondence of Hallie Flanagan, RG69, NA.
41 GMU, Leonard De Paur, Interview by Lorraine Brown, December 28, 1976, 24. In another instance of censorship, Flanagan and Philip Barber together refused to approve a play in 1936 called *Black Souls,* which was scheduled for the Negro Youth Theatre with Venzuella Jones directing. "This script focused on the wholesale raping of colored girls by a plantation overlord, and seemed to Mr. Barber and myself, rather too clinical for our project. They said that they felt both of us were afraid of sex" (see Flanagan, "Record of Interviews," April 23 to Monday April 27, 1936, General Correspondence of the National Office, RG69, NA). In a memo from

Barber to E. H. Englehorn, business director, on the subject of the Negro Youth Theatre, Barber says that *Black Souls* was rehearsed for quite a long time but that it had been approved by the previous director of New York, Elmer Rice:

> I did not approve it any time (a reading of the script would be very instructive) but as almost all of the persons on the project had a relief status and as a dismissal of a group of negroes at the time might have caused serious political reactions, I hesitated to disband Miss Jones' group and leaned over backwards. (Philip Barber to E. H. Englehorn, January 20, 1937, Correspondence of New York City, RG69, NA)

42 Ralf Coleman saw Allison in Boston years later. At that time Allison wanted nothing to do with the theatre. See GMU, Ralf Coleman, November 21, 1975, tape side A.

43 Flanagan's production record printed in *Arena* lists thirty new productions of black drama, i.e., plays specifically written for Negro units (or adapted, such as *Swing Mikado* and *Macbeth*), and twenty-five revivals. I estimate that approximately 20 percent of the playwrights were blacks. See Flanagan, *Arena,* 392–3, 428–9.

44 Hatch–Billops Collection, Maude George, "Washington Intercollegiate Club of Chicago," *The Book of Achievement: The World Over Featuring the Negro in Chicago: 1779–1929,* 129.

45 Hatch–Billops Collection, Jack Cooper, "The Negro Runs Riot with the Stage," *The Book of Achievement: The World Over Featuring the Negro in Chicago: 1779–1929,* 33.

46 The Pekin was a forerunner for other black theatres: Howard in Washington, D.C. (1910), New Lincoln and Lafayette in New York (1914, 1915), Colonial in Baltimore (1916), Attucks in Norfolk, Virginia (1919). See Edward A. Robinson, "The Pekin: The Genesis of American Black Theater," *Black American Literature Forum* (Winter 1982): 136–8.

47 Flanagan, *Arena,* 134.

48 T. W. Stevens to Flanagan, January 31, 1936, Regional Reports, RG69, NA, 2.

49 Flanagan, April 30–May 6, 1936, National Office General Correspondence, RG69, NA.

50 Richard Wright, *American Hunger* (1944; New York: Harper & Row, 1977), 113–14.

51 Hatch–Billops Collection, Theodore Ward, Interview by Camille Billops, April 7, 1974, 10.

52 Ibid.

53 Harry Minturn to Hallie Flanagan, March 5, 1938, Regional Office Chronological Correspondence, RG69, NA; F. T. Lane to Shirley Graham, Regional Office Chronological Correspondence, January 22, 1938, RG69, NA.

54 LCFTP, Production Notebook, *Big White Fog,* in *Midwest Daily Record,* April 13, 1938. See also Ward's clipping file in the New York Public

Library, Lincoln Center, for further biographical information. Wright brought together in the South Side Writers' Club about twenty people for weekly meetings to read their work. Michel Fabre claims they wanted to be seen as the heirs of the Harlem Renaissance, but they were certainly a more politically committed group than the New York writers (see Michel Fabre, *The Unfinished Quest of Richard Wright,* trans. Isabel Barzun [New York: Morrow, 1973], 128). Although Wright was further to the left than most of the group, all were "as dedicated to the art of writing as Wright was himself. They were equally as strident against racism, exploitation, and oppression, and they sought to cultivate a literature that would counteract the stereotypes of blacks already prevalent" (see Addison Gayle, *Richard Wright: Ordeal of a Native Son* [New York: Anchor, 1980], 85). For another description of this group of young black writers coming of age in Chicago in the 1930s, see Margaret Walker Alexander, "Richard Wright," in *New Letters* 38.2 (December 1971): 182–202.

55 GMU, Arnold Sundgaard, Interview by John O'Connor, September 5, 1976, 27–8.

56 Hatch–Billops Collection, Theodore Ward, Interview by Camille Billops, April 7, 1976, 15. The play *Big White Fog* must be set in the context of the Great Migration, in which some dreams of freedom were fulfilled and others disappointed. See James R. Grossman, *Land of Hope: Chicago, Black Southerners and the Great Migration* (Chicago: University of Chicago Press, 1989).

57 Theodore Ward, *Big White Fog,* in James V. Hatch, ed., *Black Theater, U.S.A. Forty-Five Plays by Black Americans, 1847–1974* (New York: Free Press, 1974), 283. Subsequent quotations will be cited from this text.

58 Minturn to Flanagan, March 5, 1938, Regional Office Chronological Correspondence, RG69, NA.

59 Kathy A. Perkins, "The Unknown Career of Shirley Graham," *Freedomways* 25.1 (1985): 10. I am indebted to this article for the facts of Graham's life. There is some uncertainty about what position Graham actually held in the FTP. Perkins claims that Kondolf offered her the directorship of the Chicago Negro unit, however this is not supported by the records. Marie Merrill and Charles DeSheim headed the company, jointly, at least for a time.

60 Shirley Graham to Mrs. Harriett Gibbs Marshall, November 27, 1937; Washington Conservatory of Music Manuscript; Moorland–Spingarn Research Center, Howard University.

61 Graham to Minturn, February 5, 1938, Regional Office Chronological Correspondence, RG69, NA. Further quotations of Graham's about this episode are from this letter.

62 Minturn to J. Howard Miller, January 21, 1938, Narrative Reports, RG69, NA.

63 LCFTP, Production Notebook, *Big White Fog,* 3, 5.

64 Minturn to Miller, January 28, 1938, Narrative Reports, RG69, NA.

65 A. C. MacNeal, Executive Secretary of NAACP to Graham, January 22,

1938, Regional Office Chronological Correspondence, RG69, NA; S. B. Danley, Manager Illinois State Employment Service to Graham, January 6, 1938, Regional Office Chronological Correspondence, RG69, NA; Graham to E. Kendell Davis, January 24, 1938, Regional Office Chronological Correspondence, RG69, NA.

66 Ernest B'. Price to Minturn, February 2, 1938, Regional Office Chronological Correspondence, RG69, NA.

67 Graham to Minturn, February 5, 1938, Regional Office Chronological Correspondence, RG69, NA.

68 F. T. Lane to Graham, January 22, 1938, Regional Office Chronological Correspondence, RG69, NA.

69 Minturn to Flanagan, March 5, 1938, Regional Office Chronological Correspondence, RG69, NA.

70 Ewing had directed two other productions in the legitimate theatre unit in 1937. *Big White Fog* was her directing debut for the Negro unit.

71 GMU, Theodore Ward, Interview by Lorraine Brown, August 13, 1976, 6.

72 GMU, Leonard De Paur, Interview by Lorraine Brown, December 28, 1976, 8–10.

73 GMU, Theodore Ward, Interview by Lorraine Brown, August 13, 1976, 7.

74 Minturn to Miller, April 9, 1938, Narrative Reports, RG69, NA; Miller to Minturn, May 7, 1938, Narrative Reports, RG69, NA.

75 The reader's report on *Big White Fog,* by Converse Tyler, criticized its wordiness (as did many reviewers) and suggested that it should be cut but, with these reservations, recommended it as an "interesting social document." It is significant that there is no mention of the politically sensitive material, no reference to the "Communist" solution, nor to the bleak depiction of the black family. See LCFTP, Playreader Report, *Big White Fog,* Converse Tyler.

76 LCFTP, Production Notebook, *Big White Fog,* Paul T. Gilbert, "Race Problem Theme of *Big White Fog,*" *Herald and Examiner,* April 8, 1938, 16.

77 LCFTP, Production Notebook, *Big White Fog,* Charles Collins, the Chicago *Tribune,* April 8, 1938, 14.

78 Flanagan, *Arena,* 143.

79 LCFTP, Production Notebook, *Big White Fog,* Gail Borden, *Chicago Daily Times,* April 8, 1938, 17.

80 Minturn to Flanagan, March 5, 1938, Regional Office Chronological Correspondence, RG69, NA.

81 Minturn to Miller, May 31, 1938, Narrative Reports, RG69, NA.

82 GMU, Theodore Ward, Interview by Lorraine Brown, August 13, 1976, 8.

83 Hatch–Billops Collection, Theodore Ward, Interview by Camille Billops, April 7, 1976, 27–8.

84 GMU, Theodore Ward, Interview by Lorraine Brown, August 13, 1976, 8.

85 Hatch–Billops Collection, Theodore Ward, Interview by Camille Billops, April 7, 1976, 28.

86 GMU, Leonard De Paur, Interview by Lorraine Brown, December 28, 1976, 22.

87 Gordon, "From 'Uncle Tom's Cabin' to 'Stevedore,' " 23.
88 Doris Abramson, *Negro Playwrights in the American Theater, 1925–1959* (New York: Columbia University Press, 1969), 116. For reviews of the 1940 production, see clipping file, Theodore Ward, the Theatre Collection, New York Public Library, Lincoln Center.
89 Langston Hughes, Introduction, *Big White Fog,* in Hatch, ed., *Black Theater, U.S.A. Forty-Five Plays by Black Americans, 1847–1974,* 279–80.
90 Hazel V. Carby, *Reconstructing Womanhood: The Emergence of the Afro-American Woman Writer* (Oxford University Press, 1987), 166.

4. The Unpredictable Audience

1 James Weldon Johnson, quoted in editorial, "The Opportunity Dinner," *Opportunity* 3.30 (June 1925): 177; Sterling Brown, "Our Literary Audience," *Opportunity* 8.2 (February 1930): 61.
2 William Stahl, Conference of State Directors of the Eastern Region, April 29, 1937, General Correspondence National Office, RG69, NA, 6.
3 Hallie Flanagan, Conference of State Directors of the Eastern Region, April 19, 1937, General Correspondence National Office, RG69, NA, 6.
4 GMU, Leonard De Paur, Interview by Lorraine Brown, December 28, 1976, 12.
5 GMU, Philip Barber, Interview by Round Table, November 11, 1976, 83.
6 Hallie Flanagan, *Arena: The Story of the Federal Theatre* (1940; New York: Limelight, 1985), 279. She called Los Angeles the "clearest and least expensive plan under which we ever worked" (274).
7 LCFTP, Editorial, "The People's Theatre Grows Stronger," *Federal Theatre* 1.6 (May 1936): 6.
8 GMU, Howard Miller, Interview by Bert Holland, January 1976, 21. Miller thought the key to the lack of political controversy in Los Angeles had something to do with the Play Bureau. Run by Georgia Fink, the bureau simply wouldn't accept anything "objectionable":

> Fink was a Catholic and if a play had anything wrong with it at all, she was doubtful. She was a great woman, she had a sense of moral values. One of the reasons I think we got less criticism out here for some of our productions was that Fink rode herd on what we produced. It took her audition or a hell of an argument from my office to produce a play. Everything had to go through the play bureau and if there was objectionable material – because by this time, not true perhaps the first year, but as we got moving, we began to run into public criticism that comes as a result of it being a government theater and everybody thought they had a great stake in it. (13)

9 GMU, Irwin Rhodes, Interview by Lorraine Brown, February 26, 1977, 15.
10 A memo sent to research workers sets out the questions to the survey as follows:

1. Is this the first Federal Theatre play you have seen?
2. Do you go to the theatre often? If not why not?
3. Are you enjoying this play?
4. What kind of play do you prefer?
5. Which do you prefer plays or movies?
6. Would you like to have a permanent Federal Theatre?
7. Should the Federal Theatre charge admission? How much?
8. Criticisms and Suggestions:
   Name   Address   Occupation

In addition your review should include:

1. Critical estimate of direction, acting, scenery, lighting, costumes and make-up.
2. Concrete suggestions for improvement.
3. Analysis of audience reaction.
(LCFTP, An Inter-Play Bureau Memorandum, September 23, 1936)

11 Audience Survey, General Subject File, RG69, NA.
12 LCFTP, "The Audience Research Department: An Outline of Its Functions and Work to Date."
13 GMU, Hiram Sherman, Interview by Karen Wickre and Jean Maddox, April 18, 1978, 22.
14 Tom Pinkerton, "Report Audience Survey," National Play Bureau Audience Survey Reports, RG69, NA.
15 Audience Survey, National Service Bureau, RG69, NA, 1. Both the audience surveys for *Noah* and for *Sweet Land* include requests for musicals. See National Play Bureau, Audience Survey Reports, RG69, NA.
16 LCFTP, Cyrilla P. Lindner, Audience Survey, *Ah, Wilderness,* March 15, 1938, 6.
17 Audience Survey, National Service Bureau, RG69, NA, 2.
18 Harold Bolton to Irwin Rubenstein, General Subject File, February 25, 1938, RG69, NA.
19 James Weldon Johnson, "The Dilemma of the Negro Author," *American Mercury* 15 (December 1928): 477, 481.
20 See Thomas D. Pawley, "The Black Theatre Audience," in Errol Hill, ed., *The Theater of Black Americans II: The Presenters/The Participators* (Englewood Cliffs, NJ: Prentice-Hall, 1980), 109–19; Lawrence W. Levine, *Highbrow/Lowbrow: The Emergence of Cultural Hierarchy in America* (Cambridge, MA: Harvard University Press, 1988).
21 W. E. B. Du Bois, "The Colored Audience," *Crisis* 12.5 (September 1916): 217.
22 Randolph Edmonds, "Not Many of Your People Come Here: A Discussion of Segregation in the Theatre," *Messenger* 10.3 (March 1928): 70.
23 Langston Hughes, *The Big Sea: An Autobiography* (1940; New York: Hill & Wang, 1984), 258–9.

24 Editorial, "Do Negroes Want High Class Anything," *Messenger* 7.1 (January 1925): 21.
25 Lovett Fort-Whiteman, "Drama," *Messenger* 5.4 (April 1923): 671.
26 GMU, Carlton Moss, Interview by Lorraine Brown, August 6, 1976, 15–16.
27 LCFTP, Audience Survey, *Sweet Land; Turpentine.*
28 Audience Survey, *Sweet Land,* February 16, 1937, National Play Bureau, RG69, NA, 13.
29 Philip Barber, "The Old Year and the New," *Federal Theatre* 2.4 (April 1937): 9.
30 Regional Conference of the Eastern Region, March 2, 1938, General Correspondence National Office, RG69, NA.
31 Roi Ottley, *Amsterdam News,* Negro Press Clippings, April 18, 1936, Press Releases of the Department of Information, RG69, NA.
32 GMU, Robert Littell, "Every One Likes Chocolate," *Vogue* (November 1, 1936): 127.
33 John Houseman, *Run-Through* (New York: Simon & Schuster, 1972), 201.
34 Pierre de Rohan, *Federal Theatre* 1.6 (April 1936): 23.
35 Edward Lawson, *"Androcles and the Lion," Opportunity* 17.1 (January 1939): 15.
36 GMU, Edward Dudley, Jr., Interview by Lorraine Brown, October 27, 1977, 7.
37 Dutton Ferguson to Edward Lawson, February 7, 1939, Press Releases of Department of Information, RG69, NA.
38 Lawson, *"Androcles and the Lion,"* 15.
39 Flanagan to Elmer Anderson Carter, January 27, 1939, WPA Central Files, 211.2 (Drama), NA.
40 "Lafayette Incident Rebuke to Cultural Pride of Community," Press Releases of Department of Information, RG69, NA.
41 LCFTP, Playreading Report, *Turpentine,* October 22, 1936, Spiegel; March 30, 1937, Kuttner; April 3, 1937, Ayres.
42 LCFTP, Playreading Report, *Brother Mose,* William H. J. Ely to Kate Lawson, April 7, 1936.
43 LCFTP, Playreading Reports, *The Trial of Dr. Beck,* June 29, 1937, Converse Tyler; May 25, 1937, Byrne; May 3, 1937, Abel Plenn.
44 Emmet Lavery to Roy Wilkins, April 14, 1939, General Correspondence National Office, RG69, NA; Emmet Lavery to Hallie Flanagan, March 28, 1939, General Correspondence National Office, RG69, NA. It seems that Cohen was popular with other Negro companies – with the actors, though not with black script readers. In the same letter from Lavery to Flanagan, Lavery reports that objections by a "very good Negro reader in the Bureau [National Service Bureau]" had been made in Hartford over another Cohen play, *Scarlet Sister Mary,* "but once again the acting company involved seemed to like the play very much."
45 Emmet Lavery to Roy Wilkins, April 14, 1939, General Correspondence National Office, RG69, NA.

46 Roy Wilkins to Emmet Lavery, April 15, 1939, General Correspondence National Office, RG69, NA.

47 " 'Brother Mose' Proves Hit as Hudson WPA Production," *Dispatch,* May 5, 1937, Vassar College Collection of Press Clippings, RG69, NA.

48 LCFTP, "Negro Drama at Empire Records Hit This Week," *Salem Evening News,* March 29, 1938.

49 LCFTP, Production Notebook, Ralf Coleman, *Brother Mose,* 3.

50 LCFTP, Ralf Coleman, Audio Tape, November 21, 1975.

51 Hatch–Billops Collection, Ralf Coleman, Interview by Paula Singer, November 24, 1972, 14, 2–3, 9.

52 LCFTP, Ralf Coleman, Audio Tape, November 21, 1975.

53 Edward Lawson, November 21, 1936, Press Releases of Department of Information, RG69, NA.

54 Hatch–Billops Collection, Ralf Coleman, Interview by Paula Singer, November 24, 1972, 11.

55 Edward Lawson, November 21, 1936, Press Releases of Department of Information, RG69, NA.

56 Leonard L. Gallagher to Hallie Flanagan, November 28, 1936, General Correspondence National Office, RG69, NA. "The Negro group have been rehearsing this play and they are very anxious to produce it. I have seen several good rehearsals and I am sure they will give a very amusing performance. It is entirely different from anything they have done up here and it is their desire to keep away from Negro folk lore plays."

57 Hiram Motherwell to Flanagan, December 2, 1936, WPA Central Files, 211.2 (Drama), NA.

58 Hatch–Billops Collection, Ralf Coleman, Interview by Paula Singer, November 24, 1972, 21–2, 11, 10.

59 Theophilus Lewis, "Theatre," *Messenger* 6.12 (December 1924): 380.

60 Lewis, "Theatre," *Messenger* 6.9 (September 1924): 291.

5. Acting Properly

1 W. S. Gilbert and Arthur Sullivan, *Authentic Libretti of the Gilbert and Sullivan Operas* (New York: Bass, 1935).

2 Eugene O'Neill, "Eugene O'Neill on the Negro Actor," *Messenger* 7.1 (January 1925): 17.

3 W. E. B. Du Bois, "The Drama Among Black Folk," *Crisis* 12.4 (August 1916): 169.

4 Alain Locke, "The Negro and the American Stage," *Theatre Arts Monthly* 10.2 (February 1926): 112, 113, 116.

5 Theophilus Lewis, "Same Old Blues," *Messenger* 7.1 (January 1925): 15, 62.

6 Lewis, "The Theater," *Messenger* 8.9 (September 1926): 279; Lewis, "Same Old Blues," 15.

7 The two actors could not have been more different. Gilpin had spent a lifetime in the theatre; Robeson had accidently fallen into a role. In 1896, Gilpin had joined the Perkus and Davis Great Southern Minstrel Barn

Storming Aggregation, and when it went bankrupt he joined the Gilmore Canadian Jubilee Singers in 1903; in 1905, he acted with the Williams and Walker Company and then joined the Pekin Players in Chicago. After that he played vaudeville in the South. In between his work in the theatre, he was a printer, barber, and Pullman porter. And the story goes that he was an elevator man at Macy's when he was tapped to perform in *Emperor Jones*. See "Men of the Month," *Crisis* 21.4 (February 1921): 171–2, and Paul Robeson, "Reflections on O'Neill's Plays," *Opportunity* 2.24 (December 1924): 368.

8   Lewis, "The Theater," *Messenger* 8.11 (November 1926): 334.
9   Arthur Gelb and Barbara Gelb, *O'Neill* (New York: Harper, 1962), 449.
10   GMU, Carlton Moss, Interview by Lorraine Brown, August 6, 1976, 44–5.
11   Hallie Flanagan wrote that she was glad that she had kept the Seattle Negro unit open:

> Now that company has improved and what morale Ed O'Connor has built up. There is a sense of things happening, plays being written, a crowded schedule, with the negro company just closing in *Mississippi Rainbow,* reviving *Dunbar* for me, and playing this afternoon to their usual crowded Saturday matinee in *Little Black Sambo.*
>
> However, the weakness, here, as elsewhere, is standard. "Man is changed by his living but not fast enough." These actors, most of them tough old professionals, trained in vaudeville and tab shows, need retraining in diction, voice, movement. Sambo and Dunbar both need speed, fresh costumes, a better staging. As usual our small projects haven't enough other-than-labor money. (Flanagan to Miller, February 25, 1939, WPA Central Files, 211.2 (Drama), NA, 2)

12   Regional Conference of the Eastern Region, March 2, 1938, General Correspondence National Office, RG69, NA.
13   Gilmor Brown to Hallie Flanagan, February 20, 1936, Regional Correspondence, RG69, NA.
14   GMU, Esther Porter Lane, Interview by John O'Conner and Karen Wickre, n.d., 23.
15   Los Angeles was the second largest project with 1,530 people employed at one point, including 545 actors, six theaters in Los Angeles, with nine different units in Los Angeles alone – modern, vaudeville, Yiddish, education, Negro, experimental, religious, marionnette, and children's theaters. See GMU, *Citizen News,* August 21, 1936, J. Howard Miller Collection.
16   GMU, Dale Wasserman, Interview by Mae Mallory Krulak, May 30, 1976, 27–8.
17   LCFTP, "Gilmor Brown Starts 9 Federal Theater Projects."
18   GMU, Max Pollock, Interview by Lorraine Brown, March 8, 1976, 4–6.
19   Carl Combs, "Negro Project Players Transfer 'Macbeth' to Voodoo Land at Mayan," *Citizen News,* July 17, 1937, Vassar College Collection Press Clippings, RG69, NA; LCFTP, Audience Survey, *Macbeth,* August 1937.
20   W. E. Oliver, "Uncle Sam's Players Turned 'Macbeth' into Witch Party,"

Express, July 15, 1937, Vassar College Collection Press Clippings, RG69, NA.

21 LCFTP, Audience Survey, *Macbeth,* August 1937.

22 Some teachers did not like the unconventional rendition according to audience surveys taken at the Greek Theatre performance. "Play not suited to negro cast. It is too 'highbrow' for negroes" – (A drama teacher). "It was not a Shakespearean production" – (A director of a College Theatre). "I do not like this type of play – do not like negro actors" – (A teacher). See LCFTP, Audience Survey, Cyrilla Lindner, *Macbeth,* Greek Theatre, Los Angeles.

23 "Federal Players Here Call Mass Demand for More Jobs," April 22, 1938, Press Releases of Department of Information, RG69, NA.

24 The longest run of any production on the Los Angeles Negro unit before *Run, Little Chillun* was *Black Empire,* which ran 48 nights; by 1939, *Run, Little Chillun* played for 181 performances.

25 M. R. Glenn to Mr. Dutton Ferguson, June 28, 1939, Press Releases of Department of Information, RG69, NA.

26 In conversations with the author, both James Hatch and Lorraine Brown, who interviewed Muse, mentioned how impossible it was to get a word in edgewise.

27 GMU, Clarence Muse, Interview by Lorraine Brown, n.d., 6–7.

28 Ibid., 7.

29 LCFTP, Production Notebook, *Run, Little Chillun,* Clarence Muse, Director's Report, 5–6.

30 LCFTP, Production Notebook, *Run, Little Chillun,* review, *California Eagle,* July 28, 1938, 32–35. The same point is made in the *Metropolitan Press* with the contrast to *Porgy and Bess:* " 'Run, Little Chillun' " is in form somewhat like 'Porgy and Bess,' but the latter was a white man's idea of the Negro, while the former is a colored man's own conception." See LCFTP, Production Notebook, *Run, Little Chillun,* 36.

31 LCFTP, Production Notebook, *Run, Little Chillun, Daily News,* July 23, 1938, 37–8; *Saturday Night,* August 13, 1938, 45; *Jewish Community Press,* July 29, 1938, 48.

32 LCFTP, Production Notebook, *Run, Little Chillun,* 54.

33 See Houston A. Baker, Jr., *Modernism and the Harlem Renaissance* (Chicago: University of Chicago Press, 1987), 15–47.

34 Allen Woll, *Black Musical Theatre: From Coontown to Dreamgirls* (Baton Rouge: Louisiana State University Press, 1989), 179; Minturn to Flanagan, December 28, 1938, Correspondence with State FTP Officials, RG69, NA.

35 Woll, *Black Musical Theatre,* 178.

36 Nathan Huggins, *Harlem Renaissance* (New York: Oxford University Press, 1971), 278.

37 Leslie Baily, *The Gilbert and Sullivan Book* (London: Spring Books, 1952), 418–19.

38 It was said of Minturn that he was "only good in his own special field, which is that of stock direction. Even here, he has to work entirely in his

own way. After a long period of friction, I have had to take Helen Dupee off his project as he seems very unhappy when any method other than his own is suggested, even for promotional purposes. This does not mean that he is not doing a fine job at the Blackstone Theatre where the business is steadily building" (Thomas Wood Stevens to Flanagan, April 14, 1936, WPA Central Files, 211.2 (Drama), NA). After the demise of the FTP, Minturn would help organize a Negro Light Opera Company with members from the *Swing Mikado* cast. See Correspondence of National Office with FTP Personnel, RG69, NA.

39 LCFTP, Production Notebook, *Swing Mikado,* 66.

40 Ibid., Nahum Daniel Brascher, "The Mikado," Chicago *Defender,* October 1, 1938, 55.

41 "Narrative Report of Events Leading to Dismissal of John McGee as Regional and State Director of Federal Theatre Project," General Correspondence National Office, RG69, NA.

42 LCFTP, Production Notebook, *Swing Mikado,* Nahum Daniel Brascher, "The Mikado," Chicago *Defender,* October 1, 1938, 54; Claudia Cassidy, "The Mikado," *Journal of Commerce,* September 26, 1938, 49.

43 "Report of Meeting Called by Mr. Minturn," December 5, 1938, General Correspondence National Office, RG69, NA.

44 LCFTP, Production Notebook, *Swing Mikado,* Lloyd Lewis, "Mikado Malayed," *Chicago Daily News,* September 26, 1938, 40.

45 Hallie Flanagan, February 9, 1939, General Correspondence National Office, RG69, NA.

46 LCFTP, Production Notebook, *Swing Mikado,* Ben Burns, "WPA Negro Unit Swings *The Mikado,*" *Daily Record,* September 27, 1938, 51.

47 Flanagan to Minturn, January 4, 1939, WPA Central Files, 211.2 (Drama), NA.

48 Minturn to Flanagan, December 28, 1938, Correspondence with State FTP Officials, RG69, NA. He goes on:

> There are other considerations which are important in connection with any proposed private production of the *Mikado*. In the first place, a private producer may so change and re-arrange the production and, for the sake of economy, may so reduce the size of the cast, that a production in New York City may be as much a failure as it has been a success in Chicago. If the production in New York City is to be with some of the people who are used by the Federal Theatre in Chicago, and the production in New York proves to be a failure, then much of the value of the public acclaim which has been given this production in Chicago will be lost. Further, there is a great difference in the public reaction to plays in New York as compared to Chicago as is evidenced by the recent showing of *Prologue to Glory*. This play, a great success in New York City, was a financial failure in Chicago. The same may well be true of the *Mikado,* particularly if it is changed to meet the needs of a private producer.

49 "Dismissal of John McGee," General Correspondence National Office, RG69, NA.

50 "Report of Meeting Called by Mr. Harry Minturn," General Correspondence National Office, RG69, NA.

51 See Stephen M. Vallillo, "The Battle of the Black *Mikados*," *Black American Literature Forum* (Winter 1982): 154.

52 Joseph Boskin, *Sambo: The Rise and Demise of an American Jester* (Oxford University Press, 1986), 169.

53 Huggins, *Harlem Renaissance*, 262.

Afterword

1 Quoted in Theodore Kornweibel, Jr., *No Crystal Stair: Black Life and the Messenger, 1917–1928* (Westport CT: Greenwood, 1975), 275; Richard Schechner, "Intercultural Themes," in Bonnie Marranca and Gautam Dasgupta, eds., *Interculturalism and Performance* (New York: PAJ Publications, 1991), 309.

2 GMU, Leonard De Paur, Interview by Lorraine Brown, December 2, 1976, 38.

3 Anne Cooke, "Third Moscow Theatre Festival," *Opportunity* 14.2 (February 1936): 59.

4 GMU, Thomas Anderson, Interview by Lorraine Brown, May 24, 1978, 10.

5 Cecelia Cabaniss Saunders to Hallie Flanagan, August 2, 1938, Correspondence of Hallie Flanagan, RG69, NA.

6 Prepared by the Negro Arts Committee Federal Arts Council, a committee endorsed by the Brotherhood of Sleeping Car porters, the NAACP, the International Workers Order, the National Negro Congress, the Theatre Arts Committe, the Urban League of New York, Alain Locke, and Miss Ernestine Rose, the librarian at the 135th St. branch of the New York City Library; see "The Negro and Federal Project No. I for New York City," 1939, General Correspondence National Office, RG69, NA.

This was not the only attempt to force the FTP into hiring black supervisors. In 1939, a group of black administrators wrote to Colonel F. C. Harrington, the administrator of the WPA in New York, protesting the relatively few blacks connected to the state administrations. There were no black women in Washington above the status of secretary, few clerical workers, even fewer professional employees connected to the state administrations; as well there was little opportunity for skilled employment on construction projects or for foremen and supervisors. Further, since there was no operating race relations unit, any complaints made against administrators were reviewed by them, clearly not an arrangement conducive to bringing suits. They asked for a committee to be empowered to look after the demands and needs of blacks and to form a race relations unit that would handle complaints and urge minority hiring; see letters from Alfred Smith, Employment Division; T. Arnold Hill, Professional and Service

Division; James A. Atkins, Specialist Education Among Negroes, Division of Education; Sterling Brown, Editor, Negro Affairs, Federal Writers' Project; Dutton Ferguson, Special Assistant Information Service; Eugene Holmes, Federal Writers' Project; John W. Whitten, Former Junior Race Relations Officer, Employment Division, to Colonel F. C. Harrington, June 23, 1939, Department of Information, Negro Press Correspondence, RG69, NA.

7   Flanagan to Charles Taylor, December 22, 1938, Correspondence of Hallie Flanagan, RG69, NA; Taylor to Flanagan, December 27, 1938, Correspondence of Hallie Flanagan, RG69, NA.

8   Paul Carter Harrison, "The (R)evolution of Black Theatre," *American Theatre* 6.7 (October 1987): 31.

9   Larry Neal, "The Black Arts Movement," *Drama Review* 12.4 (Summer 1968): 29.

10   Ibid., 39.

11   Interview, "August Wilson's America: A Conversation with Bill Moyers," *American Theatre* 6.3 (June 1989): 16–17.

12   Ibid., 56.

13   Lindsay Patterson, "Black Theatre: The Search Goes On," in Errol Hill, ed., *The Theater of Black Americans II: The Presenters/The Participators* (Englewood Cliffs, NJ: Prentice-Hall, 1980), 148, 152.

14   Harry Newman, "Holding Back: The Theatre's Resistance to Non-Traditional Casting," *Drama Review* 33 (Fall 1989): 23.

15   Richard Hornby, "Interracial Casting," *Hudson Review* 42.3 (Autumn 1989): 460.

16   Frank Lentricchia, *Criticism and Social Change* (Chicago: University of Chicago Press, 1978), 16.

17   Ibid., 161.

18   Schechner, "Intercultural Themes," 313, 308.

19   Diana Taylor, "Transculturating Transculturalism," in Marranca and Dasgupta, eds., *Interculturalism and Performance,* 72.

Index

Abbey Theatre, 33, 35, 49, 60
Actors' Equity, 31, 203, 213n.55
African Grove Theatre, 56, 59, 141
Aldridge, Ira, 56, 175
Allen, Robert C., 31, 32
All God's Chillun Got Wings, 11
Allison, Hughes, 108, 110, 158; *see also*
    Trial of Dr. Beck, The and *Panyared*
American National Theater, xi, 5, 10,
    44–5, 49, 212n.32
Androcles and the Lion, 100, 152, 155, 179;
    photograph of, 142
Apollo Theatre, 50, 71–2
Atkinson, Brooks, 44
audience surveys, 142, 144–6, 151, 166,
    167, 179, 230–31n.10
authenticity, 5, 10–16, 20, 50, 186, 194–5,
    203, 209n.23
Awkward, Michael, 9

Baker, George Pierce, 30, 34, 65, 219n.37;
    see also Drama 47 Workshop
Baker, Houston A., Jr., 19–20, 186
Barber, Philip, 30, 43, 98, 99, 108, 143,
    151–52, 226n.41
Bernstein, Barton, 23
Big White Fog, xv, 89, 91, 94, 100, 151,
    168, 179, 182, 183, 195, 201; booking
    of, 120–1, 125, 127, 128; communism
    and, 133–4; community responses
    and, 122–6; Du Bois and, 120; Kay
    Ewing and, 122, 127; Flanagan on,
    130, 132; Shirley Graham and, 122–4,

127, 129; Langston Hughes on, 134;
Hal Kopel and, 124; New York pro-
    duction of, 133; photographs of, 92–3;
    plot of, 117–26; reviews of, 129–31;
South side production of, 131–3; *see*
    also Ward, Theodore
black arts movement, 16, 200
Black Empire, 170, 179; photograph of, 172
blackface, *see* minstrelsy
black journalism, 223n.75
Black Souls, 226–7n.41
the black syndicate, 58
Bledsoe, Jules, 148–9, 155
Boskin, Joseph, 195
Brer Rabbit, 177–8, 183
Broadway, 6, 31, 17, 58, 59, 75, 203
Brother Mose, 160–1
Brown, Gilmor, 31
Brown, Lorraine, xii
Brown, Maurice, 33
Brown, Sterling, 61, 62, 104, 136
Browne, Theodore, 177
Burke, Kenneth, 1, 18, 203
Bush, Anita, 58

Carby, Hazel, 50
Carolina Players, 86, 101, 217n.24
Chicago *Defender,* 52, 111
Chicago Little Theatre, 33
City Projects Council, 99
Civil Rights Movement, 200
Clark, Maurice, 7
Cohen, Octavus Roy, 159

239

Coleman, Ralf, 160, 162–5, 183
color-blind casting, 203
Come Seven, 159–60
communism and the theatre, 196, 219*n*.43
community theatre, *see* noncommercial
    theatre
Conjure Man Dies, 98, 156, 197
Cooke, Anne, 61
Crisis, 51, 53, 70; *see also* Du Bois, W. E. B.
cultural politics, 9, 11, 15, 18; "the people"
    and, 12, 14, 16, 27, 136; racial identity
    and, 204–5, 207*n*.1, 208*n*.13

De Paur, Leonard, 44, 88, 106, 109–10,
    128, 133, 141, 196–7, 224*n*.9
De Sheim, Charles, 113–15
Did Adam Sin, 112
Dies Committee on Un-American Activi-
    ties, *see* Negro units of the Federal
    Theatre Project
Douglass, Frederick, *see* minstrelsy
Drama 47 workshop, 30, 31, 33, 86
Du Bois, W. E. B., xv, 8, 12, 53, 54,
    218*n*.33; actors and, 173; African cul-
    ture and, 80; art and propaganda and,
    64–5, 94, 134; black audiences and,
    147, 149; black theatre and, 62, 198;
    Crisis and, 51, 85; essentialism and,
    10, 12, 14; Ethiopianism and, 82, 84,
    219*n*.38; folk and, 83; KRIGWA and,
    67–8, 70, 75; minstrelsy and, 57;
    NAACP and, 85; national separatism
    and, 6, 8; *The New Negro* and, 63–4;
    noncommercial theatre and, 6, 202;
    pageants and, 65–7; "talented tenth"
    and, 14, 15

Edmunds, Randolph, 148–9
Edward, Harry, 97–9
Emperor Jones, 11, 15, 59, 101, 148–50,
    155, 176
Ethiopia, 41
Ethiopianism, 66, 70; *see also* Du Bois,
    W. E. B.; Randolph, A. Philip; and
    Owen, Chandler
Ethiopian Players, 60
Everyman, 113

Federal Arts Projects, xv, 10; cultural poli-
    cies of, 2, 21–2, 24; organization of, 1,
    25–6; popular art and, 27, 42
Federal Theatre Project, 3; audience sur-
    veys of, xiii, 5; budget of, 1, 2; com-
    munism and, 42, 196; culture and, 34;
    federalism and, 35; New York City
    units of, 41, 43; oral interviews of, xii,
    xiii; regionalism and, 38–9; structure
    of, 2–4, 7, 198, 213*n*.55, 230*n*.8;
    vaudeville and, 208*n*.5; Yiddish unit
    of, 178; *see also* Negro units of the Fed-
    eral Theatre Project
Ferber, Edna, 59
Fisher, Rudolph, 98
Fisk Jubilee Choir, 50
Flanagan, Hallie, 12, 202; audiences and,
    37–8, 152; biography of, 29–31; cul-
    ture of "the people" and, 23, 36, 39,
    140; Negro units and, 45, 96, 156,
    191, 226*n*.41; noncommercial theatre
    and, 33, 37, 42, 60; politics and, 3, 6,
    13, 36, 40; relationship to black com-
    munity and, xiv, xv, 45–6
the folk, 40, 83; *see also* Du Bois, W. E. B.;
    Johnson, Charles; Lewis, Theophilus;
    Locke, Alain; Negro units of the Fed-
    eral Theatre Project; Owen, Chandler;
    and Randolph, A. Philip
Fort-Whitman, Lovett, 150–1

Gates, Henry Louis, Jr., 9
George Mason University, xi,xii
Gilbert, W. S., 187–8
Gilpin, Charles, 59, 104, 171, 175, 176,
    233–4*n*.7
Gilpin Players, 58
Gilroy, Paul, 9
Gold in the Hills, 163
Graham, Otis, 23
Graham, Shirley, 59, 121, 122; *see also* Ne-
    gro units of the Federal Theatre Proj-
    ect, Chicago unit
Gramsci, Antonio, 18
Great Migration, 52, 134–5
Green Pastures, 116, 163, 176
Green, Paul, 17, 59, 100, 104, 162,
    217*n*.24; *In Abraham's Bosom,* 101–3,

164, 225*n*.23; response of black critics to, 101–3

Gregory, Montgomery, 86, 101

Grinnell College, 29, 30

Haiti, 7, 156; photograph of, cover and p. vi

Hall, Stuart, 12, 13

Harlem Cultural Committee, 159

Harlem Renaissance, 10, 15, 83, 85, 201, 202

Harrison, Paul Carter, 200

Hayes, Roland, 80

hegemony, 16–20

Held, David, 12, 13

Hill, Abram, 106

Hopkins, Harry, xv, 2, 13, 23, 152, 191, 192; on censorship, 40; on culture, 23, 27, 202; social work and, 26, 211*n*.14; *Spending to Save,* 27

Hot Mikado, 194; *see also Swing Mikado*

Houseman, John, 3, 96–8, 100, 153, 154, 197, 224*n*.9

Howard Players, 86

Huggins, Nathan, 188, 195

Hughes, Langston, 81, 105, 148–9, 221–2*n*.70; *see also Big White Fog*

hybridization, xvi, 9, 10, 205–6

Hymn to the Rising Sun, 89, 113, 114, 116; photograph of, 91

Ickes, Harold, 25

In Black America, 188

Intercollegiate Association, 86

It Can't Happen Here, 144, 177

James, Burton, 177–8

James, Florence, 177–8

jazz, *see* Johnson, Charles

Jericho, 162

Johnson, Charles, xv, 12, 54, 94, 152, 201, 222*n*.71; the folk and, 83; Langston Hughes and, 81; on ideas of culture, 81–4; on jazz, 83, 223*n*.76; on literature, 51, 75–6; on national identity, 82; *Opportunity* and, 51; George Schuyler and, 81; stereotypes and, 81

Johnson, Hall, xvi, 169, 181; *see also Run, Little Chillun*

Johnson, James Weldon, 51, 57, 136, 147, 165

Jones, Alfred Haworth, 35

Kennedy, Adrienne, 202

Koch, Frederick, 31, 34, 86, 101, 217*n*.24

Kondolf, George, 121

Kruger, Loren, 43

Lafayette Players, 58, 179, 181

Lafayette Theater, 4, 58, 72, 183, 197, 224*n*.7

Lavery, Emmett, 107, 159–60

Lee, Spike, 84

Lentricchia, Frank, 17, 203–4

Levine, Lawrence, 31, 147

Lewis, Theophilus, 51, 53, 54, 167, 203; on actors, 175, 176; on audience, 75, 166; on the folk, 83; on KRIGWA, 70–1; on noncommercial black theatre, 74–5, 104, 166; on popular theatre, 72–3

liberal rhetoric, 21, 22, 23

Liberty Deferred, 89, 106–8, 201; *see also* Hill, Abram, and Silvera, John

Lincoln Theatre, 58, 72–3, 149

Little Black Sambo, 177

little theatres, *see* noncommercial theatre

Locke, Alain, 49, 53, 134, 152, 201, 220–1*n*.63; on actors, 154, 173–5; on Africa, 80, 85; on the arts, 51, 94; commercialism and, 86, 223*n*.76; on communism, 89; Federal Theatre Project and, 87; folk plays and, 88–9, 173; Intercollegiate Association and, 71; modernism and, 70, 80; the natural and, 70; noncommerical theatre and, 86; the primitive and, 15, 76, 80, 85; separatism and, 80; social realism and, 85, 222*n*.75; university theatres and, 86; *see also* Du Bois, W. E. B.

Los Angeles Art Festival, 206

Los Angeles Theatre Center, 206

Lysistrata, 177

Mabie, E. C., 31, 34

Macbeth, 4, 16, 98, 152–4, 170, 175, 179, 191; photographs of, 141, 171

McClendon, Rose, 3, 89, 96–7, 162, 224–5*n*.11
McGee, John, 189, 192
Mathews, Jane De Hart, 50
Merrill, Marie, 113
Messenger, 51, 53, 68, 70, 85
middle-class theatre, 136
The Mikado, 168, 187–9
Miller, Claude, 179
Miller, Howard, 35, 43, 144, 180
minstrelsy, 5, 8, 52, 54, 175, 216–7*n*.17; Frederick Douglass and, 57; in the nineteenth century, 56–8, 216*n*.16
Minturn, Harry, 120, 122, 189, 235–6*n*.38
Moley, Raymond, 26
Moscow Art Theatre, 33, 35, 49, 59
Moss, Carlton, 96, 97, 98, 108, 158, 176–7
Motts, Robert T., 111
movies, 33, 34
Mumford, Lewis, 24
Muse, Clarence, 162, 169, 181, 183–4

National Archives, xii
National Association for the Advancement of Colored People (NAACP), 25, 52, 53, 222*n*.71; *see also* Du Bois, W. E. B.
National Ethiopian Art Theatre, 70, 74
National Negro Theatre, 5–8, 10, 20, 46, 49, 54–6, 60–2, 94, 100, 167
Natural Man, 177, 179; *see also* Theodore Browne
Neal, Larry, 200–1
Negro Arts Committee, 198–9, 237*n*.6
Negro Dramatists Laboratory, 105
Negro units of the Federal Theatre Project, xi, xii, 3, 4, 5, 19, 22, 35, 48, 87; actors in, 154, 160, 168, 170–1, 180–1, 186, 189, 191–3; audiences of, 4, 5, 8, 136–8, 141–3, 145, 147, 150, 152, 155, 164, 165–7, 203; Boston unit of, 160, 162–5; Chicago unit of, 7, 17, 59, 94, 111, 187–95; choosing directors of, 93–7; choosing plays of, 48; cultural politics of, 62, 94–5; development of playwrights and, 104–10; Dies Committee on Un-American Activities and, 42, 199; first idea of, xvi, xv; folk plays of, 163, 165; Harlem unit of, 16, 95–8, 155, 196–9; hiring and, 25, 237–8*n*.6; Los Angeles unit

of, 153, 145–6, 178–82, 234*n*.15; minstrelsy and, 58–9; New Jersey units of, 157, 158–61; noncommercial theatre and, 33, 47, 49, 59, 74–5, 86; photographs of, 137, 138; playreaders and, 156–60, 226*n*.36; Seattle unit of, 177–8, 181, 234*n*.11; theatrical stereotypes and, 94; vaudeville and, 177; Richard Wright and, 113–15
New Deal, 1, 8, 17, 23
New Negro, xv, 16, 53, 62–4, 84
New York City, 33
Nigger, 59
Noah, 177, 179
noncommercial theatre, 31, 32, 34, 88; *see also* Du Bois, W. E. B.; Flanagan, Hallie; Lewis, Theophilus; Locke, Alain; and Negro units of the Federal Theatre Project
Norton Anthology of African American Literature, 84

O'Connor, John, xii
O'Neil, Raymond, 60
O'Neill, Eugene, 11, 59, 100–1, 104–5, 149, 164, 171–2, 176
Opportunity, 51, 53, 70, 85
Owen, Chandler, 51, 54, 68, 85, 219*n*.43; Ethiopianism and, 70; folk and, 83; race and, 69; uplift and, 69

pageants, 42, 219*n*.37; *see also* Du Bois, W. E. B.
Panyared, 89, 108–10, 112; *see also* Allison, Hughes
Pekin Theatre, 58, 111
Pells, Richard, 42
Perkins, Kathy A., 121
Perry, Edward, 97
Peters, Paul, 88
Poggi, Jack, 32
Pollock, Max, 179
Popular Front, xv
Porgy and Bess, 59
postmodern, xvi, 10
Provincetown Players, 33

racial uplift, 8, 62
Randolph, A. Philip, 51, 54, 68, 82, 85,

196, 199–200, 219*n*.43; Ethiopianism and, 70; folk and, 83; race and, 69; uplift and, 69
resident stock company, 32
Rhodes, Irwin, 43
Rice, Elmer, 34, 41, 43
Robeson, Paul, 59, 104, 175, 176
Rogin, Michael, 7
Roll, Sweet Chariot, 101, 162
Romey and Julie, 113
Roosevelt, Franklin Delano, 17, 22, 27, 35
Run, Little Chillun, xvi, 168, 169, 179, 181, 182, 191, 195; photographs of, 169, 170; plot of, 184; reviews of, 185–6

Schechner, Richard, 196, 205
Schlesinger, Arthur, 22, 25
Schubert Theatres, 33
Schuyler, George, 51, 53, 54, 81, 82, 221–2*n*.70
Sellars, Peter, 206
Shakespeare, William, 4, 34, 49, 56, 104, 154, 155, 175, 179, 197
Shange, Ntozake, 202
Shaw, George Bernard, 4, 100
Sheldon, Edward, 59
Showboat, 59
Silvera, John, 106
Sing For Your Supper, 43
Sklar, George, 88
slave narratives, 50
Smith, Gus, 98, 99
social realism, 15
South Side Writers' Club, 115, 116, 228*n*.54
Stevedore, 88, 89, 163, 164; photograph of, 90
Stott, William, 13
Sullivan, Arthur, 187
Sundgaard, Arnold, 116
Susman, Warren, 21, 24
Sweet Land, 89, 100, 118, 151, 156, 201; photograph of, 90

Swing Mikado, xvi, 4, 168, 170, 187–95, 197, 236*n*.48; photographs of, 139, 140, 173, 174; reviews of, 190–1; *see also Hot Mikado* and *The Mikado*

Theatre Union, 88
Torrence, Ridgely, 59
Trial of Dr. Beck, The, 108, 110, 158–60
Turpentine, 89, 98, 106, 118, 151, 152, 156–7, 179, 197, 201

university theatre, *see* noncommercial theatre
Urban League, 51, 52, 222*n*.71

vaudeville, *see* Federal Theatre Project and Negro units of the Federal Theatre Project
voodoo *Macbeth, see Macbeth*

Walker, George, 51, 58, 175
Walk Together, Chillun, 98, 151, 152, 160
Ward, Theodore, xv, 94, 100, 115, 135; life of, 116–17; *see also Big White Fog*
Wasserman, Dale, 178
Welles, Orson, 97, 153, 154, 197
West, Cornel, 9, 84–5
Wilkins, Roy, 160
Williams, Bert, 57, 58, 175, 176
Williams, Raymond, 18, 210*n*.27
Wilson, August, 201–2
Wilson, Frank, 98, 160, 161, 162
Wolfe, George C., 202
working-class theatre, 88
Works Progress Administration, 1, 26
Wright, Richard, 17, 116, 135, 223*n*.74; *see also* Negro units of the Federal Theatre Project

Yiddish theatre, 7, 54

Zorn, George, 105

Continued from the front of book

64. Elisa New, *The Regenerate Lyric: Theology and Innovation in American Poetry*

63. Edwin S. Redkey, *A Grand Army of Black Men: Letters from African-American Soldiers in the Union Army, 1861–1865*

62. Victoria Harrison, *Elizabeth Bishop's Poetics of Intimacy*

61. Edwin Sill Fussell, *The Catholic Side of Henry James*

60. Thomas Gustafson, *Representative Words: Politics, Literature, and the American Language, 1776–1865*

59. Peter Quartermain, *Disjunctive Poetics: From Gertrude Stein and Louis Zukovsky to Susan Howe*

58. Paul Giles, *American Catholic Arts and Fictions: Culture, Ideology, Aesthetics*

57. Ann-Janine Morey, *Religion and Sexuality in American Literature*

56. Philip M. Weinstein, *Faulkner's Subject: A Cosmos No One Owns*

55. Stephen Fender, *Sea Changes: British Emigration and American Literature*

54. Peter Stoneley, *Mark Twain and the Feminine Aesthetic*

53. Joel Porte, *In Respect to Egotism: Studies in American Romantic Writing*

52. Charles Swann, *Nathaniel Hawthorne: Tradition and Revolution*

51. Ronald Bush (ed.), *T. S. Eliot: The Modernist in History*

50. Russell Goodman, *American Philosophy and the Romantic Tradition*

49. Eric J. Sundquist (ed.), *Frederick Douglass: New Literary and Historical Essays*

48. Susan Stanford Friedman, *Penelope's Web: Gender, Modernity, H.D.'s Fiction*

47. Timothy Redman, *Ezra Pound and Italian Fascism*

46. Ezra Greenspan, *Walt Whitman and the American Reader*

45. Michael Oriard, *Sporting with the Gods: The Rhetoric of Play and Game in American Culture*

44. Stephen Fredman, *Poet's Prose: The Crisis in American Verse, Second Edition*

43. David C. Miller, *Dark Eden: The Swamp in Nineteenth-Century American Culture*

42. Susan K. Harris, *19th-Century American Women's Novels: Interpretive Strategies*

41. Susan Manning, *The Puritan-Provincial Vision: Scottish and American Literature in the Nineteenth Century*

40. Richard Godden, *Fictions of Capital: Essays on the American Novel from James to Mailer*

39. John Limon, *The Place of Fiction in the Time of Science: A Disciplinary History of American Writing*

38. Douglas Anderson, *A House Undivided: Domesticity and Community in American Literature*

37. Charles Altieri, *Painterly Abstraction in Modernist American Poetry*

36. John P. McWilliams, Jr., *The American Epic: Transforming a Genre, 1770–1860*

35. Michael Davidson, *The San Francisco Renaissance: Poetics and Community at Mid-Century*

34. Eric Sigg, *The American T. S. Eliot: A Study of the Early Writings*

33. Robert S. Levine, *Conspiracy and Romance: Studies in Brockden Brown, Cooper, Hawthorne, and Melville*

32. Alfred Habegger, *Henry James and the "Woman Business"*

31. Tony Tanner, *Scenes of Nature, Signs of Man*

30. David Halliburton, *The Color of the Sky: A Study of Stephen Crane*

29. Steven Gould Axelrod and Helen Deese (eds.), *Robert Lowell: Essays on the Poetry*

28. Robert Lawson-Peebles, *Landscape and Written Expression in Revolutionary America: The World Turned Upside Down*

27. Warren Motley, *The American Abraham: James Fenimore Cooper and the Frontier Patriarch*

26. Lyn Keller, *Re-making It New: Contemporary American Poetry and the Modernist Tradition*

25. Margaret Holley, *The Poetry of Marianne Moore: A Study in Voice and Value*

24. Lothar Hönnighausen, *William Faulkner: The Art of Stylization in His Early Graphic and Literary Work*

23. George Dekker, *The American Historical Romance*

22. Brenda Murphy, *American Realism and American Drama, 1880–1940*

21. Brook Thomas, *Cross-examinations of Law and Literature: Cooper, Hawthorne and Melville*

20. Jerome Loving, *Emily Dickinson: The Poet on the Second Story*

19. Richard Gray, *Writing the South: Ideas of an American Region*

18. Karen E. Rowe, *Saint and Singer: Edward Taylor's Typology and the Poetics of Meditation*

17. Ann Kibbey, *The Interpretation of Material Shapes in Puritanism: A Study of Rhetoric, Prejudice, and Violence*

16. Sacvan Bercovitch and Myra Jehlen (eds.), *Ideology and Classic American Literature*

15. Lawrence Buell, *New England Literary Culture: From Revolution through Renaissance*

14. Paul Giles, *Hart Crane: The Contexts of "The Bridge"*

13. Albert Gelpi (ed.), *Wallace Stevens: The Poetics of Modernism*

12. Albert J. von Frank, *The Sacred Game: Provincialism and Frontier Consciousness in American Literature, 1630–1860*

11. David Wyatt, *The Fall into Eden: Landscape and Imagination in California*

10. Elizabeth McKinsey, *Niagara Falls: Icon of the American Sublime*

9. Barton Levi St. Armand, *Emily Dickinson and Her Culture: The Soul's Society*

8. Mitchell Breitwieser, *Cotton Mather and Benjamin Franklin: The Price of Representative Personality*

7. Peter Conn, *The Divided Mind: Ideology and Imagination in America, 1898–1917*

6. Marjorie Perloff, *The Dance of the Intellect: Studies in Poetry of the Pound Tradition*

The following titles are out of print:

5. Stephen Fredman, *Poet's Prose: The Crisis in American Verse,* first edition

4. Patricia Caldwell, *The Puritan Conversion Narrative: The Beginnings of American Expression*

3. John McWilliams, Jr., *Hawthorne, Melville, and the American Character: A Looking-Glass Business*

2. Charles Altieri, *Self and Sensibility in Contemporary American Poetry*

1. Robert Zaller, *The Cliffs of Solitude: A Reading of Robinson Jeffers*